SHARPY: MY STORY

SHARPY
My Story

Graeme Sharp
with Darren Griffiths

MAINSTREAM
PUBLISHING
EDINBURGH AND LONDON

First published in Great Britain in 2006 by
MAINSTREAM PUBLISHING COMPANY
(EDINBURGH) LTD
7 Albany Street
Edinburgh EH1 3UG

ISBN 978 1 84596 201 2 (from January 2007)
ISBN 1 84596 201 X

A catalogue record for this book is available
from the British Library

Typeset in Cheltenham and Univers

Printed in Great Britain by
William Clowes Ltd, Beccles, Suffolk

Acknowledgements

As you are about to discover, I enjoyed a long and eventful career in professional football, but I wouldn't have managed it without the following people.

I'd like to thank my mum and dad, May and Jim, who have been with me every step of the way. I am also grateful for the support that my mother-in-law and late father-in-law, Rosemary and John, have given my wife Ann Marie and me over the years. I would also like to thank my co-author, Darren Griffiths, whose help with this book has been invaluable.

As for the actual football, I am indebted to Bill Livingston, Davie Wilson, Gordon Lee and Colin Harvey, who were all very influential in making me into the player I became.

Finally, and most importantly, without the love and support of my wife and my children, Chris and Emma, none of it would have been possible or worthwhile . . .

Contents

FOREWORD
by Andy Gray

I am delighted to have this opportunity to say a few words about my great pal Sharpy. When I first joined Everton back in 1983, I knew that I'd been a bit of a hero of his when he was younger, which just goes to show how much older than him I am! Sharpy and I hit it off straight away and we have been big mates ever since.

Sharpy is an easy guy to get on with and in our case I think it's true what they say . . . opposites do attract! He is generally a quiet family man, whereas a lot of people would probably consider me to be a bit of a nutter, but there is huge mutual respect between us: we really enjoy each other's company and always have done, and both coming from Glasgow, initially we at least had something in common. We both learned our craft in the rough-and-tough world of Scottish amateur football. It shaped Graeme and me, as well as countless other professional footballers, and the lessons we learned served us very well. Those ash pitches! Goodness me, if you took a tumble on those, you knew about it!

That was where Sharpy learned the art of being a centre-forward, although I am chuffed to bits if he believes that I contributed to his development when we teamed up at Everton. He wasn't a great goalscorer at the time, but he was a scorer of great goals. He was a very good centre-forward, but maybe he just needed to take his game forward so that he could reach the next level. He undoubtedly did so and he certainly became a great goalscorer – as his record shows beyond any doubt.

When I first arrived at Goodison, I actually played alongside Adrian Heath because Sharpy had a knee injury, but we soon forged a fabulous partnership and we had some brilliant times. We had two years of the very best football of our lives. The famous night when we defeated Bayern Munich will live with us forever and I am sure that Sharpy will go into that game in far more detail in this book. Another game that I will never tire of recalling is the 2–1 win at Tottenham Hotspur in 1985 that edged us closer to Everton's first League Championship success in 15 years. Tottenham had more home games left than we did and the match at White Hart Lane was billed as a possible Championship decider.

It was a cracking game and Sharpy and I had a rare old tussle with Paul Miller and Graham Roberts. They were a very physical central defensive pairing and gave us just the sort of challenge that we relished. We knew that we could play, but we were also fully prepared to mix it and stand up to be counted when the going got tough . . . in fact, we enjoyed it! Not many defenders looked forward to playing against Sharp and Gray! We knew that if the physical stuff started, then not many of them could live with us.

That was a special night at Tottenham and there were plenty more besides. The FA Cup final in 1984 when we both scored against Watford at Wembley was terrific.

As well as winning big football matches, we also knew how to celebrate! We had some wonderful evenings and, even now, I love getting back together with Sharpy and the rest of the boys from our magnificent team because the atmosphere between us is as good now as it was then. The reunion nights are a different class. The football's not bad either!

I was delighted to play alongside Sharpy again at Goodison Park before Howard Kendall's testimonial in August 2006. And who set me up to score at the Gwladys Street end? You've guessed it . . . my mate!

We also play a bit of golf together and we love the annual Scots against the English tournament that we take part in every year at The Belfry. A gang of us ex-professionals get together and play under Ryder Cup rules. It's terrific fun. Nobody wants to lose, I can assure you . . . especially Messrs Sharp and Gray.

During my playing career, I was very fortunate to line up alongside three phenomenal front men. I was with Brian Little when I was a kid at Aston Villa, I had John Richards later on when I was with Wolves, then Sharpy at Everton.

There is no doubt that Sharpy is one of the all-time great Everton centre-forwards and he thoroughly deserved every bit of success that came his way. He really is a smashing lad. I am great friends with him and Ann Marie, and it's been an absolute pleasure to know them.

Andy Gray

NO ORDINARY NIGHT

We were shattered, but elated.

Goodison Park was rocking to the sound of 50,000 celebrating supporters. As a professional footballer, it didn't get much better than this. We'd taken on one of Europe's finest teams, given them a one-goal start and then fought back to win. For the first time in the club's history, Everton had won through to a European final. The victory over Bayern Munich would soon be labelled Goodison's Greatest Night.

At the time, we were happy enough to celebrate a famous success. We didn't stop to think about how we had just been propelled towards legendary status and I never dreamed that supporters would still be eager to discuss the events of that night 20 years later. There is no doubt about it: 24 April 1985 was no ordinary night!

We'd earned a 0–0 draw in the first leg in Munich and so it was winner takes all as we approached the second leg of our European Cup-Winners' Cup semi-final. We stayed in the St George's Hotel on Lime Street opposite the city's main railway station and stuck to the same routine as every midweek match. We would train in the morning, then be ferried to the hotel in the afternoon for some sleep and some food. In those days, we'd have steak or fish for our lunch and maybe some tea and toast early evening, if any of the lads fancied it.

We boarded the team bus at quarter to six for the short journey to Goodison Park. There was nothing out of the ordinary about the journey . . . until we approached the stadium. We couldn't get the bus anywhere near it because of the masses of fans strewn all over the streets.

The sight of so many Everton supporters took my breath away and made me realise, if I hadn't already, just what a big occasion this really was. We were carrying the hopes and dreams of so many people into this one football match. The magnificent Everton fans had never seen their team contest a European final and this was their best ever chance of it happening. We were within touching distance of creating history.

The driver somehow managed to negotiate his way through the throngs, with some help from the police and the roar as we got off the bus to walk the few yards into the stadium was incredible.

When we were in the dressing-room at Goodison, we could always tell just how big the crowd was by the noise and on this occasion we could tell the place was rocking. I swear the dressing-room was vibrating because of the volume out on the terraces and in the stands.

We went out onto the pitch about half an hour before the kick-off for a bit of a warm-up and the crowd was deafening. Goodison was already jam-packed to the rafters and I remember thinking that although some of our opponents were experienced internationals, they must surely be fazed by the cracking atmosphere. It was a perfect stage for the night of drama that was about to unfold.

We were stunned when the experienced German centre-forward Dieter Hoeness gave Bayern the lead after 27 minutes. There was no panic after their goal, but there was a worry that we'd maybe given ourselves too high a mountain to climb. Make no mistake about it: we were up against a very good team and we now needed to score at least two goals to win the tie.

There was a physical edge to the contest, but then you'd expect nothing else because this was a semi-final. We could play football as well as any other team on the Continent, but we could also look after ourselves, or 'mix it', as we called it, when the going got tough. There wasn't a team in the world that could ever intimidate us, and we were right up for the battle and the challenge that lay ahead.

Sitting in the dressing-room at half-time, I looked at the men around me and not for one moment did I consider that we wouldn't emerge victorious. We were more than teammates, we were close friends and comrades. I had progressed through the reserve team with Gary Stevens and Kevin Ratcliffe. Andy Gray had been my boyhood hero and now he was a striking colleague. Kevin Sheedy, Peter Reid and Neville Southall were great mates of mine, who also happened to be vying for the Footballer of the Year accolade. These were men who I would have trusted with my life. We had come through so much together, but we were facing our biggest 45 minutes ever.

Although we were a goal behind, manager Howard Kendall was playing it cool. 'Keep playing the way you are and the Gwladys Street will suck one in for us,' he joked.

The second half was the stuff of dreams.

One of their defenders, Hans Pflugler, was kicking lumps out of us and I thought, I'm not having this, and started to give him some back. There were elbows flying and high tackles going in all over the place. Goodison Park was no place for the faint-hearted.

The lads at the back played some high balls up towards me and Andy and the Bayern defenders didn't care for it too much. Andy and Pflugler had a real set-to that ended in both of them being booked – an amazing statistic from that night is that they were, in fact, the only two cautions handed out by referee Mr Fredriksson all night.

Andy also had a go at Norbert Eder and left the big defender with his nose all over his face. He had to go off for some treatment and when he came back on, the first chance Andy got he whacked him again.

Bayern Munich were no angels themselves. They had players

who were not averse to making late challenges, but we battered them into submission and by the end of the game they had, quite literally, had enough.

I was fortunate enough to score the equaliser in the 48th minute and Andy squeezed home our second goal to leave the Germans shell-shocked. Trevor Steven wrapped it all up with an excellent finish four minutes from time and Goodison exploded when Mr Fredriksson brought the match to an end.

The dressing-room and then the players' lounge at Goodison were transformed into party venues. Usually the stewards were keen to get everybody out of the place at a certain time so the stadium could be locked up, but that night there was no chance. People were singing and dancing on the tables. It was fantastic.

I was just so happy that my dad was there to share this moment with me. He'd been with me every step of the way from Boys' Brigade matches through to amateur football with Eastercraigs and Dumbarton, and he'd seen most of my reserve and first-team games for Everton. He always got so much pleasure from seeing me do well, as any father would, and he was a proud man that night. My wife, Ann Marie, was there too, as were other members of our respective families.

From Goodison Park, we all made our way to a place called the Lido, in Ainsdale, to carry on the party. They stayed open late for us. It was terrific in there, with the singing and the dancing, but I remember looking across the room and seeing Ann Marie's uncle fast asleep on one of the chairs. It was pandemonium all around and yet he was dead to the world. At least he had a smile on his face.

I was one of the last to leave and what a sight greeted me when I put the key in the door at my home. There were people strewn all over the place. I had to step over countless bodies to make my way up the stairs. My side of the bed was just about the only available space left in the entire house.

We couldn't continue the celebrations the next day because

we had to play Norwich City in a First Division match on the Saturday, but what a night it had been. At some point during the evening I paused for reflection and I couldn't help but let my mind drift back to the days when I kicked a case-ball up and down the streets of Stepps, a small town on the edge of Glasgow. From there to the glory of Goodison had been a long, eventful journey with no shortage of trials and tribulations along the way, but that night I knew everything had been worthwhile . . .

ONE
GLASGOW YEARS

The small village of Cardowan, just outside Glasgow, is a place with an unspectacular history. The only entry it ever gets in any Scottish timeline dates back to 1932 when there was an explosion at the local colliery that claimed several lives. But Cardowan is where I entered the world on 16 October 1960. I was actually born at home, the third son of Jim and May Sharp and a younger brother for Andrew and Richard.

The five of us didn't stay in Cardowan long after I arrived and my early childhood was spent in a place called Millerston, which is north of the River Clyde and only a couple of miles down the road from the place of my birth. We lived in a council house in Millerston until I was about 11 years old and then, like most families I suppose, my mother and father bettered themselves and bought their own place on Ballaig Crescent in Stepps, about five miles from the city centre. Our first three homes were quite close together – there is no more than three miles between them.

My first school was Stepps Primary and from a young age, I was always capable of holding my own in lessons. I was forever kicking a ball about but never to the detriment of my class work – my mum and dad saw to that. Regardless of where I lived or studied, the one constant was my love of football.

When Richard was in his final class at the same primary school as me in Stepps and I was no more than seven years old, I got called up to play in his school football team, even though he and his peers were some four years older than me. It was my first experience of anything like an organised game of football – it was certainly the first time I had played in a strictly 11-a-side match because the games we played in the playground and outside our houses were a free-for-all with anyone and everyone joining in. I can even remember the kit that the school team wore: it was a yellow top, similar in style to the away jersey that Everton often wore in the 1970s. I only played one game at that level and then it was back to my own age group.

Prior to that I had only played football in the streets of the surrounding area or in the local park. I had developed a love for the game from a very early age and I would watch it on television as often as I could – when I wasn't playing myself.

I became a member of the 190th Boys' Brigade Troop in Stepps because I discovered they had a football team, which meant I could play more organised matches. In all honesty, the other activities at BBs didn't really interest me one jot, but the fact that the football was good and, in my eyes, 'proper' was a big enough incentive for me to go along.

We had a smashing little team. We had a fixture every Saturday morning and it was my first regular football. But as I began to play more often, I was developing a hatred of losing.

There was one game at Glasgow's famous Alexandra Park where we were up against a team that was far superior to our own. We were losing 9–0 when I lost my rag completely. My dad always tried to come and watch my matches, but on the rare occasions that he couldn't make it my mum would step in and it was sod's law that she was there that day.

When the ninth goal went in, I had just about had enough. I felt that the rest of the lads weren't overly concerned about the game and had merely accepted that the opposition were much the better side. When another boy and I kicked off (again), I turned around to face my own teammates, dribbled the ball through the lot of them and whacked it past my own goalkeeper!

That made it 10–0 and I just carried on straight off the pitch and back to the dressing-room. I was so angry.

Of course, my mum was absolutely mortified and couldn't understand what I'd done! That led, not unreasonably, to my first-ever suspension. The Boys' Brigade took a very dim view of my behaviour and I was banned for the next three games.

I was only ten years old at the time and, I tell you what, it taught me a lesson because it was very frustrating getting up on a Saturday morning and not being able to play any football. I soon understood that I'd been totally out of order and realised just how important football was becoming in my life.

I am often asked if I was aware of my own footballing ability at this stage. I think people always assume that anyone who makes it to the top of the profession has been a superstar at every level he's ever played at. But I genuinely can't recall being particularly better than the rest when I was a primary school pupil. In fact, when I look back on those days now I recall there being an awful lot of very good players: it would have been difficult for any one boy to stand out from the crowd. We played in every single spare minute that we could and there were lots and lots of very good games. It was football at school playtime and dinnertime. Afterwards, it was a rush home, a quick change and then off to the local park to play again. Some of the matches would go on for hours and goodness knows how we ever kept score – if we even bothered! We all loved playing football.

We would play until it was almost too dark to see the ball, but I always knew when my time was up because my dad would come out of the house, stand at the gate and blow a whistle. It was a piercing blast and when I heard it I knew that was me done for the night! Our house in Millerston was at the top of a hill and the park that we played in was just at the bottom, so it was nice and handy for me. But once that whistle went, regardless of the state of play, it was off up the hill to bed. There was no indication of added time for me!

It saddens me that you just don't see as many young

lads playing street football any more. You often hear the sentimentalists bemoaning the fact that youngsters can learn a great deal about the game by playing football in the streets. And they are right. There are no two ways about it: if you learn to control a football on the uneven pitches provided by local parks, or even in streets and alleyways, then it can only be good.

Dad worked in the newspaper industry as a sub-editor for the business section of the *Glasgow Herald*. He generally worked the nightshift, leaving the house at about 6 p.m. and coming back home the following morning, but if he ever worked in the afternoon, I used to love going with him to his office. He'd leave me in the sports department, which was great, and I'd pore over all the football stories and pictures that came in. And there was the odd perk to his job, like the time he took me to Ibrox to watch Glasgow Rangers from the press box. In those days, journalists would watch the games from high up in the Ibrox roof. It was an amazing vantage point for someone like me, who was a Rangers fan anyway.

I actually considered pursuing a career in the media and I suppose it's quite ironic that I watch Everton now from the various press boxes in the Premiership, offering my views for the radio.

Like most 'Gers supporters, I went to watch them as often as I could, although my own playing commitments made it more difficult as I got a bit older. One of my proudest days was travelling to Easter Road in Edinburgh, home to Hibernian, to watch my team play. My brother Richard was in the Rangers side that day and although it was the only senior first-team appearance he ever made, he is still able to say that he played for the club we all loved.

Strangely enough, my dad was not a big football fan until we started to play ourselves. Andrew wasn't interested either, but Richard and I would go to games whenever we could. My dad took me to Parkhead when I was only six years old to see

Rangers take on Aberdeen in the semi-final of the Scottish Cup. We were in the Jungle end, which was absolutely jam-packed by the time we got there. I couldn't even see the pitch, so my dad hoisted me onto his shoulders and kept me up there for the entire 90 minutes! Thankfully Rangers won and went on to beat Celtic in the final.

My favourite player then was a little winger called Willie Henderson. He was only 5 ft 4 in. tall, but what a player he was. He had unbelievable skill and made over 400 appearances for Rangers. I think I took to him more than the others because I used to watch Rangers from a vantage point on the halfway line opposite the main stand, so I would always see Willie really close up. In fact, before I was a centre-forward, I played wide left, so I had an affinity for the wingers anyway. Ironically, Richard's favourite player was the big centre-forward Colin Stein. Many years later during my testimonial year at Everton, Willie Henderson came down to speak at one of the dinners my committee had organised, which was a great honour for me.

Since I was playing every weekend, I wasn't an Ibrox regular, but if ever there was a midweek fixture then my dad would take me – until I reached a certain age when I was allowed to go on my own . . . although never to an Old Firm game! I had to be a lot older to run the gauntlet that was a Rangers versus Celtic match. In those days, these games could be absolute mayhem. There was a genuine hatred between the rival fans and skirmishes took place all over Glasgow on Old Firm days. They were violent confrontations and I would imagine the scenes were similar to those on the streets of Belfast in the 1970s.

Even as youngsters we were always aware that there was some sort of religious divide in Glasgow. Some of my friends from the local area went to a different school, St Josephs, because they were Catholic and the rivalry at our football matches could be quite fierce. It was as though we were playing out a Rangers versus Celtic match – Protestants against Catholics. They were matches that we all desperately wanted to win, even though we were only primary school kids. When we played at St Josephs, we would change into our kit at our own school and walk the five-minute journey to get to their pitch. Whichever team was at home had tremendous backing because the rest of the pupils were allowed out early to watch the game. It was incredible and, don't forget, I'm talking about seven- and eight-year-old children. But once the game was over and the two teams had gone their separate ways, we would meet up in the usual way for a street kickabout.

There was rivalry, for sure, but there certainly weren't any grudges and I don't recall there being any real problems. Not from my point of view, anyway, although there were undoubtedly some people in Glasgow who took the religious rivalry a step further.

From Stepps Primary, children had a choice of senior schools, dependent largely on how they had performed, and so I moved on to Coatbridge High, a good school with an excellent reputation. My parents were pleased and it was an early indication to me of the value of a good education.

Mum and Dad always taught us three boys what was right and what was wrong and although we were encouraged in everything we did, we also had to toe the line. For example, we were never allowed to play out on a Sunday. If it was sunny we could maybe kick a ball about in the back garden but that was it. There was no playing in the park or the street. It would drive me mad. I used to go to Sunday school to relieve the boredom, although I hated it because I would see some of the other lads playing football. In the end, I stopped going.

Once I moved to Coatbridge, I found myself amongst some more very good footballers. The school kids came from all over the Lanarkshire area and there was always speculation amongst us about who would get into the team. I knew that the competition would be stiff because I was always aware of the best players from other districts, whose names would be bandied about, and there were some excellent boys at Coatbridge. I just went along to the training sessions with the intention of doing the best I could and, although this might sound big-headed, it soon became apparent that I was the best player in my year.

Once again I was part of a very good side. There were some great players in our team. Davie Brand went on to play for Airdrie and two boys, James Sexton and Peter Shields, had trials for Ipswich Town.

We played on a Saturday morning and the teacher who took the team was called Paddy Gardner. He was terrific and had a great influence on me. And I felt he was the best choice to take the school team because he loved his football so much. He had so much enthusiasm that it couldn't fail to rub off on the young lads in his team.

I was playing well and I started to acknowledge that perhaps I did have something about me and that a career in the game might not be such a bad idea. Playing for Coatbridge got me noticed by the district selectors and then the Lanarkshire county side called me up. I went for county trials without actually getting a game, but I was soon playing on both Saturday and Sunday.

The amateur football scene in and around Glasgow was famous for the strength of its football teams and for the number of players it produced. Drumchapel Amateurs, Eastercraigs, Harmony Row, Celtic Boys Club, Celtic Amateurs: they were all good clubs with reputations to match.

The team that wanted me was Celtic Amateurs, which was a Sunday team. My brother Richard played for them for a while. They had two teams – Under-16 and Under-14 – and I initially played for the younger team.

Unfortunately the club disbanded, although I was very quickly offered a trial with Eastercraigs. I was delighted because they were one of the best amateur teams around. The problem was that they played on a Saturday afternoon, which meant two games in one day for me. It was Coatbridge in the morning and then Eastercraigs in the afternoon. I loved it at first – the more football the better, as far as I was concerned

– but it soon became apparent that it was too much for a young lad to take on board. Something had to give and I eventually told the school that I couldn't play for them. I figured that the good-quality amateur football I was getting with Eastercraigs was far better for my development. Coatbridge weren't happy about it and told me that they were prepared to invoke a rule that stated if a boy doesn't play for his school team then he is not permitted to play for anyone else. It got a bit messy, but I stood my ground and eventually got my own way. However, there was a sting in the tail because although they agreed to let me play for Eastercraigs, they asked me back to help them win the final of the Scottish Schools Cup. It was to be played at Lesser Hampden, which is adjacent to the main stadium. My first reaction was to refuse because it wouldn't have been fair on whoever had to miss out to accommodate me, but Coatbridge were insistent and I reluctantly agreed. I played against John McDonald that day, who went on to have a good career with Rangers. We beat the opposition and I scored a hat-trick. It was my last game for the school, so at least I went out on a high! Even so, I actually didn't feel overly pleased about the whole thing and tried to give my medal to the boy I had replaced. He was gutted at missing out after playing in all the previous rounds, and he didn't want the medal.

Back at Eastercraigs, Bernie Slaven was a teammate. He went on to play for Middlesbrough and the Republic of Ireland. Maurice Johnston also played for the club later, as did John Hannah. John never made a living out of football, but he's done OK for himself and is now a famous actor after getting his big break in *Four Weddings and A Funeral*.

We played in a very good, tough, competitive league, the best league in the region by far. All the teams were from Glasgow or the surrounding area and you would always see scouts from clubs from all over Scotland and England watching the games, looking out for players.

I owe a lot to the coach, Bill Livingston, who was always

encouraging me to continue with my studies whilst still taking my football as seriously as I could. He looked like Compo from *Last of the Summer Wine*! He wore a similar cloth hat and wellington boots and was a fabulous man. He is an Eastercraigs legend! His training sessions were strict, but everything he did was designed to benefit young footballers. Bill was the man who persuaded me to play up front as I'd primarily been a midfielder when I first joined Eastercraigs.

A lot of our games were played on a famous arena in Glasgow called '50 Pitches' which was, quite literally, a massive expanse of land with 50 football pitches marked out. It was a truly amazing sight when they were all being used. The area is not too far away from Ibrox, but, like a lot of open ground in the cities these days, the space has been developed and there are only a couple of the pitches left now.

We weren't playing on grass, by the way! The pitches were all made of ash. I tell my son, Chris, how spoiled he was playing his junior football on grass! You can only imagine what state we'd be in after 90 minutes – my dad used to make me scrub myself with a wire brush in the bath before he'd let me anywhere near my bed sheets. We went through a lot of Dettol in those days because we picked up so many cuts and grazes from the pitches. We were so delighted every time we reached any sort of cup final because they were played on grass. That was a big enough incentive in itself, let alone the chance to win a trophy.

But I loved it. For the first time, I was involved with a football club that had a structure to it. We trained twice a week and, although we were strictly amateur, the approach and the organisation of Eastercraigs was very professional. They had high standards and they fully expected all their young players to adhere to them. There was a discipline, too. Your boots had to be clean when you turned up for training and matches and you had to be properly attired at all times. We even had our own Eastercraigs FC sports bags for our gear. They wouldn't stand for unruly behaviour or foul and abusive language on or off the pitch, and they were great for me.

The training was very hard, though, and it was too much for some lads. A few of the pals I had played alongside in the street games and at school came along for trials, but most of them couldn't handle the toughness of the training and simply packed it in.

We did a lot of physical, non-football training, like running and weightlifting, and, there was no doubt about it, you had to be dedicated. I gave up quite a lot to make it as a player with Eastercraigs. I was training and playing while my pals were doing the sort of recreational things boys normally do between the age of 14 and 17. I'm not saying that I thoroughly enjoyed it all the time, but I knew that it had to be done and that sacrifices had to made if I was to achieve my dream of being a professional footballer.

My dad always made sure that my education came first, but he knew just how beneficial playing for a team like Eastercraigs was for me. He spoke to the club and explained that he wanted my studies to come first and, to be fair, they understood that if I had exams to take or to prepare for, then I would miss the odd training session.

The manager was an older man called John Murray and he had a good group of lads. Most of the boys came from the inner areas of Glasgow, like the Gorbals, Castlemilk and Easterhouse, so the competition was tough . . . in every sense of the word! Football was a way out for a lot of the lads. Some of them inevitably came from rough and tough backgrounds, but the discipline that the likes of Eastercraigs instilled did a lot of them the power of good. Not all of them, obviously, but the amateur football clubs in Glasgow helped a lot of youngsters over the years.

Some of the other teams in the league didn't have our discipline ethic, but we were encouraged to always maintain our standards, even in the face of provocation. Many of the opposing teams did provocation very well, so it was a very good learning process for me.

We were a fine side, but so were most of the others and there weren't too many convincing victories for any team in the matches. They were generally very close, hard-fought affairs, though I did manage to score five goals in one game when we thrashed Celtic Boys Club, of all teams.

It saddens me that the amateur game in Scotland just isn't the same any more. The leagues provided an abundance of footballers that went on to have good professional careers – many of them even went all the way through to the full international set-up. At the moment, the Scotland team isn't doing too well, although things are certainly looking brighter under Walter Smith, and when I hear people discussing the connection between underachievement at that level and the dearth of good amateur football teams, I find it impossible to disagree.

It's not just in Scotland, either, that amateur football is struggling. It's the same all over. There are too many other things for kids to do with their time now. But it was definitely the way forward for me and for countless others.

As I progressed through the Eastercraigs teams, I established a reputation for myself as a bit of a goalscorer and I was invited to go for trials with Aston Villa. I went down with another lad and stayed at the club hostel while I was training, but I didn't enjoy it. Brian Little was a Villa player, as was Gordon Cowans. In all honesty, I can't recall too much about my time there – other than that Little used to bring his dog to training! I suppose Andy Gray must have been there, too, because it was 1976, although I have to say I don't remember seeing him! He must have been away from the club that week because even if I didn't see him I would have heard him!

I trained with Villa for a week, then went home to Glasgow and never heard another word from them. I wasn't overly concerned because I genuinely didn't enjoy being at the place and it didn't put me off because I was constantly being linked with other clubs. I always thought my chance would come again. Of course I was envious of the lads who were signing schoolboy forms for this club or that, but I just knuckled down and got on with things. I was still at school, don't forget, so there wasn't time for me to mope about and dwell on what might have been.

Anyway, Bill Livingston told my dad that it wouldn't be long before a professional club came in for me. Rangers were interested, but my dad was adamant that I wasn't going there. He felt that I wouldn't get a proper chance; that I would get lost in the system. His opinion had been formed after my brother's experience there. If anything, Richard probably had more natural ability than me. He signed for Rangers because he idolised the club but, although he did well for the reserves, he never got the chance he deserved. My dad decided that the same thing wouldn't happen to me.

Anyway, I was 17 years old when I went with Eastercraigs on an end-of-season trip to America. It had been a terrific trip for a group of young lads. We'd won all six of the matches that we'd played, we'd seen New York and Philadelphia and I was dying to tell Dad all about it. My dad collected me from the airport when I returned, but he did all the talking. 'We're going to the North British Hotel in George Square,' he said.

'Why?' I asked.

'We're meeting Dumbarton,' he replied.

TWO

DUMBARTON DAYS

Although the actual approach from Dumbarton came somewhat out of the blue, I don't suppose it should have been that much of a surprise because during the previous season Alan McKay, a scout from the club, had been at virtually every match that Eastercraigs had played. He was a regular face on the amateur circuit and it transpired that he had been having regular conversations with my dad and had hinted that Dumbarton were very keen to sign me.

So my dad and I went to the North British Hotel to meet Alec Wright, who was the club's general manager. I was hardly involved in any of the discussions: it was mainly Alec and Dad thrashing out what was best for me. They agreed that I should put pen to paper on a two-year deal as a part-time professional for the princely sum of £35 per week, with a signing-on fee of £750, which my dad negotiated for me. It was that simple.

On 10 July 1978, I received an official letter from Dumbarton Football Club confirming my registration as a professional footballer with the Scottish Football Association. The club were in the First Division at the time, the structure having changed in Scotland following the introduction of the Premier League. I was 17 and was still at school after deciding to stay on for an extra year to do Highers. In all honesty, though, it rapidly became a waste of my time. My heart just wasn't in it. I now knew exactly what I wanted to do with my life and I really thought I'd taken the first important step. My attention was now switching to

Boghead. (Dumbarton was a great little football club, but it had the most unromantically named ground anywhere in Britain!)

The school didn't view professional football as a suitably secure career for a young boy and, to a certain extent, they were probably right. The careers teacher even arranged a job interview for me with the Royal Bank of Scotland. It was the only interview I have ever attended. I didn't want the job and I think the guy at the bank could tell – I didn't get it. I was determined to make it as a professional and was putting more into my football than my schoolwork, though at the end of the academic year I still managed to pass my Higher exams. To be fair, most of the teachers took a genuine interest in my career and would always ask me on the Monday how I'd done. It was strange when I broke into the first team because the staff at the school would tell me they'd read about me in the papers!

And so I duly reported for pre-season training with Dumbarton in the summer. We trained on a Monday and a Thursday because the club was still predominantly part time. From the family house in Stepps, I had to get a bus into the centre of Glasgow and then walk through to Queen Street station to get a train to Dumbarton. It was about an hour there and an hour back, but I didn't mind one bit.

I was a bit insecure when I first went along to Boghead. I really didn't think I had any right to be there amongst some of the senior professional footballers who had played at the highest level and were winding down their careers. You must remember this was my very first experience of open-age football. Up until then, I had always been amongst lads of a similar age to me and now, suddenly, I was pitting my wits against some wily old pros who had forgotten more about the game of football than I thought at that time I would ever learn.

Pat McCluskey was in the Dumbarton team when I first joined the club and, in my eyes, he'd seen and done it all. He'd played hundreds of games for Celtic alongside the likes of Jimmy Johnstone, Billy McNeill, Danny McGrain, Kenny Dalglish and

Bobby Lennox. I'd read about him in the papers and watched him on television and now I was expected to slot in right alongside him.

Graham Fyfe, a former teammate of my hero Willie Henderson, was also in the side. My brother Richard and I used to cheer him on from the terraces of Ibrox when he was with Rangers. It was no wonder that I was a little bit overawed at the prospect of mixing with these players. I was a naturally quiet lad who lacked a bit of confidence and I seriously doubted my credentials during the first few weeks.

Davie Wilson was the manager and Stan Anderson was his assistant. Davie was another Rangers legend who I admired. He'd been a winger at Ibrox and his record of 157 goals in 373 appearances was astonishing for a wide man. He won leagues and cups with Rangers and also represented Scotland 22 times.

It was a weird experience, mixing so closely with men that my brother and I had read about in *Shoot!*. I used to buy the magazine every Saturday morning without fail and I would love reading all about the English game and the big-name players. Every Scottish kid had a favourite English team and, even though I'd had an unhappy week there, mine was Aston Villa.

The most successful team at that time was Liverpool and consequently a lot of my friends had adopted them as their English favourites. I had a great day in school the day after Aston Villa defeated them 5–1 at Villa Park one evening in December 1976!

I was very much a new kid on the block at Dumbarton and although I had always considered the training at Eastercraigs to be difficult, this was another level. Davie and Stan had us running up and down every hill they could find! I was a slender lad at 17, with very little strength or power, and I found the going very testing. We'd go on unbelievably long cross-country runs, where we'd be crossing streams and jumping over brooks, and I'd be thinking to myself, what on earth have I let myself in for here?

There was plenty of weight training as well, and we did lots of running and sprinting around the track that surrounded the pitch at Boghead. I kept at it, though, and I quickly reaped the rewards of putting in the effort. After making my first-ever appearance for Dumbarton as a substitute in a friendly against a team called Clachnacuddin, I started the season in the reserves and I did OK, scoring a few goals and generally playing quite well.

Stan always took the reserves. He was a hard man who had been on the coaching staff at Rangers. He was a real disciplinarian, a sergeant major-type who could shout and scream when he needed to. He was like Archie Knox, who was at Manchester United with Sir Alex Ferguson, Rangers and Everton with Walter Smith and is now Under-21 team coach for Scotland.

My debut for Dumbarton came against Raith Rovers on 3 December 1978, but if I thought I'd made it there was a painful shock in store. Not long after this I got my first serious injury playing for the reserves when an old professional who'd been around a bit did me late in the game. I had scored a goal early on and he was marking me. He knew what he was doing. As I ran towards the ball shaping to get a header in, he stepped back and threw his head at mine, catching me full in the face. I went down, out cold and didn't come round until I was in the dressing-room. The first thing I did after I regained consciousness was throw up everywhere. The diagnosis was a fractured cheekbone.

I couldn't see out of my right eye so I was taken straight to Glasgow Royal Infirmary, where I stayed overnight. I had an operation the next day, which involved inserting a wire into my face to support the cheekbone.

I was devastated because I felt that I was really beginning to make an impression at Dumbarton and here I was out of action for four months. My misery was compounded when I received a call-up letter from the SFA, informing me that I had been selected to represent Scotland at Under-18 level. There was no way I could go; it was a massive blow. Walter Smith, still a player at the time, was then the assistant coach and others in the squad included Everton's Joe McBride, and Ralph Milne, who played for Dundee United and Manchester United.

Don't forget, I was still at school, so had to take six weeks off while I recovered. The club were great, though, and assured me that I would still get my chance. This was music to my dad's ears. This was the very reason he had arranged for me to join them in the first place: they treated youngsters in the correct manner, were never afraid to give them a chance and would then never stand in their way if they had an opportunity to better themselves.

Just before I joined the club, they had sold Ian Wallace to Coventry City. He ended up making a £1 million move to Nottingham Forest. Tom McAdam had left the club to join Dundee United and later played over 200 games for Celtic. Murdo McLeod was another well-known old boy, so I gathered that I'd get an opportunity far quicker than I would at one of the bigger clubs.

Dumbarton were true to their word and, after patiently regaining my fitness, I did become a part of the first team. I went on my first pre-season tour in the summer of 1979. The club went to Ireland and, for an impressionable teenager from Glasgow, it was an eye-opener, I can tell you. We stayed in a lovely hotel right by the sea.

One night, a couple of the lads had some girls in their room – they shouldn't have done, of course – and somebody shouted that Davie Wilson was coming along the corridor. The girls were hastily bundled out of the window – fortunately we were only on the second floor! It was all harmless fun and the lads were single, but it was all new to me.

The young players naturally spent time together and one night, after we'd been out, while we were going back to our rooms, we bumped into Paddy McCluskey. That was it! He insisted we come back to his room for a few drinks and, before we knew it, we'd knocked back more than was good for us.

So of course we didn't hear Davie Wilson the first time he knocked on Paddy's door. But we did the second time, when he almost broke it down. He was standing outside the room, ranting and raving at Paddy. All he had on was a white hotel towel around his waist. We had obviously woken him up.

Paddy was getting both barrels and we young lads soon sobered up when he and Davie started brawling on the floor. We just looked at each other and sneaked out of the door as the two senior men traded punches. It blew over very quickly – both were experienced football men and there were no grudges harboured. It was my first taste of trouble on tour . . . but it was by no means the last!

I liked Paddy a lot – even though he was a Celtic man! He knew I needed some assistance in coming out of my shell and looked after me a bit. He found out that I was travelling to and from training by public transport, so he organised lifts for me. It was a generous offer that led to some smashing afternoons in his company.

Paddy lived in Airdrie, so we would either stop off at a nice little pub on the main dual carriageway, or we would carry on into Glasgow and go to the Waterloo. Joe and Tommy Coyle were teammates who lived in the Gorbals in Glasgow, so they were often with us, and they could certainly drink! (Their little brother, Owen, used to come and watch us play. He later had a good pro career himself with Airdrie and Bolton Wanderers amongst others.) And, of course, because my dad worked nights, it was reasonably safe getting into the house without my parents knowing what I'd been up to.

It was all part of an initiation process for me and I was enjoying myself, until the lads decided to vary things a bit one Thursday when we went to a different pub in Glasgow called the Horseshoe. It was approaching 10 p.m. when I got a tap on my shoulder.

It was my dad! He was doing his nightshift at *The Herald* and had popped out for a quick pint on his break.

He'd done so much to get me where I was and there I stood, rather the worse for wear, on a Thursday night with a pint in my hand. Still, he was great about it. Dad knew that I was in good hands with people like Paddy and Graham Fyfe, and he also knew me well enough to understand that I was never going to cause any bother or drink too much. The Thursday ritual never got out of hand and it was great because it made me feel much more a part of the team. We were a good side then and there was a terrific atmosphere at the club.

I achieved two Highers, in maths and modern studies, and decided to go back to school in September to sit the two that I'd failed – English and French. Eventually, though, I didn't see the point in taking those two subjects again and I left school altogether. Davie Wilson asked me to go down to Boghead a lot more often to do extra training and to work on various aspects of my game. One of my early matches for The Sons (Dumbarton's nickname) was a Scottish Cup fourth-round tie at home against Clydebank. I scored twice in the 3–1 win. There's nothing particularly remarkable in that, but when I was researching this book I discovered, amazingly, that Dumbarton haven't beaten a fellow Scottish League club at home in the Cup since that game!

That win put us into the quarter-finals and the local people started thinking about the glamour of Hampden Park. Dumbarton hadn't been in the Scottish Cup final for 82 years at the time, so the excitement was understandable. We were paired with Partick Thistle in the fifth round – it was the talk of the town for weeks ahead of the game.

Partick, of course, are the third-biggest team in Glasgow and at that time they were one of the best in Scotland. We were a fairly young team with few inhibitions and we really thought we could turn them over.

The atmosphere was fabulous and the 6,000 fans that squeezed into Boghead represented the biggest crowd I'd played in front of. I was marked by John Marr, an experienced old professional, but I did well against him, even though I didn't manage to score. It was a massive game for me and I was bitterly disappointed that we lost 1–0. Alan Rough, later to become an international teammate of mine, was man of the match, and we were by far the better side. Roughie had made some unbelievable saves before Partick broke away with only five minutes left to score the winner.

We had a very good side and had seen some fine results, and were often tipped for promotion to the SPL.

I scored twice in a 4–1 drubbing of Berwick Rangers and got another couple a fortnight later when we defeated Dunfermline 3–1. Indeed a 4–0 win over Hamilton Academical on the last Saturday of 1979 actually sent us to the top of the First Division, but we soon fell away. We only managed to win one of the following eight games, a 2–0 victory away at Berwick, when I scored both goals. The pitch on which we played was in the most dreadful condition and the match was in doubt in the morning. The surface was rock hard that game!

I still made my way to Boghead on public transport from time to time and it was while on the bus from Glasgow that a Dumbarton fan asked me if I thought the Berwick game would go ahead. I had to confess to him that until I got to the ground to meet the team coach I really wouldn't know. When I got confirmation that the game was on, I gave the guy a couple of tickets. He still had another long journey ahead of him and I thought about him when we got to Berwick to discover that the referee was inspecting the pitch, but thankfully the match went ahead as scheduled. The fan turned out to be a guy called Jim McAllister, who later wrote a book on the history of the club.

At one stage, Dumbarton had three teenage strikers in their line-up (Brian Gallagher and Ray Blair were the other two). Needless to say, we attracted a fair amount of interest and it wasn't long before we were being linked with bigger and better things.

Funnily enough, one report in a Scottish paper suggested that

John Barnwell, the manager of Wolves, was poised to sign me as an understudy for . . . Andy Gray! The same article mentioned that Notts County and Manchester United had also been to Boghead to run the rule over me. And another story indicated that Aston Villa were weighing me up as a possible replacement for the recently sold . . . Andy Gray!

My dad kept a scrapbook of newspaper cuttings from all the matches I played with Dumbarton and he pasted in all the speculation stories, too. Bristol City, Manchester City and Stoke City watched me one night and apparently Barnsley had a bid turned down.

Davie Wilson was quoted in one of the local papers as saying, 'I don't think Graeme is as good as Andy Gray in the air just yet, but that could come. His skill and speed on the ground are as good as Andy's.' At the time I was a teenager and was just trying to make my way in the game, whereas Andy had recently moved from Aston Villa to Wolves for a British record fee of £1.5 million. Davie believed in building his players up a bit! He would say anything to get Dumbarton in the papers. We had Boghead re-seeded once and when a local reporter asked Davie about it, he said, 'It's just like Wembley!'

I was always well aware that there were a number of teams monitoring my progress. My name appeared in the Sunday papers in Scotland linked with moves to Aston Villa (again), Rangers and Celtic. Even Arsenal were mentioned at one stage and I must admit the thought of signing for them and moving to London did startle me a wee bit! But whether or not there was anything in half of it, I never knew. I was just content to concentrate on my game and keep scoring goals for Dumbarton. I honestly never seriously contemplated what might lie ahead in the future.

Aberdeen actually invited me for a week-long trial, which I enjoyed. They used to train on an ash pitch opposite Pittodrie. The club put me up in a hotel in the centre of town and Alex Ferguson, the manager at the time, used to pick me up each morning to go to the ground, where we changed for training. Willie Miller was there then and so were Neale Cooper, Alex McLeish and Jim Leighton. I heard that Aberdeen wanted to buy me but nothing came of it and it never crossed my mind to ask why they never followed up their interest. Maybe there was a problem with the fee. Had Aberdeen made me an offer, then I would have gone there, but I was too busy playing to get involved in my own future.

When one Saturday I turned up eager to play a Scottish Cup tie against Ayr United at Boghead, I was stunned to hear Davie Wilson say that I wouldn't be included in the team. I was livid and demanded to know why. He told me that it had been a board decision, which perplexed me even more. It turned out the club didn't want me to play because they knew before I did that I had been invited to Aston Villa for a trial and didn't want the deal scuppered by any injury to me. I wasn't bothered about the prospect of Dumbarton missing out on a potential transfer fee, I just wanted to play in the Cup tie. I told them that if they didn't let me play against Ayr United then there was no way I would be going to Aston Villa. The problem was eventually resolved about 45 minutes before the match when they reluctantly agreed to let me play.

Looking back, I can fully understand their point of view – selling an asset can be a lifeline for smaller clubs – but at the time I had no appreciation of the economics of the game: I just saw a big match ahead of me in which I was desperate to play.

So I went to Aston Villa again and this time I enjoyed the week I spent there. It went far better than the trial I had endured a few years earlier and I did well. Ron Saunders was the manager and I trained with the first team. I recall one particular session when I joined in some shooting practice against goalkeeper Jimmy Rimmer, who had previously played for Manchester United. I scored with virtually every shot and Peter Withe was very complimentary about my finishing ability. At the end of the week, I was full of confidence. I knew that I'd done OK and felt that I had held my own with a team that was in the English First Division. Once the trial was over, I was called into Ron's office, along with Davie Wilson and his assistant, Sean Fallon, and he asked me how I thought it had gone. I told him I'd enjoyed it. He said that he'd had good reports about me and that he wanted me to sign for his team.

He assured me that the two clubs would sort everything out and I returned to Dumbarton believing that I was poised to join Aston Villa. But that was the last I heard from them. I don't know whether the two clubs got together and couldn't agree on a deal or if Ron Saunders changed his mind. I just carried on at Dumbarton where I had left off.

I played against Arbroath one night in March 1980 at Boghead and scored our goal in a 2–1 defeat. We had the next day off and so I stayed in bed most of the morning only to be woken by my dad, who informed me that Davie Wilson had been on the phone asking me to report to Boghead immediately. Dad hadn't asked why, but we jumped into his car and went to the ground, where we were told that Davie was in the boardroom. When we walked in, Davie was on the telephone. After a few minutes, he passed the receiver to me, saying, 'It's Gordon Lee, the manager of Everton and he wants to talk to you.'

THREE

A BLUE BOY

I can remember sitting in Davie Wilson's Boghead office as if it was yesterday. I was 19 years old and I had just been informed that the manager of one of the biggest and most famous clubs in England wanted to speak to me. I tried to sound confident, but I don't think it worked.

'Hello, Mr Lee,' I just managed to get out.

Gordon told me that he'd watched me the previous night against Arbroath and, although he'd left before I scored my goal, he had liked what he'd seen. He asked me to travel to Merseyside and I agreed, assuming that he wanted me to have a trial so that he could take a closer look. It came out of the blue because Everton had not been one of the teams I had been linked with in the newspapers, but I was happy to travel south and give it a go.

My dad had enlisted the help of his friend Jim Morris, who had a car, and the following morning the three of us set off for Liverpool. Davie Wilson and Sean Fallon had travelled down separately and we all met at Bellefield, Everton's training ground in the West Derby district of the city. I was introduced to Harry Cooke, the chief scout. It transpired he had watched me many times without the press in Scotland getting wind of it. Of course Gordon Lee was also there to meet us. Bellefield looked fantastic to me. I'd never seen a training complex like it.

Gordon never asked me to train, he just showed me around the place and suggested moving on to Goodison Park for a look around there, too. Believe it or not, I still thought this was the prelude to a trial invitation. It never occurred to me that I was about to sign for one of the most famous football clubs in England.

We ate in one of the lounges, which again impressed me – I had never seen a restaurant inside a football stadium before! The hospitality was fabulous. After a very good meal, we moved into the office of the secretary, Jim Greenwood, who later became a very good friend of mine. He was sitting with Davie and Sean, who had, unbeknown to me, agreed a transfer fee of £125,000. Gordon Lee came in and made some polite conversation before shoving a contract in front of me.

I was a naive teenager and I didn't know what to do. I looked at my dad for assistance and Gordon wisely left the two of us alone for five minutes.

'This is what you have always wanted,' said Dad. 'It seems like a smashing football club and, although you'll be leaving home for the first time, it seems like an ideal opportunity for you.'

The wage I'd been offered was £120 a week with a £15,000 signing-on fee that would be payable in three instalments over the period of the three-year deal. That was brilliant money for me, though that really wasn't the issue. It was all about the opportunity that lay in front of me. My dad made his point and then left the decision to me. I signed the contract.

I was an Everton player, subject to me passing a medical. Not for a second did I think that the medical arranged for the following week would frighten the life out of me.

Everything had all happened so quickly that it still hadn't sunk in by the time we got back home to Glasgow that night. In fact, I fell fast asleep in Jim's car as we headed back up the road. I was hanging out with a group of mates the following day and they refused to believe that I had signed for Everton until they read about it in the papers.

Someone else who couldn't quite believe it was Ron Saunders, who was furious with Dumbarton for letting me sign for Everton. He claimed the club had sold me to the highest bidder and accused Dumbarton of being unprofessional. 'It was a disgraceful way for Dumbarton to do business,' he said at the time. 'As far as I was concerned, a deal had been done and then they told me it's off because they had a higher bid.'

'The last contact I had with Ron Saunders was three weeks ago,' Davie Wilson replied. 'Everton made a bid that was the best for Dumbarton and the player wanted to join them. What am I supposed to do?'

The general manager, Alex Wright, was a touch more sympathetic towards Villa's plight. 'We had agreed a deal, but Everton stepped in with a better offer. When that happens, you are duty-bound to listen, especially when you're surviving on gates of 2,000. I tried to phone Saunders but couldn't get hold of him. We regret the way we had to do the deal.'

It all looked a bit messy, I must admit, but I had no view on it. I considered the wheeling and dealing to have nothing to do with me. As far as I was concerned, the first concrete offer I got came from Everton.

Gordon Lee refused to enter into the transfer debate other than to say, 'He is enthusiastic and clearly has potential. I've been looking for a young striker like Graeme because I think we need one.'

He obviously didn't want me to get too carried away.

There were a couple of months of the 1979–80 season to go and Gordon gave me two weeks to return home to Glasgow to sort myself out before I had to report for training at Bellefield. I didn't have too much to arrange, but it gave Everton the chance to sort out some digs for me and finalise that medical I considered to be a mere formality.

I was very wrong.

I did the usual tests at Bellefield and then had some scans at a private clinic in Rodney Street in the centre of Liverpool. Jim McGregor was the physiotherapist at the time and he came with me. When the results for the scan came back, they showed an abnormality with my heart. I was devastated. I thought my career might be over before it had really begun and there was a real panic at the club and for me personally. The scans had detected a slight heart murmur and I had to go to an old hospital in the south of the city called Sefton General for tests. It was a really worrying time. I was on my own a long way from home and this was a massive setback for me. I was obviously speaking to my mum and dad every day and when I told them about the tests, they were probably even more worried about it than I was. Everton were great about the whole scenario. Gordon Lee told me not to worry. He said that, as they were spending money on me, they had to be absolutely sure that everything was OK. There was a two-day wait for the results and it was an incredible relief when they came back giving me the all-clear. They were the longest two days of my life.

I quickly put the whole episode behind me and started training with my new teammates. However, the insecurities that had plagued me during my early days with Eastercraigs and then again at Dumbarton soon came back to haunt me. When I looked around at the rest of the lads at Bellefield, I convinced myself that I was out of my depth and that I had no right to be there. I really didn't think I was good enough. I would see seasoned professionals like Asa Hartford, Bob Latchford, Mike Lyons and John Gidman and be completely fazed by their presence. I couldn't envisage myself ever getting ahead of my peers and taking my place in the first team alongside these people.

There were two dressing-rooms at Bellefield, just as there are today: one for the senior first-team professionals and one for the young players. I may have cost £125,000, but I was in with the youngsters.

They were a great set of lads. I used to spend time with Paul Lodge, Brian Quinn, Dean Kelly, Brian Burrows, Joe McBride and Steve McMahon. Whenever I didn't go home to Glasgow for the weekend, I would join those boys for a Saturday night out, though this didn't happen too often because I was going back home as regularly as I possibly could: I was homesick.

I played for the reserves and my dad would invariably come down from Scotland to watch the games. The Central League was regionalised, so all matches took place in the North-West, which suited me fine. My dad would watch me play and as soon as the match was over it was a shower, then into his car and straight back up to Glasgow.

After Saturday home fixtures, we would pull up outside my parents' house at about half-nine in the evening and I'd stay up there until the next day, when I'd get a teatime train back to Liverpool Lime Street. They were fleeting visits and I couldn't do too much when I was there, but it was a fix for me. Anyone who has ever suffered from homesickness will know exactly what I mean. It's an unpleasant experience and at times it nearly defeated me.

My first-ever appearance in the famous royal-blue shirt of Everton was for the reserves in a Central League win against Blackpool on 8 April 1980 at Goodison Park. We won 3–0, but I didn't score; nor did I when we beat Bolton at Burnden Park by the same score four days later. Thankfully I finally got off the mark with my new club with our goal in a 2–1 defeat at Stoke City. I followed it up with another in the next game – a 3–3 draw with Derby County – when Garry Stanley and Kevin Richardson also scored.

Any danger of me getting carried away was dispelled when I next hit the target. We defeated Wolves at Molineux by a single goal to nil and I was our goalscorer; however, the headline in the *Daily Post* the following day read: 'Shaw breaks the deadlock.' Within the short summary, it was reported: 'Fifteen minutes from time, Everton scored the game's only goal when Shaw headed home from a corner.'

The local paper had got my surname completely wrong. It still went into my dad's scrapbook, although he scribbled out the references to 'Shaw' and wrote 'Sharp' on the page in blue biro.

I also grabbed a brace against Leeds United at Goodison in a 5–2 win, but the next day the papers made more of our fifth goal, described as a 'brilliant solo effort by Kevin Ratcliffe'. He was never one for scoring ordinary goals!

It was good experience because, unlike these days, the second teams played their matches at the club stadium, so I got to play at the likes of Burnden Park, Stoke City's Victoria Ground and the Baseball Ground. It was a valuable education for me because I was playing against some experienced players and I was picking up little bits and pieces as I went along. I had nowhere near mastered the centre-forward's art and there was not much of me in a physical sense. I was always naturally fit, but I was also still rather slender in build.

And I was also young of mind. I still missed Glasgow enormously. The loneliness I had felt initially in Merseyside was now also exacerbated by the fact that I had a very good reason indeed for wanting to spend time back home: Ann Marie Taylor.

I had met Ann Marie when I was at Dumbarton, but I probably didn't realise how keen on one another we were until I moved down south. We'd write to each other all the time and although she came to Liverpool on the odd occasion, it was easier for me to travel back home with my dad after the reserve games.

Colin Harvey took most of my early Everton training and, as it was the first time in my life that I had done any full-time training, I found the going tough. We'd train hard in the morning and then Colin would keep some of us back in the afternoon to work on one or two things. I was a professional footballer and I was enjoying the actual work, but it was hard and the homesickness didn't help. I never thought for a moment that Gordon Lee would have me in mind, which, looking back, is a bit strange because the first team weren't scoring goals.

As the end of the season loomed, the first team played

Brighton and Hove Albion away and Gordon invited me to travel to the game with the squad. I just assumed that he was giving me a taste. I knew in my heart that I should have been nowhere near the first team, so I went there viewing it as a little bonus that I should enjoy as much as possible. Anyway, when we got to our hotel, Gordon pulled me to one side and told me that I would be the substitute. There was only one player allowed on the bench in those days and I was delighted to have the opportunity. I remember sitting on the sidelines, watching the match, thinking that just a few months earlier I'd only ever seen English football on the television. I warmed up a few times along the touchline, but I don't think that even the travelling Everton supporters knew exactly who I was.

My big moment came in the 70th minute when Gordon told me that I would be going on for Bob Latchford. I ran onto the field and the first thing I got was a whack from Brighton centre-half Peter Suddaby. He'd been around and as an introduction to the First Division he decided to give me a good old-fashioned right hook! The ball was at the other end of the field when he clouted me and I couldn't believe it. The incident shocked me and did nothing to ease the feeling that I was way out of my depth at this level. If his intention was to intimidate me, it worked a treat. I was too young and inexperienced to even consider giving him a bit back.

It wasn't just a lack of confidence on my part either. Physically I wasn't ready for the rigours of the First Division and I just wasn't a good enough footballer yet. I knew there were a few things that I had to work on, yet I found myself in the starting eleven for the very first time when we played Nottingham Forest at the City Ground the following week. Gordon clearly felt that it was a convenient time to see what I could do, the club having secured First Division safety at the end of a very poor campaign. I took Bob Latchford's place in the team, which went some way to spoiling the news earlier that week that he'd been recalled by England.

I couldn't believe that I would be playing a football match against a team managed by Brian Clough, though that game didn't go too well for me either. We lost 1–0, but nevertheless I had some first-team experience under my belt. Everton finished that 1979–80 campaign in a disappointing 19th position.

Before I could head back home for the eight-week summer break, there was a youth tournament in Gronigan, Holland, to take part in. We had a good team and we won the competition.

In the event, those subsequent two summer months back in Glasgow almost stretched to a lifetime because as the time for me to return to Merseyside drew nearer I just didn't want to go back down. I had really enjoyed being home again and I'm not exaggerating when I say that I was dreading the start of the new season.

Even though I now had two senior appearances to my name, I was still racked with self-doubt. The two games I had been involved in had been meaningless end-of-season matches and I hadn't read too much into my inclusion. Graeme Sharp and Everton just didn't seem right.

But I knew that I had to try and work through the self-doubt and I knew that I had a fantastic opportunity. My dad was always pointing out that it wasn't that far away – the train only took a few hours – and that he'd be down regularly. Another problem though, a big problem, was that I wasn't happy in the digs the club had sorted out for me. I was staying with a family in Score Lane in Childwall with three other youth players. The family was nice, but I just couldn't settle. Their regime didn't suit me. At night we'd get a pot of tea and three biscuits to share, which, as there were four of us, meant someone had to miss out. We soon started to make our own catering arrangements and would sneak out of the house at night and go to the local chippy for a big feed. We'd finish the food off back in the house and then throw the wrappers away the following morning on the way to training.

As luck would have it, when I reported back after that first summer break, I couldn't get into the house because the family was away on holiday. It was the excuse I needed to tell the club that I wanted to leave the place anyway and they put me up in a hotel by Greenbank Park while they sorted out some new accommodation.

Ray Minshull looked after all the young players' needs and he knew all the landladies that Everton used. He fixed me up with a family who lived in Town Row, West Derby, just two minutes from the training ground, and as soon as I went round there I took to the place. A lovely down-to-earth couple, Jimmy and Betty Duvall, ran the house. It was a genuine Liverpool family home and that was just what I needed. I felt settled straight away and it made a big difference.

Imre Varadi was also staying there at the time. He was an established first-team player and a real character. Compared to me, he was a real Jack the Lad. He had his own flash car and despite his exotic name, he is as cockney as Alf Garnett. But he was good to me.

One night during the season, we got some tickets to watch Liverpool play a European tie at Anfield. We left before the end so we could avoid the rush and cross Stanley Park to get to Imre's car, which was parked at Goodison. I was injured at the time with an ankle problem and as we cut through the park a group of six lads stopped us.

'What time is it?' one of them asked. That line usually meant a bit of trouble and with our accents we had no chance. Imre answered them in an accent straight off the River Thames. To my absolute horror, the gang promptly pulled out knives from their pockets and asked us how much money we had. We didn't hesitate. We ran as fast as we could. Bad ankle or not, I sprinted through the park with Imre and thankfully we had more pace then they did.

I must have done something right after coming back from my first summer break because I travelled with the first team to Marbella for the pre-season trip and I did fairly well. We played one friendly against a side called Castillas, which was basically Real Madrid's second team, and I played alongside Bob Latchford. We lost 2–1 and I scored our goal with a good shot from 20 yards after Asa Hartford had set me up. Bob was getting kicked all over the place by their centre-half throughout the game and as he came in for more and more punishment, I began to feel a bit disillusioned about him. I had him down as a tough 'take no prisoners' type of centre-forward and here he was, receiving rough treatment from a Spanish reserve-team player.

I should have known better! Very late in the game Bob caught this lad with an almighty whack as he attempted to clear the ball. Only Bob knew whether it was intentional or not, but it clearly had the desired effect. When I saw the lad around the hotel the following day on crutches, I knew that Bob was all right and could more than look after himself.

My other lasting memory of that trip was foolishly accepting a lift from Gordon Lee from the hotel to the training ground in a little Fiat he had borrowed from someone. Gordon drove out of the hotel and through the local lanes . . . all on the wrong side of the road! He paid no attention to the speed bumps, so I banged my head on the roof of the car every time he went over one. I thought he knew he was driving on the wrong side of the road and that he was doing it because there were few other vehicles about, but as he turned onto a main road we spotted a whole load of cars coming right towards us. I was screaming when he finally took evasive action and manoeuvred the Fiat into the correct lane!

I obviously made an impression myself on that tour and when we returned I managed to score my first-ever first-team goal at Goodison Park against the Dutch side Excelsior. I came on as a substitute and found the net with a last-minute header to seal a 4–0 win. All I'd done was ice the cake, but it was a very special moment for me.

My summer form was reasonable, although I was still surprised when Everton went to Sunderland for the 1980–81

First Division opener and I was in the starting line-up. We had a young side that day. The *Liverpool Echo* took a group photo as we left Bellefield for the North-east and in the caption we were called the 'Young Guns'.

We were soon shot down! Sunderland were newly promoted, Roker Park was absolutely bouncing and they beat us 3–1 in front of over 32,000 fans, which was, by some distance, the biggest gate I had ever played in front of. Big Sam Allardyce, who is currently managing Bolton Wanderers in the Premiership, was marking me. He must have done a good job because I was back on the bench for the next match, replaced by Peter Eastoe. I may have been young, but I was realistic: Gordon had shown a bit of faith in me, but I knew that I was some way off being ready to fight for a regular place. I was quite content to drop back down to the reserves with Colin Harvey and learn my trade.

Colin is a fabulous man, but he was hard taskmaster. He demanded 100 per cent from his players in everything they did and he would regularly fly off the handle. I have already mentioned that I scored for the reserves at Derby County in one of my early games, but on that occasion we had let a 3–1 lead slip to draw 3–3. Colin was absolutely furious and went ballistic in the dressing-room. It was frightening; it really was. He saved the worst of his tirade for Garry Stanley, who really got a tongue-lashing. We could only sit there and listen to Colin let off steam. We all skulked off into the showers, where the deathly silence was broken when Garry piped up, 'Has anyone got any conditioner?'

Colin went into orbit again. He stormed in, fully clothed, and grabbed Garry. 'Conditioner?' he screamed. 'Fucking conditioner? I'll give you conditioner, you fucking posing get.'

I didn't even finish washing: I just got out, got dried and dressed, and got on the coach!

But that was Colin. He knew that there was no way he could ever let senior professionals take any sort of liberty when there were youngsters in his team.

He had been a wonderful player himself and you could see it during the training sessions. His touch was still sublime and his awareness was second to none. I would have dearly loved to watch him in his prime. To this day, Evertonians speak in revered tones about the midfield trio of Colin Harvey, Alan Ball and Howard Kendall that played together when the club won the 1970 League Championship.

Colin would kick you in training if he felt that a game needed livening up. There was never an easy day with him. After the training sessions, he would organise five-a-side games and when he divided the lads into teams, nobody wanted to be on his side because there was too much pressure to win. You knew you'd have to work your socks off and even if the other team were winning, Colin would just keep playing the game until his own side had pulled it back. As soon as his team took the lead, he'd blow the whistle to end the game.

He pushed us exceptionally hard and it was often quite easy to resent him for it. After a hard morning's session, he would select certain players to come back after lunch for more work and, at times, it was awful. The other lads would be getting changed and going off to play snooker whilst half a dozen of us would work on possession, movement, shooting and the like. I tended to be an afternoon regular and I sometimes felt that Colin was deliberately picking on me. I could never say that I disliked the man because, even then, I had far too much respect for him, but I did think that he was giving me an unnecessarily hard time.

I didn't know any better, of course. I hadn't realised then that Colin cared too much about the game and too much about young footballers to do anything that wasn't beneficial.

Colin was a clever man. He could gauge the moods of the young players and after noting some dissent in my attitude when I was asked to do extra work, he took me to one side and told me that if he didn't think I had a chance of making it, then he wouldn't waste his time with me. He knew that sometimes we didn't like what we were doing, but he stressed that it was all for our benefit and, of course, he was right. But I still wasn't getting a look-in at first-team level.

At one stage, there was speculation that I was poised to move back to Scotland and join Hearts. In the same story, it was suggested that Gordon Lee had already lined up John Deehan at West Bromwich Albion as a replacement for me. Ian Wallace and Peter Withe were other names bandied about, which merely added to my general frustration.

A lad called Paul Maguire was actually about to sign for Everton from Shrewsbury Town for a fee of £260,000 when, at the eleventh hour, he failed the medical and the deal broke down.

Ironically, I was feeling a lot more settled off the pitch living with Jimmy and Betty, though I was still heading north whenever I could. If we didn't have a game at the weekend, Colin would have us at Bellefield on the Saturday morning for a training session and when it was over big George Wood, the goalkeeper, would drop me off at Wigan station on his way home to Parbold. That was something else to tell my pals back in Glasgow – I had a Scottish international goalkeeper as a chauffeur! Woody was a great lad, but I wouldn't have been quite so comfortable in the passenger seat had I known just how short-sighted he was. One day, one of the lads – and I can't remember who it was now – put on Woody's glasses for a laugh: he couldn't see anything! They had really strong lenses.

As tough as Colin was, he was wise enough to know that I was still a young lad living away from home and from time to time he would take me to one side on a Friday and give me the weekend off if we had no match.

When I wasn't going back up the road, I would watch the first team as often as possible. I remember on one of these weekends seeing Kevin Ratcliffe, later to become such a close friend, getting sent off in the FA Cup against Manchester City when he head-butted Tommy Hutchison.

Sometimes the reserves would kick off at 2 p.m. somewhere

in the local area and we would rush back to Goodison to catch the last 20 minutes or so of the first-team match. I would also watch the midweek games when I could.

While I was scoring goals and, in my opinion, playing well for the reserves, the first team were struggling. They were flirting with relegation and, if the newspapers were to be believed, Gordon was fighting for his job. I always had a lot of time for Gordon Lee and I still have. He is a genuinely nice man – if anything, he was perhaps too nice to be a football manager. He looked after me and always called me into his office to make sure that everything was OK. Like Colin, he knew the importance of allowing me to make the odd trip back to Scotland. I'll always be grateful to him for giving me the opportunity to play for Everton and I still enjoy his company when I meet him on the golf circuit these days.

But back in the spring of 1981 he needed someone to score the goals that would win him some football matches after losing six and drawing one of the previous seven, so he put me into the squad to play Middlesbrough at Goodison. I started on the bench but came on after only 22 minutes to replace Garry Stanley. It was the best I had felt in a first-team match. I changed the game a bit when I came on after getting brought down by Tony McAndrew for a penalty just before half-time, which Asa Hartford converted. We won 4–1, but the crowd of just over 15,000 was a reflection of how poorly the team was doing.

My appearance wasn't the most notable event of the day, though, because the referee collapsed in a heap with just 45 seconds gone after turning his ankle and one of the linesmen had to take over.

I got my first senior Goodison start a week later against Stoke City in our last home fixture of the season. It was a terrible afternoon and I didn't play at all well. The crowd were booing and chanting, 'Lee out, Lee out,' and we lost 1–0. Adrian Heath – Inchy – of all people scored the only goal. We were poor and that was it as far as my season went. I played no part in the last two matches.

Gordon's position had long been under threat and when we travelled away on the team coach, some wag from the team would always put Gloria Gaynor's 'I Will Survive' on the stereo. Sadly he didn't survive. The board took the decision to dispense with his services. We finished the season in 15th place.

There was a trip to Japan at the end of the season to take part in the Kirin Cup and since Gordon was sacked before it started, we left England under the charge of the new manager. I hadn't really expected to be on the trip, but I was selected and it gave me my first taste of travel with Howard Kendall.

FOUR

THE EVERTON BREAKTHROUGH

Howard Kendall had been a terrific player for Everton in the late '60s and early '70s and he was a popular choice amongst the fans as Gordon's replacement.

The Japanese trip in May 1981 was tremendous. It was the ideal way for Howard to get to know all the players and vice versa. We all met at Bellefield and Howard introduced himself in the dressing-room. We then jetted off from Manchester airport.

Alan Irvine, the assistant manager at Everton at the moment, was in the squad. Alan had just joined us from Queen's Park – in fact, his signing was a bizarre event. Gordon Lee had been interested in him for a long time, but Queen's Park had refused to let him go until the end of the season. They were an amateur side with rock-solid principles and they took the view that had Alan been allowed to leave whilst under contract, it might have opened the floodgates for other clubs to handpick their players.

Alan was actually at Goodison for transfer talks on the day Gordon was sacked. They were in a meeting when Gordon was called away to be informed of his impending dismissal. To his eternal credit, Gordon told Alan what had happened but still urged him to sign for Everton because it was the right move for him. That was a typical example of Gordon's integrity. It would have been easy for him to badmouth Everton, but, even though he was leaving, his natural instinct was to do the right thing for the club. Alan always maintains that Gordon's behaviour persuaded him to sign for Everton when he had 22 other clubs vying for his attention.

Japan is a fabulous place. We were taking part in the Kirin Cup in Tokyo along with the national team, China and Inter Milan, so it was quite a high-profile tour. We wanted to win, but it was an end-of-season trip so we hoped we'd get the opportunity to let our hair down and enjoy a bit of free time together – but this would depend on the new manager.

We didn't really know Howard, of course, but he made his mark on us straight away. He said he wanted us to win our three games but that there would be plenty of time for us to get out and about and enjoy the delights of Tokyo. In the event, we drew with Japan and beat China, but we were hammered 4–1 by Inter.

Alan Irvine played his first game in an Everton shirt against Inter and he was clearly keen to impress both the new manager and his new teammates. Every time he got the ball, he tried to take on the Italians virtually on his own, but they were having none of it and were queuing up to kick lumps out of him. They were volleying him all over the place.

I was still a little bit overawed in the company of my teammates, but we had some great nights out and I got to know a bit more about them – and, crucially, we all got to know more about Howard. He was brilliant on that tour because although he was new to the job and he obviously wanted to impress upon us that he was the boss and that we'd be doing things his way, he wasn't afraid to let us have some leisure time. He knew we'd just completed a long and difficult season and he knew the value of good team spirit. He treated us like adults and just pointed out that as we were representing Everton Football Club we had to behave ourselves. We didn't let him down.

When we reported back for pre-season training at Bellefield, there was a big shock for me. We were aware that we'd done badly the previous season and expected Howard to bring in some fresh faces, but we didn't envisage him signing *seven* new players for the forthcoming 1981–82 campaign, including two centre-forwards.

Mike Ferguson and Alan Biley came in and instantly moved above me in the pecking order. They were joined by two goalkeepers (Neville Southall and Jim Arnold), two midfielders (Alan Ainscow and Mickey Thomas) and one defender (Mike Walsh). The local press lapped it up and christened them 'The Magnificent Seven'.

Mickey Thomas came in from Manchester United – John Gidman went the other way – and was a really bubbly character and was just the same as he is now: daft as a brush! He drove to training in a flash car, a 2.8 litre Ford Capri, but only lasted 11 games before he was on his way again. He'd been named in the reserve team to play at Newcastle United one evening, but after seeing his name on the teamsheet pinned to the wall at Bellefield the day before the game he declared that he had no intention of going. He insisted for the rest of the day that he wouldn't be playing in the game, but we just assumed that he was letting off steam and that he'd be with us.

The following afternoon we were all sitting on the team bus outside Bellefield but were one short: Mickey hadn't shown. We waited and waited until we really had to leave for Newcastle and when we reported for a warm-down the next morning we discovered that Mickey was on the transfer list. It wasn't a surprise. Howard had no choice: he was establishing himself and he had to show that he wouldn't accept that sort of behaviour and that he wasn't going to be messed around by Mickey Thomas or anyone else.

Neville Southall, on the other hand, was very quiet when he first joined us. He lived in digs in Woolton and used to cycle to Bellefield on his bike. He'd work very hard on the training ground then cycle back home afterwards. He wasn't the best mixer in the dressing-room and he hasn't changed much over the years, although he's possibly become a bit more opinionated as he's grown older!

SHARPY

I thought the writing was on the wall for me when all these new players arrived: Peter Eastoe and Eamon O'Keefe were already first-choice strikers at the club. All my old insecurities came flooding back and I was doubtful that I had a future at the club. I had tasted a little first-team action and I'd been on the tour of Japan, but suddenly I just couldn't see myself staying at Everton.

Around this time, though, I did achieve a lifelong ambition by playing, and scoring, at Ibrox. We went to Glasgow to play against Rangers in a testimonial match for Colin Jackson. It was a pleasure for me to play because I'd watched Colin from the terraces as a youngster. A big defender, he played more than 500 matches for Rangers in a career spanning nineteen years and won eight caps for Scotland. I scored our goal in a 1–1 draw. It was fantastic for me. In my entire career that was the one and only time I ever played at Ibrox.

Despite the fact that Howard had brought a couple of new forwards into his squad, I still really enjoyed his first pre-season training session. On our first day back, which was effectively Howard's first real day in charge, there were footballs all over the place. Under Gordon Lee, the first couple of weeks were strictly fitness work and we scarcely had an opportunity to kick a ball, but with Howard it was quite the opposite. He believed that we got all the fitness we required by playing football matches. He organised competitions by splitting the whole squad into groups, with a couple of senior professionals, a couple of younger lads and some apprentices in each team, and we all threw a fiver into the kitty for the eventual winners. It was good, competitive stuff.

Although we perhaps didn't realise it at the time, we did an awful lot of running during the games as well. And even when we did basic running, it was tailored to suit individual needs. We could do the 12-minute circuit or 20 minutes at our own pace rather than to a pre-determined target. Howard was doing things his way and he had all the players on board with him immediately because we enjoyed the training regime so much.

However, once the season started, I didn't get a look-in.

I was even on the substitute's bench one night for the reserves against Manchester United, which to me seemed as clear an indication as any that Howard didn't fancy me as a player. I'd scored twice against Bolton in the previous reserves match and when I got dropped I thought to myself, 'I've got no chance here.' I was also starting to be linked to other clubs. Barnsley were rumoured to be interested in me again and so were Chesterfield. I was a touch confused by it all, although I was still too young and inexperienced to have gone knocking on Howard's door at Bellefield demanding to know what was going on or asking for a transfer. I was disillusioned, but I was still determined. I resolved to hang on in there and work as hard as I could with Colin on the training ground and in reserve matches, and that's exactly what I did, though I'd be lying if I said I wasn't worried about my situation.

Managers will always bring in their own players and if a new man at the helm doesn't like what is already there, he will ship players out: it's a fact of life in football. But I knew that Howard hadn't seen enough of me to really formulate an opinion. All I could do was hope and pray that I would eventually get a chance to show him what I could do.

I'd had a couple of substitute appearances in the first team – once when I came on for John Bailey at Stoke City when we lost 3–1 and again at Goodison for Alan Ainscow when we lost 1–0 to Manchester City – but I didn't really show much in either of those games and couldn't say with any justification that I deserved a run in Howard's team. Nevertheless I was playing well for the reserves and I was scoring goals.

A starting place finally arrived when we played Notts County at Meadow Lane. I think all Howard's other strikers were either injured or suspended. Ironically, he played himself in that game. It was a pleasure to be in the same team as Howard because he was so gifted even then; you could plainly see that Howard was still an extremely talented footballer. We all knew about the Harvey–Kendall–Ball trio that had done so well for Everton and we had seen just what a player he was in training. Whenever he joined us, he was often the best player on the pitch. He'd be pinging balls all over the place. He was still very fit. When he first took over, he'd told us that his intention was to stop playing, but Mick Heaton, his assistant, and Colin Harvey were always on at him to pull on a shirt and give himself a game. They persuaded him that he would still be capable of doing a job for the team. As player–manager, he only played four games for the first team, but we won three and drew the other, which tells you just how influential he could be.

At Notts County, I scored my first senior goal for Everton and what a lucky one it was! I hit a left-foot shot from about 25 yards and it deflected off Pedro Richards then squirmed past Raddy Avramovic, who really should have saved it. But it found the net and it got me up and running.

I played up front alongside Alan Biley, who scored our first goal in the 2–2 draw, and I thought we could have developed our partnership, but his own stay at Everton was nearing its end.

I kept my place for the next match, away against Arsenal, and although we lost 1–0 we were very unlucky on the day because we played really well. I had a good late chance saved by Pat Jennings. On the bus back to Merseyside, however, Howard had a right go at Alan about his performance. I couldn't believe it because Howard had brought Alan to the club and here he was giving him the dressing down of his life. Alan only played three more games for Everton after that.

Alan was a lovely lad, to be fair to him. He breezed in with his Rod Stewart-style hairdo and he had bags of confidence, but he was a down-to-earth guy. He actually got off to a good start at Everton when he scored in the opening two games of the season. The fans were desperate for a hero to replace Bob

Latchford and for a short while it looked as though Alan could be the one.

That rather fortuitous goal at Meadow Lane set me off. It was good that I had managed to score because Howard had thought about giving me a run in the side – although I didn't know that at the time. Had I not scored goals, then the pressure would have mounted on me very quickly. Goals can change everything. They can turn football matches on their head and they can make a young player's career. That was certainly the case with me. I was originally only in the team because Mick Ferguson was injured, but, even when he was fit, I kept him out of the starting eleven, which was a big boost for me.

A fortnight after the Notts County match, I scored my first League goal at Goodison Park against Swansea City. It was an incredible moment for me. Swansea had a really experienced side, with Alan Curtis, Robbie James, Leighton James and John Mahoney joined by ex-Everton players Dai Davies, Garry Stanley, Neil Robinson and Bob Latchford. I can recall my goal clearly: Howard played a great pass to Trevor Ross, who crossed the ball over for me to head past Davies.

The match was Howard's first at Goodison as a player since he had left the club in 1974 and so there was a lot of newspaper coverage, but the boss remained tight-lipped afterwards. He had no choice . . . he'd needed stitches in the inside of his mouth after taking a whack during the game.

I was up and running at last and I got my first regular run in the team.

We'd had an inconsistent start to the season, but after I broke into the team we had a good run of results (pure coincidence, I'm sure). The goal that really got Graeme Sharp noticed, and the one I still get asked about even now, was a volley past Ray Clemence against Tottenham at Goodison in November 1981. The game was televised by Granada and was the featured match on the Sunday afternoon football programme *Scotsport* on Scottish television. I remember that because it was one the few games that my dad couldn't make, so he watched it on television. Even though I say so myself, my goal was a cracker. It dropped over my shoulder and I volleyed it past Clemence from about 25 yards. It was a nice time to score a goal like that because I was still making a name for myself and that sure got me noticed. I asked the television lads to play it back for me over and over again after the match. I was young and felt confident, and trying my luck on the volley from so far out seemed the natural thing for me to do. That was the goal that made the Everton fans sit up and think that maybe I did have something about me.

Just like teams can often look back through history and select a pivotal match that changed their fortunes, so do footballers and that goal certainly altered a few things for me. To fire a rocket past a goalkeeper as experienced and well known as Clemence catapulted me into the spotlight. He said afterwards,'[I] only just saw the lad's shot, never mind reach it!'

Once again, my surname helped and I found myself being dubbed 'Sharp Shooter' or 'Razor Sharp'. My dad still devoured the papers, but he was filling the scrapbooks a lot faster than in the old days. Everything I had worked so hard for seemed to be sliding into place. I was re-enacting the passes I had made and the goals I had scored in the streets of Glasgow all those years before, only now they weren't on cobbles but at Highbury, Maine Road, White Hart Lane, Stamford Bridge and, of course, Goodison Park.

I was making waves in the First Division and making headlines in the papers, but it didn't change me as a person, I'm pleased to say. It was obviously nice to read about myself in the newspapers or watch myself on television, but I could still jump a bus into town on my day off . . . and often did without being recognised. I smile when I think about those days because I cannot imagine a young Premiership footballer standing at a bus stop, waiting for a lift into Liverpool city centre to do a bit of shopping. I can just envisage the chaos if James McFadden or Leon Osman walked out of Bellefield and caught the number 13 into town!

I was very pleased after a goalless draw with West Ham at Goodison Park at the end of February when their manager, John Lyall, told Howard that Billy Bonds had been very impressed with me. Apparently, *big* Billy wasn't one for dishing out praise too freely. It gave me the lift that I needed because I'd missed a few chances in that game and it was our third 0–0 draw in succession. But we were a young side and we were all still developing.

It helped me enormously that I was still living at Jim and Betty's at this time. Jim was a season-ticket holder and sometimes we'd share a taxi to the games. Even when I was scoring spectacular goals I couldn't get above my station if I'd been inclined to because Jim and Betty were so down to earth: they would have clipped me around the ear! I can't stress enough how much they helped me to settle on Merseyside.

Alan Irvine stayed at the house for a while and Kevin Richardson was in digs just around the corner, so we'd all go out for nights on the town after the games and I began to really feel at home. I was maturing as a person – moving away from home always helps an individual to grow up – and I was maturing as a footballer.

Paul Lodge was still a good pal, as were Steve McMahon and Joe McBride, and I was enjoying life. It's like anything: once you make a breakthrough and put your foot in the door, you can mix more freely with those around you and you have the belief to move forward and progress. That's what was happening to me and it was exhilarating.

My trips back up to Glasgow were becoming less frequent and Ann Marie would sometimes come down and stay. I was finding the success I was enjoying on the football pitch the best cure for homesickness. My dad still came to as many matches as he possibly could, but I didn't go back with him as regularly as I had done when I first joined Everton. He was content with that, though, because he knew full well that if I wasn't desperate to get back to Glasgow, then I must be feeling much happier.

SHARPY

People talk about my partnership with Inchy that season, but Howard initially signed him as a midfield player. My favoured partner was in actual fact Peter Eastoe. I really enjoyed playing alongside him. He was a far better footballer than a lot of people gave him credit for and I don't think he'd interpret it as an insult if I said he was a poor man's Kenny Dalglish. Kenny was one of the best in the world and Peter had a few of his traits. He could shield the ball superbly well, hold it up when he got it and he had a terrific touch. We had a very good partnership.

When Inchy first arrived, he struggled to make an impression. He'd been signed from Stoke City for big money – £700,000 – and I think the punters expected more from him than they were seeing. He confided in me that the level of expectation was a bit much for him. He'd come from a club that, with all due respect, was nowhere near as big as Everton and he couldn't adapt to the hunger for football in Liverpool. He claimed that he was getting it everywhere he went, every minute of the day, and it took some getting used to. Howard had worked with him at Stoke, where they had been teammates, and he knew that Inchy could operate up front. When he moved forward, he was an instant success and we did so well that Peter Eastoe couldn't get back in.

Just as it had with Peter, my partnership with Inchy developed naturally. We got on very well off the field and we didn't have to work at it too much on the pitch either. He was an intelligent footballer and would play off me and pick up my flicks and headers. This was a new role for me, in some respects, because Peter had been the main striker in the past and it was my job to feed off him.

We had some smashing games during that 1981–82 season, none more so than the one against Manchester United with whom we shared six goals at Goodison that April. United were a big club and we always wanted to beat them. I remember scoring one and setting up the other two, one each for Inchy and Mike Lyons.

Lyonsy was as big an Evertonian as you are ever likely to meet and, as well as scoring against United that day, he also played in goal. Neville had to leave the field in the last minute after being injured and, as we all looked at each other to see who would be brave enough to take his gloves, up stepped Lyonsy. I didn't expect anything less – he would have done anything for the Everton cause.

Lyonsy has always been very good to me. Back then, he tried to bring me on by including me in the dressing-room banter, which was passing me by at times. I found it difficult to join in when the stick was flying around – particularly when it came from the Scousers in the squad. Lyonsy also gave me a great piece of advice when I was becoming a bit disillusioned at not getting a first-team opportunity. He told me that the hardest thing in football was trying to force your way out of the reserve team – I soon knew what he meant.

He also spotted during one game against Arsenal that I had been too much in awe of David O'Leary. It was only my second first-team start and when Lyonsy pulled me after the game, I had to agree with him. I had always rated O'Leary very highly and I was apprehensive facing him. Lyonsy assured me that it was only natural but pointed out that I should have more confidence in myself.

I'd been involved in some right ding-dong tussles with big Lyonsy during training. Colin Harvey used to organise first team versus the reserves matches and they were hard games. There was no way you would pull out of tackles like you'd be expected to today. I think Lyonsy respected me for that and always told Howard that he didn't fancy playing against me, which was a compliment. He was the captain of the first team and he looked out for me because he'd seen that I could do it in training.

The midweek home fixture with Nottingham Forest towards the end of April was a real red-letter day for me. At lunchtime, I found out that I had been included in the Scotland Under-21 squad to face England at Maine Road in a European Championship qualifier and in the evening I shot both Everton goals past Peter Shilton in a 2–1 win to earn a huge bottle of champagne from the match sponsors as their man of the match. Those goals started a run of seven in the last six matches of the season that left me on a total of fifteen. I always set that number as my target for every League season. I never classed myself as a Gary Lineker or an Ian Rush, who would both regularly get 30 goals, but I always tried to at least reach my own personal target and it was exceedingly gratifying to do so at the end of my first full season. Only Steve McMahon played more games than me during 1981–82 and I received a nice personal boost when I won that year's *Liverpool Echo* Everton Player of the Year award. The local paper selected a man of the match after every game and then totted up their totals at the end of the season. Graeme Souness received the Liverpool award and, in the words of the *Echo*, I was the 'runaway winner' at Everton with nine nominations. Lyonsy and Big Nev were joint second with four each.

We finished in eighth position in the table and, after having struggled against relegation the previous two seasons, that represented success. The only disappointment really had been our FA Cup exit at West Ham in the third round. We had been 1–2 down when I got tripped up by Ray Stewart in the very last minute to win us a penalty. Trevor Ross stepped up . . . and missed. It was a terrible way to go out. Still, I was just excited to have played in the FA Cup. I knew all about the magic of the competition and there I was playing in it. It was part of a thrilling new experience and I loved it.

And I was learning all the time. For example, after the West Ham FA Cup defeat, I realised that I was laying the ball off too quickly. I wasn't keeping hold of it long enough to consider my options and at times it was putting the team under pressure. I had been a one-touch player at Dumbarton, but I soon realised the importance of retaining possession. Colin Harvey had helped me with that aspect of my game and overall I was reasonably pleased with my progress as an Everton player. I was becoming increasingly confident and felt more like an established professional. But I still had a slight build and there were times when I could be bullied out of games. If anything, I was too honest a player. If I got kicked from pillar to post by a centre-half, I just assumed that it was part and parcel of being a centre-forward and I wouldn't give it back. Until we played Leeds United at Goodison.

I was being marked by Kenny Burns and I thought that as a fellow Scot he wouldn't give me too hard a time. I couldn't have been more wrong. He caught me early in the game and I had every reason to believe he was going to do so again. My dad had always warned me that this type of thing would happen and he stressed the importance of looking after myself properly on the pitch. 'Don't be bullied, son,' he'd say. 'You've got to stand up for yourself.'

His words rang in my head after Burns had caught me again and when a long high ball came towards us, I caught him right on the bridge of his nose with my elbow.

Play continued before the ball eventually went out for a corner at the Gwladys Street end and when I turned around, Burns was still flat out on the halfway line with his nose all over his face. The Leeds trainer patched him up and I thought the first thing he would do would be to seek retribution, but he never came near me. My dad's advice had been good. I was learning quickly. We beat Leeds 1–0. I scored the goal and they got relegated at the end of the season. It was a pivotal moment for me and I decided there and then that I wouldn't be intimated by anyone any more.

My end to the season was quite spectacular. I was on a run that all strikers dream about. Not only was I scoring, but they were also all good goals – the type that made headlines. I blasted in the goal against Leeds, for example, from 30 yards, past John Lukic. It seemed that Howard was talking me up after every game and I was full to the brim with confidence. I scored twice on the last day in a 2–1 against Aston Villa and signed off with another man of the match award. What a year!

SHARPY

I had started the season counting the strikers ahead of me in the manager's plans and by the end of it I was the club's leading scorer, having pushed summer signings Alan Biley and Mick Ferguson out of the first-team frame and onto the transfer list. I didn't want the campaign to come to an end and I couldn't wait for the end-of-season trip because I felt much more a part of the club now. When I discovered that we were travelling to Israel, it couldn't come quickly enough.

We were based in Tel Aviv and our hotel was right on the beach. It is a lovely city, but the sights and sounds of fighter jets crossing the sky at the time to and from south Lebanon was slightly unnerving.

We had ended the season strongly, we knew we'd done well and, sure enough, Howard encouraged us to enjoy ourselves and unwind. He reminded us that we were representing the football club so we were to avoid any unsavoury publicity, but he gave us plenty of opportunity to have a good time. We played a local team, but it was a low-profile match and I can't even remember the score.

I shared a room with Inchy on the trip and although we'd been out one night until the small hours, we were thoroughly determined to be up at 10 a.m. for the trip of a lifetime: the Everton party was being taken to Jerusalem. It was something that I, for one, was really looking forward to. It was an outing that I didn't want to miss.

Inchy and I duly woke up at ten o'clock . . . then realised it was ten o'clock at night. We'd not only missed the trip, we'd also slept through the whole day and most of the next evening. I couldn't understand why it was dark outside when my watch said ten o'clock. When it dawned on us what had happened, we were absolutely gutted and we took some unmerciful stick from the lads. Howard also fined us and we had to pay for the first few rounds of drinks. Before leaving for Israel, I'd told all my family that I would be going to Jerusalem and I was so embarrassed when I was forced to confess on our return home. But what a fabulous trip it was.

Jim Greenwood, the club secretary, came with us and he was a tremendous man. Some of the directors were there as well: Jack Search, Bill Scott, Alan Waterworth, David Newton and Sir Philip Carter. They were a great group of men. The hotel approached them on our last morning and offered us a massive farewell party, which of course they gratefully accepted. The hotel staff promptly decorated the place in Everton colours, had banners specially made, ordered a sumptuous banquet and filled the shelves with fine wine and champagne. The night was going like a dream and we were being royally looked after until the hotel manager handed Jim Greenwood the bill for the entire event. Jim's face went pale when he looked at the figure at the bottom of the bill and he passed it to the directors.

'Pay it,' they said. 'It's been a wonderful evening, so pay it.'

That was so typical of the atmosphere within the football club at the time. Howard should take a lot of credit for the fact that the whole club was being run in such a warm and friendly manner. He knew that Jim and the directors would be good tourists and would join in with the lads. Bill Scott used to play golf with the boys and then we'd share a few drinks in the clubhouse afterwards. It was very good for morale: there was none of the 'us' and 'them' attitude. Everyone, and I mean everyone, got on with each other. We were all looking forward to the new 1982–83 season with real confidence.

I'd finished the previous campaign very well and was determined to keep it going in the summer friendlies. I had also decided that I quite fancied a change of image and opted for a perm, which was very fashionable at the time. (Actually, it wasn't a perm, it was a demi-wave, though I didn't really know the difference, if I'm being honest – even when I did, I would never have tried to explain it to anyone in Glasgow!) Some of the other Everton lads, like Kevin Richardson (Richo), Inchy and I think Bails (although he will claim that his was natural), had one done and I just thought, 'Why not?' I'd never been anywhere near brave enough to have anything like it done before and it didn't look too bad when it was first done. Although, as it grew, it got a bit wild!

In pre-season, we went to Belgium for a four-team tournament and acquitted ourselves reasonably well. I scored two goals in a 4–3 defeat against Lokeren and I found the net 24 hours later when we secured third place in the mini-tournament with a fine 2–1 win over Italian outfit Genoa. On our return home, I added a couple more in pre-season friendlies during a stroll against Witton Albion and then converted a penalty in a 6–1 win at Wigan Athletic.

The team spirit amongst the lads was first class and it had most certainly been helped by Howard's first summer signing: Andy King. Kingy was a huge character, a typical cockney. He never shut up, but he had the most amazing skill. He could do incredible tricks with a ball at his feet. I remember one afternoon after training he set the apprentices a challenge: he bet them that he could juggle a football longer than they could and, to give them a fighting chance, he said he'd do his juggling sitting down. The young kids snapped up his offer and Kingy stood to lose a few quid. We all gathered round to watch, but the outcome was never in doubt: Kingy sat down, started juggling the ball and just kept it going and going. He was still juggling long after the last apprentice had lost control. It was amazing to see! He was a really bubbly lad to have around. Kingy had spent four seasons with Everton in the late '70s and it was unfortunate for him that this second spell at Everton didn't really work out, although the injuries he picked up contributed to that. He was transferred to Wolves at the end of 1983–84.

The other new signing, Kevin Sheedy from Liverpool, was just the opposite – in character anyway. We thought he was a rather strange signing because he'd got nowhere near the first team at Anfield. He was a very shy, reserved lad. But as soon as we were training with him every day, we saw why Howard had picked him up. What a left foot! He had great ability and could put the ball on a sixpence. He was a centre-forward's dream and over the years I developed a terrific working partnership with him. Whenever he got the ball onto his left foot in a wide position, I knew instinctively where he would cross it. Nine times out ten, Sheeds would put it just where I wanted it.

We now had the makings of a quality midfield. Steve McMahon was, of course, still in there as well. He had everything. A measure of his ability was that Colin Harvey had rated him very highly from an early age. He broke into the first-team frame at the same time as Paul Lodge, but Macca had more tenacity about him and stood out. He never saw eye to eye with Howard, though, and he didn't get the contract offer he felt he deserved, which ultimately led to his departure at the end of the season. It was a big loss for us when he moved to Aston Villa.

He was still a regular in the team in 1982–83 and we made a solid enough start – though we lost to newly promoted Watford on day one – winning five and drawing two of our opening eleven matches, including a 5–0 thumping of Aston Villa, when I kept up my excellent record against them by scoring two more goals. They were European champions by then, of course, which is a measure of the quality of our display against them.

Another game that sticks in the mind was a 1–1 home draw with Norwich City when Alan Irvine scored a cracking goal for us. I was having a right old battle with Steve Walford and, of all people, Dave Watson, who later became not only a colleague at Everton but also a very good friend. I was determined to look after myself. I'd had a couple of clatterings from Waggy before I gave him one back with my elbow. Walford was outraged and rushed over to shove me to the ground. He was booked, I wasn't.

Waggy, who needed four stitches in the wound on his cheek, said afterwards that it was just one of those things, which was typical of him. He dished it out and took it back in equal measure. He was as hard as nails and I was glad that he was on my side a couple of years later: I wouldn't have liked to face him too often, knowing that he might have been looking for retribution. But

Walford and the Norwich manager, Ken Brown, both had a go at me in the papers the next day.

I wasn't exactly the sort of striker who would go out to rough up a defender without good reason. If I got kicked, I considered it part and parcel of the position I was playing in, but if it happened again I would warn the centre-half that I would be giving him some back. I genuinely didn't want to play that way, but sometimes you had no option. I was never going to allow myself to be kicked out of games or get battered from pillar to post: I learned to give as good as I got and, as my career progressed, opposition players realised that.

The team was moving along nicely . . . and then we met Liverpool.

I speak a bit more in-depth about that fateful day later in the book, but, suffice to say, it was an excruciating afternoon for everybody connected with Everton Football Club: we lost at home to Liverpool 5–0. It was a devastating setback. I was particularly down about it because though I was playing regularly, my goalscoring record wasn't as good as I'd have liked and it worried me a bit.

When Howard brought David Johnson back to the club, I had another striking partner. I was looking forward to learning from such a decorated professional and, for his part, Johnno was relishing teaming up alongside me. Or at least he said he was! When he spoke to the press boys, he told them: 'I've watched Graeme against Liverpool and there is no doubt he has everything you need, as long as he remembers not to start thinking that he's made it. No matter how many goals he's scored, he needs to be always looking for more. I hope I hit it off with Graeme as well as I did with Trevor Whymark at Ipswich and Kenny [Dalglish] at Liverpool.'

Johnno had won European cups with Liverpool and he'd played for England, but he would be the first to admit that his second spell at Goodison wasn't a success. He didn't score goals and the crowd got on his back. He was a great professional and he used to have arguments with Howard about the way the team were playing. Johnno thought we were too direct at times and I think he had a point.

Some of the fans just couldn't forgive Johnno for achieving success at Liverpool. You have to remember that these were tough times for our supporters: they hadn't enjoyed success since the team won the Championship in 1970 and our barren run coincided with a purple patch for our neighbours from across the park. Our fans were frustrated with us – even Kevin Ratcliffe took some unmerciful terrace flak. He had been introduced as a left-back, but he didn't exactly excel in that position and he only began to win the fans over when he moved infield to centre-half, which came about because Howard had lost patience with Billy Wright.

Billy was, by human nature, a large-framed lad, but Howard believed that he could have lost some weight if he had really applied himself to the task. Billy's weight, if anything, went up rather than down and Howard dropped him from the team in December 1982 and put Rats in his place. Rats never looked back and Billy never played for Everton again. 'Billy's failed a fatness test' was Howard's famous line.

Rats and Mark Higgins (Higgy) formed an excellent partnership. I remember seeing Higgy getting pain-killing injections into his groin before a match at West Ham. It was the first time I'd seen anything like it. He would go to any lengths to play for Everton.

Thankfully, that 5–0 thrashing from Liverpool didn't knock us back too much and we steadied ourselves and got some good results.

We battered Luton Town 5–0 at Goodison, where John Bailey scored a goal from inside his own half. Jake Findlay was in goal for Luton and Bails had possession for us and lumped it forward. It was meant for me, but Bails hit it too hard so I never even bothered going for it. Instead, I watched as it bounced up and sailed over Findlay into the net. 'Pelé tried it once, but he missed!' quipped Bails after the game.

That should have really set the alarm bells off for me – Everton winning a game 5–0 without me scoring and John Bailey getting one!

Terry Curran played for us in that game after joining us on loan from Sheffield United. He was a maverick player who couldn't seem to settle anywhere, but our punters loved him. He was fantastic and was overflowing with self-confidence every time he pulled on the blue shirt. He played very well, creating goals and scoring them, and the fans urged Howard to make the signing permanent. For one reason or another, we couldn't get Terry until the following season and when he did come back I thought he was bloody awful! As far as I could see, he couldn't do a thing right! But back in 1982–83, he was a real breath of fresh air.

As was another new signing at whom many people had raised their eyebrows: Peter Reid. He didn't exactly arrive at Goodison Park with a clean bill of health behind him. Gordon Lee had tried to sign him from Bolton a few years earlier for very big money, but Reidy had broken his leg and the deal fell through. After that, nobody would take a chance on him until Howard virtually stole him for £60,000.

We knew that he could play, but we also knew that he was injury prone and we weren't convinced that Reidy could help us move to the next level. The doubters thought they'd been proved right when he picked up another injury after playing only ten games for us, but Reidy would prove them all dramatically wrong in the fullness of time.

My lack of goals in the middle third of the campaign was a source of real irritation to me. My record at one stage was a single goal from 18 matches, which by any standards is not good enough. Howard stood by me and I didn't miss many games, but I was concerned that I would be regarded as a one-season wonder. Howard assured me that as long as I was contributing to the team then I had no worries about my place in the side. I had always considered myself to be more than just a goalscorer so Howard's words were nice to hear, but I still craved a return to the scoring form I'd enjoyed the previous season.

But the goals had dried up for me. Also, Johnno and I didn't hit it off as a striking pair. Some people said I was suffering from the 'second season' syndrome and that defenders knew a bit more about me, but I'm not so sure.

I was doing OK in practice sessions, though throughout my Everton career I could never hope to reconstruct any lost confidence on the training ground because of one man. Neville Southall was a nightmare to train with because he was so difficult to score past! With all due respect to Jim Arnold, we were far happier doing our shooting practice against him.

Big Nev would take the mickey at times by standing on one side of his goal so that you had the rest of it to aim at. Even then he'd fling himself full length and keep the ball out. Believe me, training could be really soul destroying at times.

However, it was not finding the net on a Saturday that was getting me down at that time, but I knew I just had to work through it. Nowadays clubs employ psychologists and motivational coaches to help the players, but in those days it was just a case of plugging away by yourself and trying to put things right. It wasn't nice being reminded in the press that I was going through a barren spell, but, as I'd enjoyed all the positive headlines the previous season, I realised that I had to accept the negative ones when things weren't going according to plan.

Eventually, after just three goals from twenty-one games, I was dropped to the bench. There was no ranting or raving from either me or Howard. He merely pointed out that I needed a rest. On the face of it, I could have no complaints, but the contrast in my fortunes from one season to the next wasn't lost on me.

Thankfully my expulsion from the team lasted for just three matches. Inchy was unlucky to pick up an injury and, after missing one match completely and then having two substitute run-outs, I was back to face Nottingham Forest at Goodison. It was Reidy's debut and the game that I finally rediscovered my goal touch.

I scored two in a 3–1 win, one of which was beautifully created by Reidy. I should have had a hat-trick, but I wasn't too concerned about the late chances that went begging – I was far too relieved to be back amongst the goals – though there was another huge disappointment ahead of me later in the campaign in the shape of our FA Cup sixth-round tie with Manchester United.

We defeated Newport County, Shrewsbury and Tottenham to reach the quarter-finals and I was just beginning to dream about Wembley when we went to Old Trafford. We had a young side, but we gave them a right good game in front of a packed stadium. We thought we'd done enough to earn a replay, but then they brought on Lou Macari as a late substitute and he volleyed a cracking goal in the last minute to win the tie. What a blow!

We finished the season strongly again, including a 5–1 spanking of Luton at Kenilworth Road, and I ended with another goalscoring flurry. I bagged seven goals in the last eight games and, being the type of player who always liked to analyse each season when it finished, I was satisfied to once again reach my target of fifteen. I thought that Howard was still tinkering with his team a bit too much, but we clearly had the nucleus of a decent side.

Although 1982–83 hadn't been that good a season for me, I was playing regularly again and was happy with my form. I really felt like an Everton player.

I had no inkling of what was to follow.

FIVE
WEMBLEY GLORY

The main event of my summer of 1983 was my marriage to Ann Marie. We tied the knot in the Catholic church of St Joseph's in Cardowan, near to where I was born. The ceremony took place on 10 June 1983 and Kevin Richardson was my best man.

The subject of religion was raised at this point because, as Protestants, my parents weren't happy that I was getting married in a Catholic church. As I've already stressed, I wasn't bothered by religion one jot, but Ann Marie was a practising Catholic who attended Mass regularly, as did her parents, so I was quite content to go along with what she wanted. But my mum and dad weren't too happy with it.

Don't get me wrong, they thought the world of Ann Marie, and still do, and they were delighted that I was marrying the right girl, but they had their own beliefs and would have preferred their youngest son to walk down a Protestant aisle. Unfortunately for them, my church attendance had ended abruptly when the Stepps Boys' Brigade reluctantly accepted my transfer request many years earlier!

As I was busy earning my living some 250 miles south of Glasgow, I didn't have too much involvement in any of the wedding plans, other than the obligatory meeting with Father Herbert Flack beforehand. He is still the St Joseph's parish priest to this day, having started there back in 1972. I didn't have time for a proper stag night; I just had a few drinks with some friends from Glasgow. Paul Lodge, Kevin Richardson and a few other pals from Liverpool came up for it, too.

The night before the wedding, I went out with Ann Marie's dad, John, and her brother, who was driving us. On the approach home, we travelled along a stretch of road by Millerston called 'Three Hills', so-called because that is quite literally what it consists of. John, who, like myself, had had a few drinks, was in the passenger seat and because we could only see the lights of the car behind us when it was at the top of one of the sharp hills, he was under the incorrect impression that the driver was flashing his headlamps at us! After the third hill, John was convinced that we were being harassed by this car and when we stopped at some traffic lights, he did no more than jump out of the passenger door, march up to the vehicle behind us and punch the driver right in the face! I was laughing my head off, but Ann Marie, who later found out about it, was absolutely disgusted!

After the wedding, Ann Marie and I moved into our first house together in Ainsdale. We didn't have time for a honeymoon because I wanted us to sort everything out with regards to our new place before the season started.

When I focused my mind back on football, I relished the challenge of really starting to move on as a First Division player. I had already endured the ups and downs of life as a professional but as I had finished the previous season in a rich vein of form I fully expected to be part of Howard's plans when the new term got under way. Sure enough, I was in the starting line-up for the curtain-raiser against Stoke City at Goodison and I scored the only goal in our 1–0 victory. It was an awful game, but at least we were up and running.

Or so we thought. Subsequent results were not very good and, once again, I suffered a barren spell in front of goal. Howard had brought in Trevor Steven for the new season and we could see that he was a good player. There had been a lot of speculation about whether or not he'd join Everton from Burnley or sign for Liverpool, but in the end Howard paid big money for him. He took some time to settle, but big things were expected of him and he was straight in the team at the start of the season.

Howard was a great fan of his, but he started to struggle after making the big jump to the top flight. He was a quiet lad and he wasn't naturally a great mixer. It's difficult when you join a new club and Trevor came in without knowing a single soul. Also, and most crucially, the team wasn't playing well, so Trevor was trying to settle into an indifferent side.

I was struggling to find my scoring touch as Christmas approached but the difference this time was that I wasn't playing as well as I had done when the goals had dried up 12 months earlier. Our bad results indicated that I wasn't the only one. In fact, one of the few players to acquit himself with any sort of consistency was Alan Harper, who we'd signed from Liverpool in the summer.

I used to play against Harpo in reserve mini-derbies when I first came down from Scotland and he was always excellent. He played centre-half and sweeper, and I never got much change out of him. He was a great footballer: good on the ball and he could pass it well. It was still a bit of a surprise when Howard brought him across the park, but I knew he was a good player. He rarely had a bad game for us and was unfortunate not to play more often. The fans were a bit sceptical when he arrived because he'd only been in Liverpool's reserve team, but Harpo could play, no doubt about that, and he soon won them over.

The team was a mixture of youth and experience, with Higgy, Bails, Johnno and Kingy alongside me, Trevor, Rats and Kev Richo, but it wasn't working. We lost against teams that we were capable of beating. The likes of Ipswich, West Ham, Luton Town, Leicester City and Norwich all defeated us before the end of November and we couldn't muster a single goal against any of them.

We'd only just managed to stumble past Chesterfield over two legs in the second round of the Milk Cup. I scored the only goal at Saltergate and we then drew 2–2 at home to scrape through.

Goodison crowds were down and Howard was suddenly under pressure.

I don't think there was one single player who could look at himself and claim that he was happy with his form. I was decidedly unhappy with mine. My dad would ring me after every game that he hadn't been able to come down to see and ask me to talk him through everything in minute detail. If I hadn't done well, he'd ask me why. If I'd scored, he'd want me to describe it, likewise if I'd missed chances. He may well have seen the highlights on the television, but he still wanted a full blow-by-blow account from me. It was his way of ensuring that there were no extenuating circumstances to anything. He knew when I was up and he knew when I was down: he didn't need to ask me.

At the beginning of November, Liverpool battered us 3–0 at Anfield when Howard played me as a lone striker and we never had a shot on goal. It was embarrassing. Our self-belief was on the floor when we welcomed Coventry City to Goodison three days later for the next round of the Milk Cup. I consider that night to be one of the most significant in the club's history. Had we not won that game, the knives would have been sharpened for Howard and our famous match later in the tournament at Oxford United would never have taken place.

We went a goal behind against Coventry; it was lashing down and there were only 9,000 fans inside Goodison. We could hear all the abuse from those that had bothered to turn up and most of them were urging the board to sack Howard. Then Reidy came on as a substitute for Trevor, Inchy scored an equaliser and we were back in it. But I had turned my ankle and it was giving me serious discomfort. Had our one substitute not already been on, I would have gone off, but I had to soldier on and try to offer as much 'nuisance value' as I could. Incredibly in the very last minute, we silenced the boos when a cross came over to the back post and I did enough to head it into the net.

Just as in the previous round, we had limped through (quite literally in my case!). There was no way I was going to be able to play in the next game and so a certain Andy Gray made his debut.

In an attempt to freshen things up, Howard had gone to Wolves and returned with my boyhood idol! It was a bolt from the blue because there hadn't even been any speculation. But I was thrilled because I thought so highly of him and had looked up to him for such a long time. He breezed into the Bellefield dressing-room on his first day and went round all the lads introducing himself. There was no shyness whatsoever.

As he made his way around the room, shaking everyone's hand, I could see the lads looking him up and down and gesturing to each other. Andy had on a pair of jeans with a turned-up hem that went almost to his knees! He'd clearly got a pair that was far too long for him and his missus, instead of shortening them, had folded the hems inside the legs and ironed them! They looked ridiculous. He later confessed that he threw them straight in the bin when he got home on that first day.

He was just the sort of character we needed, though. He was terrific: a breath of fresh air. And you could hear him long before you saw him. He had an unbelievable will and a desire to win football matches and, although our fortunes didn't turn around immediately, he made sure we were never down for too long after a poor result, which is important to a group of young players.

Andy was always encouraging me. He was a great believer in strikers attacking the posts: one at the near post and one at the far post. 'Let the midfielders take the middle,' Andy would say. He was magnificent at attacking the ball at the back stick.

He was also fiercely keen to foster a positive team spirit. Andy had been around and he knew the value of a close-knit dressing-room. He didn't take long to instigate the team bonding sessions that took place in Southport on a Sunday.

Andy lived in Formby and he nominated the Falstaff pub in Southport as our regular meeting place the day after the Saturday games. We all had to be there by midday for a few beers. We'd have a great laugh and talk the game out of our systems. In those days, the bars closed on a Sunday at 3 p.m., but of course we knew where we could get a lock-in. As a newly married woman, Ann Marie wasn't too happy at my inclusion in these bonding sessions, but Andy insisted that everyone made the effort. Even Reidy used to travel over from Manchester.

Andy's recruitment helped the team to move in the right direction, but for my money, it was the promotion of Colin Harvey from reserve to first-team coach that really took us to the next level. Mick Heaton, sadly no longer with us, was a lovely man, but the feeling was he didn't have the respect of the players that Colin had. I must stress that's no slight on Mick whatsoever because he was a big part of our eventual success, but the young lads like myself, Gary Stevens, Kev Richo and Rats had all grown up with Colin. Mick was a more easy-going man, whereas if Colin told you to jump, you jumped and you never questioned why. He was great with us and he also knew how to deal with senior professionals like Andy and Reidy.

His promotion was massive for Everton. The Coventry game was a turning point for us that season, as was the game at Oxford, but I will always maintain that the elevation of Colin Harvey from the reserves to the first team was *the* main reason that we went on to achieve what we did.

He didn't come in and change things around too much, it was just his overall influence and his attention to detail that we noticed. He worked incredibly hard with individuals and he would always obtain a video of the game and then go through it painstakingly with certain players on the Monday morning. They do that now, of course, but it is called sport science. It didn't matter who you were: if Colin thought you needed to learn something from an incident in any of the games, then you'd get the Monday morning call to sit with him and watch the video. He was a forward thinker and he'd often tell the player to take the video home and watch it again to make sure he was aware of the point that was being put across.

He made subtle changes and all of a sudden we started to knit together, though it was by no means an overnight transformation. Between the middle and end of December, we played four games and didn't score a single goal – including a 3–0 whipping at Wolves, which was as bad as we played all season. Wolves were bottom of the table – by some distance, I hasten to add – but they brushed us aside. Wayne Clarke scored one of their goals. Later, when he joined Everton and we were chatting about that game, he told me, 'We were an awful side, but that was our easiest game all season. I thought you'd struggle to stay up.'

Had we been beaten at Oxford in the next round of the Milk Cup, Howard might well have been sacked, but we got the draw and it really felt as though a massive weight had been lifted, though it was a horrible game and I got kicked all over the place by their central-defenders, Malcolm Shotton and Gary Briggs. Oxford had a reputation as a giant killer and they looked as though they were going to add our scalp to their list when Kevin Brock put one on a plate for Inchy.

We lived to tell the tale and when we brought Oxford back to Goodison, we thrashed them 4–1 on a very cold and snowy night. From staring down the barrel, we suddenly found ourselves tied against Aston Villa in the Milk Cup semi-finals with a great chance of making it to Wembley.

Kev Richo and Sheeds scored our goals in a 2–0 first-leg semi-final win against Villa at Goodison – everyone remembers Kev playing with a cast on his arm. When we were two goals up, he blatantly cleared an effort off the line with his hand. Villa were understandably livid and after the game we warned Kev not to say on television that the ball had struck his hand. 'Just deny it,' we told him. 'Don't admit to anything.'

What we didn't know was that the cameras showed, beyond question, that it had been handball. So there was Kev, a young lad doing one of his first-ever television interviews, facing the camera and looking decidedly nervous. They showed the incident and, sure enough, the ball came back off his hand. When the interviewer said, 'That was a handball that you got away with,' Kev replied, 'No, it wasn't!' We were watching it and all just fell about laughing.

Down at Villa Park for the second leg, we had Kingy making one of his rare starts. He made a mistake that gave them a 1–0 lead on the night and was terrified that his error was going to cost us a place at Wembley. I hit the post and so did Inchy, but there was no more relieved man inside that stadium than Andy King when the final whistle went.

Steve McMahon was in the Villa side and I suggested to him that he must regret leaving the club now. I just lapped it all up – the scenes at the end, singing in the dressing-room, the champagne in the big bath. It took a while for it to sink in that I was actually going to play in a cup final at Wembley Stadium. And, of course, we knew we would be playing Liverpool.

The first-ever all-Merseyside League Cup final was an amazing spectacle to be a part of. I'd never even been to Wembley before – not even as a spectator – so it was an unbelievable experience to be there on the day we were making history. There was a lot of hype ahead of the game and although Liverpool were the clear favourites before the kick-off, we knew that we had a chance. Our form was excellent and even without the Cup-tied Andy Gray, we fancied ourselves. From the beginning of December through to the Milk Cup final at Wembley, we had played twenty-seven matches and lost only four of them.

We had grown as a team and, I firmly believe, we had grown as men. The promising youngsters were now very good First Division footballers and Howard was close to getting the team he had always wanted, playing in the style that he craved. And don't forget that we went to Wembley with a place in the semi-finals of the FA Cup already secured.

It was pouring with rain at Wembley and although the match ended goalless, we should have won the game. The referee, Alan Robinson, denied us a clear penalty when Alan Hansen handled a shot from Inchy. We left the field disappointed not to have won.

It was a good game and everyone was saying what a great advert it had been for Merseyside, and they were right – but we desperately wanted to win it. The only downside for us was the loss of Kevin Sheedy, who suffered a bad injury after a challenge from Phil Neal. He went on to miss the rest of the season.

The replay just three days later at Maine Road was something of an anticlimax in comparison. While we lost to a good goal from Graeme Souness, we had given them a good game and had proved that we weren't that far away from them – and they were the European champions that season. We were gutted to have lost to Liverpool, but there was definitely a feeling amongst us that we were getting closer to them. I could sense that we were really becoming a very good team indeed.

Andy had been brilliant throughout that run, even though he was unable to kick a ball because he'd played in the competition for Wolves earlier in the season. He travelled to every game and was a big figure in the dressing-room. Being the type of person he was, I imagine he must have been smouldering at the prospect of not playing against Liverpool at Wembley, but he hid it very well. He went around the dressing-room speaking in turn to all of the lads and giving us one or two bits of advice. He'd been a League Cup-final winner with Wolves at Wembley four years earlier.

Andy's actions were symptomatic of our spirit of togetherness in those days. Howard a great believer in the squad travelling together. The injured lads would always be welcome whenever we were playing away from home. Invariably those not in the team would have a night out in London or Birmingham or wherever the team was playing. It meant that it wasn't just the substitute on the bench at the game: it was every member of the squad, whether they were involved or not.

We went on to emulate our Milk Cup run in the FA Cup that season – amazing considering we had looked like anything other than potential finalists when the campaign had kicked off in January. We played Stoke City at the Victoria Ground in the third round. This was the famous occasion when Howard stopped his team talk to open the window of the dressing-room so that we could hear the fantastic noise our supporters were making. He named the team and told us to go out there and win the game not only for ourselves but also for the fans. I recall thinking that we dare not lose and, of course, we didn't: we won 2–0.

And at least we only had Gillingham in the next round. But, goodness me, what a shock they gave us. With a bit more luck, they could well have knocked us out and changed the whole story. They had Tony Cascarino in their team at the time and I was marked by Steve Bruce. We drew 0–0 at Goodison, 0–0 at Priestfield (when Cascarino hit the crossbar late on) and I was out of the side for the second replay, also at Gillingham. I was an unused substitute when we beat them quite easily 3–0.

We often struggled against lower league teams. Even when we were successful, we were never overly convincing against teams that, on paper, we should have been wiping the floor with. Teams like Newport and Chesterfield spring to mind, and there were others, but we didn't know what the problem was. Perhaps we were uptight at times, especially at Goodison, or maybe the fact that we were expected to win led to some overconfidence.

Thankfully we had no such trouble overcoming Shrewsbury in the fifth round to set up a quarter-final tie with Notts County at Meadow Lane. Everyone remembers that game for Andy's headed goal, which he converted when the ball was about an inch off the ground. I still maintain that he left a furrow in the mud with his nose!

Strangely enough, although we were doing really well, from a personal point of view, I still wasn't completely happy with my own form as the semi-final with Southampton approached. I'd played in both of the League Cup-final matches but my recent goalscoring record in the League itself was, to be frank, abysmal, though this didn't prepare me for the devastation I felt when I was left out of the team that was to play the FA Cup semi-final at Highbury. Terry Curran was in the starting eleven and I was on the bench.

I had an inkling it was coming on the day of the match. I woke up that Saturday morning in my hotel room ahead of a very big game and before I'd even finished scanning the few papers that had been left outside my door I realised that I was going to miss out. Players always had an idea about team selection because there were strong hints in the newspapers on the day of the games. There were no quotes, but I always thought Howard had given the press lads a steer with regard to his way of thinking and his plans for the game. It was the same with Scotland: in fact, it was even worse. If you read the paper, you'd more or less know the team.

I had argued with Howard on the subject because I maintained that the players should know who was in and who was out before the press. That was Howard's way of doing things, but I thought it was wrong.

Howard told me as we took the morning walk. There was always a bit of a joke amongst the lads: whoever got the call from Howard during the morning walk was going to get bad news. That day, of all days, it was my turn.

'Can I have a word, please, Graeme?' he said.

And that was it. We all knew that I wouldn't be playing in the semi-final of the FA Cup. It was a truly horrible feeling being on the periphery of the exciting build-up to the match.

Every player worth his salt that has ever started a match from the bench – especially an important match – wants his team to struggle a bit so that he can get a chance to play. I don't care what anyone says about it, that's the way it is.

After the game, which we won 1–0 in extra-time, I just didn't feel part of all the celebrations. I came on for Trevor during the extra period, but I felt out of it afterwards, as though I hadn't contributed, and I couldn't join in the singing and celebrating. Andy King, who wasn't even in the 12, felt the same. The dressing-room was bedlam and there were hundreds of Everton supporters lining the street outside the main entrance at Highbury, but I couldn't force myself to enjoy it all. It was strange because although I was pleased that Everton were going back to Wembley, I just couldn't shake the feeling that I wouldn't be a part of the final either. I really thought that I would not make the team to play Watford four weeks later.

It was a subdued Graeme Sharp that took his seat on the bus outside the ground, but the showbiz personality Ed Stewart unwittingly put a smile on my face. Ed is a massive Evertonian and he walked in front of the bus, clenching his fists and shouting out, 'Brilliant lads!' and 'Well done, boys.' He was overjoyed to see his team win a semi-final match, so much so that he didn't see a concrete lamppost by the Highbury steps and walked right into it. Smack! He fell straight to the ground. The lads were in stitches!

The boys partied all the way back up to Liverpool, but I found it tough to join them. I knew that I had eight matches to stake a claim for a Wembley place. Andy and Terry Curran were the preferred option up front, but I just had to hope for the best and wait for any opportunity that might come my way. Andy missed a 2–1 loss at Sunderland in late April, but he was straight back in for the next game and I was straight back out again.

My much-prayed-for stroke of good fortune came when poor old Terry Curran picked up a bad injury at Norwich at the end of the month. I came on for him and retained my place because he played no further part in the season. It was a real blow for him and it was too late to change the FA Cup-final programme, as it had already been printed, so in there Terry Curran was in the team and I was down as number 12.

There were four games before the final and I was 100 per cent determined to make the most of them. I scored at Aston Villa (didn't I always!) and then got a brace against Queens Park

Rangers at Goodison. I felt very much like my old self in that game and confidence flooded through my veins again. We won 3–1 with my two goals coming in the last ten minutes, but Andy was the man of the match in all the Sunday papers. One reporter summed it up by saying, 'Gray produced more fireworks in front of goal in the opening 15 minutes than many forwards manage in a month.' That was the way he was.

We terrorised Terry Fenwick and Steve Wicks, and we were unstoppable. Their centre-forward, Ian Stewart, said afterwards that Watford would spend so much time keeping an eye on Andy and me that they wouldn't have time to win the Cup final! Reading things like that gave me such a lift after I had been so disgruntled and upset about not being in the semi-final team. It was an ideal way for me to finish the League campaign after all the uncertainty I had endured during the closing stages.

But my unrest had been no secret. Once again there were rumours about me moving away from Goodison. My Cup final week was disrupted by all the transfer talk surrounding a possible move to Aberdeen. Alex Ferguson was supposed to be keen on taking me back up the road to Pittodrie and I even read somewhere that Howard was pondering signing the Sheffield United striker Keith Edwards as my replacement. Aberdeen were the top dogs in Scotland at that time, having won the European Cup-Winners' Cup and a couple of League titles, so had I not been back in favour at Everton I may have been tempted. They were looking for someone to fill Mark McGhee's boots because he was leaving for SV Hamburg. I believe that Alex came to watch our last League game that season at West Ham on the Monday before the Cup final – a ridiculous piece of scheduling, in my opinion – but I'm not too sure if he'd been impressed: it was a nothing match.

It was a dangerous one for us to play, so close to the biggest occasion of most of our lives. Trevor Brooking had announced his retirement, so there was an emotional atmosphere at Upton Park as their punters turned up to pay tribute to him. Also, and a touch more concerning for me, Billy Bonds had declared that he wanted to concentrate on coaching from the following season so it was likely to be his last match too. He clearly wanted to go out with a bang because he caught me early on with a really hefty challenge. Howard had made the decision not to risk Andy and brought in Kingy instead, but I was still in the firing line! Thankfully I came through unscathed. We won 1–0 and we were ready for Wembley five days later.

I heard that some of our fans had decided to stay in London after that West Ham match because they thought it wasn't worth going all the way home only to have to come back to London for the final later that week!

We were the clear favourites to win the Cup, even though we'd only finished five points and five places above Watford in the First Division table. We stayed at the Bellhouse Hotel in Beaconsfield, Buckinghamshire, and I roomed with Inchy. The night before the game, we played some pool, watched a bit of television and had an early night – only to be woken the next morning by the sound of hysterical laughter! At the back of the hotel, outside our rooms, was a big lawn and the comedian Freddie Starr was marching up and down in the style of Adolf Hitler! We were all watching him. He deliberately marched towards a great big hole in the lawn and fell right down it! It was a deep hole, too, because Freddie completely disappeared from view! It helped to relax us, even though we were already supremely confident that we would win the game.

Watford were a small club who had done fantastically well to be where they were. Graham Taylor said during the final build-up that his team were 'going to Wembley to enjoy it. It will be a great day out for everyone connected with the club.'

Howard picked up on that straight away. 'We are going to Wembley to win,' he said.

We'd been there a couple of months earlier, so we knew what it was like, which helped us, but, of course, the FA Cup final was, and still is, a far bigger showpiece than the League Cup final.

I remember walking out in my Cup final suit to inspect the pitch and thinking, 'Blimey, I've watched so many FA Cup finals on television and here I am, a part of it.' It was an unbelievable feeling. I had butterflies in my stomach a good hour or so before the kick-off.

Strangely enough, Watford were the better side early on and John Barnes and Maurice Johnston both had decent chances. But once we took the lead, there was only one winner. Gary Stevens blasted a shot towards goal and I was fortunate that it landed right at my feet. My first touch was good and I hit the ball with my right foot past Steve Sherwood. It was a dream come true for me. We were by far the better team after that. Andy scored a second goal and the FA Cup was ours.

If you look closely at photographs of us receiving any trophy, you will notice I always seemed to go up second behind Rats – I don't know why, I just used to follow right behind him – and the memory of all the blue banners and scarves waving at Wembley as Rats picked up the Cup still brings a lump to my throat. I knew roughly where my family and friends were, but it was impossible to pick them out so I just waved in the general direction.

The beer, the wine and the champagne flowed in the dressing-room. It was an incredible feeling. My family and Ann Marie's family had travelled down for the game and I met up with them in the players bar upstairs at Wembley. My mum and dad had their picture taken with the trophy and they were delighted. It was as much a reward for them as it was for me. They had given me unswerving support from the moment I first kicked a football in the street and I made sure that they were right there with me to celebrate the FA Cup win.

A huge party had been arranged afterwards for the players and their guests in the Royal Lancaster Hotel by Hyde Park. What I found strange was the fact that the manager and the coaching staff had to go back to the Bellhouse for a dinner laid on by the board of directors. I know that Howard was gutted at having to attend because he wanted to celebrate with the players. As soon as we got to our hotel, the wives and girlfriends went to their rooms to get ready, but the lads just stayed in our Cup final suits and went straight to the bar. We wanted to enjoy it together. And we still had the Cup with us, even though the Bellhouse party had wanted to take it! At the end of a memorable night, a few of us ended up in Stringfellows until the small hours.

There were some rough people travelling back to Merseyside on the train the following morning. There are photographs of that journey and I've since had some stick for my choice of outfit, but I thought the quarter-patterned crew-neck jumper and black leather trousers looked the part!

We had more celebratory drinks on the train and there were some Everton supporters milling around, too, on the same journey home. Bob Paisley even joined us at one point and had a drink and a photo taken with Howard. We got off at Broadgreen station and boarded the open-topped bus for the homecoming ride through the city.

The scenes were remarkable. All the lads were taken aback at the turnout. The season was over and it had been a real roller-coaster ride for both the team and for me personally.

One of the saddest tales to emerge from the year was the dreadful injury that Mark Higgins picked up. I'd known Higgy since I had arrived at the club from Dumbarton and I really liked him as a player and as a man. He'd had a few injury problems, but after he damaged his knee he was never the same again. It was a crying shame for one of football's genuine nice guys. He had been through the pain barrier so many times for Everton, but his injuries finally caught up with him. When I hear of current players missing matches for the slightest twinge, I often recall the sight of Higgy taking those injections to numb the pain so he could pull on the blue shirt. He could well have been in contention for an England place had he not been so unlucky because he was playing really, really well and it looked as though he and Rats were forming an impregnable partnership at the back.

But in football, when the door closes for one player it automatically opens for another. When Higgy's season was abruptly curtailed, Derek Mountfield took full advantage.

To be perfectly honest, I can't remember Derek joining us but I must have played against him because we tended to meet Tranmere Rovers every year in pre-season friendlies. He was young and raw and I remember thinking he was a clumsy sod on the training ground! He was all elbows and knees and he'd kick you up in the air unintentionally. I thought he was a pain in the neck at times!

After ten months of so many contrasting emotions, what we needed was a good end-of-season tour – and that's exactly what we got. Bangkok was a very popular choice amongst the lads and to go out there as the FA Cup winners made it even better. We had ten days in Bangkok itself, then a few days at the beach in Pattaya. We'd won one cup, lost in the final of another, finished seventh in the League and Howard allowed us to let our hair down. We played a game against a local team in Bangkok, but it was really a holiday for the lads.

In one bar we visited, unbelievably, there was a full-size Thai boxing ring. We were having a few beers, watching the Thai boxers knocking seven bells out of each other, and making little bets on the outcome of the bouts. John Bailey and Terry Curran were winding each other up as usual. Bails and Terry were good mates, but they were always at each other's throats, so we persuaded them to settle this latest spat inside the ring. The Thais gave them some gloves and let them get on with it. Bails had done a bit of boxing as a kid and he knew a few moves, but Terry, typically, only *thought* he could fight. It was hysterical! The Thais were betting on two English footballers in a bout in the middle of a bar in Pattaya.

Bails was bobbing and weaving and catching Terry almost at will with some sharp punches. We were winding Terry up and the more flustered he got, the more Bails picked him off. We had to stop it in the end and declare Bails the clear winner.

SHARPY

I always remember our first night over there. We were in a beautiful hotel right on the beach and we couldn't wait to freshen up and get out, but Howard instructed us all to gather in the reception area at 7 p.m. because we'd been invited to go and watch a show. That killed us. We were appalled. Some threatened not to go, but Howard was adamant that it had to be a full turnout. We met at 7 p.m. prompt and got bussed to a theatre-like complex for the show. The mood changed a bit when the curtain went up to reveal dozens of beautiful women dancing on the stage.

Or at least we thought they were women! They had all the bits and pieces on both the top and bottom halves of their bodies, and they were, in fact, our first sight of Thai lady-boys! They were performing a version of a Broadway show. We were at first bemused by it all but that turned to sheer terror when they started to leave the stage and walk amongst the audience. I was planning to start throwing punches if one of them attempted to chat me up! Ian Bishop, then a young lad on his first tour, was approached by one of them and he screamed the place down before running away as fast as he could! When Mick Heaton was propositioned, he picked up and threw the lady-boy about four rows behind. Someone had recommended the show to Howard, but he said he hadn't realised it was that kind of show . . . or had he?

All in all, we were a contented bunch of players at the end of the season. We were taking shape as a team and we felt as though we were ready to really push on and put Everton Football Club back on the map. It's true to say, though, that not one of us envisaged anything like the sort of campaign that was about to get under way . . .

SIX

THE GREATEST TEAM

Having finished the 1983–84 season so well, Howard didn't see much need for summer investment; indeed the only new face at Bellefield when we reported for pre-season training was Paul Bracewell, a player that Howard obviously knew well from their days together at Stoke City. Brace was a good footballer, who could pass the ball well, and he went on to dovetail perfectly with Reidy in one of the best central-midfield partnerships in the history of the club. We didn't know too much about him when he joined us and he wasn't exactly a big-name signing, but he more than proved his worth in the couple of years that followed.

We knew that we had the makings of a good team, but we were far from title favourites as the season started. I remember reading that we were 'one to keep an eye on', which was probably just about right.

Personally, I couldn't wait for the season to start. Having scored in the FA Cup final, I was desperate to keep my own momentum going. I never dreamed that within a month of the first whistle I would be considering my entire Everton future, or that I would arrive at Bellefield one day with a transfer request in my pocket.

On the opening day of 1984–85, we had Tottenham Hotspur at Goodison. The sun was shining as we paraded the FA Cup and the FA Youth Cup before the game. The whole place was set for a positive start.

We lost 4–1!

Inchy scored for us, but Tottenham played us off the park. The message after the game was 'Don't be too concerned' because we had a chance to put things right at West Brom just 48 hours later.

We lost 2–1!

There was still no panic, but, I must admit, I was taken aback by this calamitous opening.

Our next game was at Stamford Bridge against Chelsea on the Friday night. We had to get a result to avoid being bottom of the first printed league table of the season. The game was to be broadcast live on television and we wore our silver kit, which I never liked. Richo scored the only goal of the game and we were off the mark, but things got worse again before they got better.

We were unconvincing against Ipswich, when we drew 1–1 at Goodison, and then we managed to beat Coventry 2–1, when I scored my first goal of the season. They had Bob Latchford up front for them. He was named skipper for the day and they led 1–0 until the last 20 minutes. I was having an awful afternoon. I'd missed a sitter after Inchy had put it on a plate for me and I was booked shortly afterwards for dissent. Thankfully, after Trevor Steven had equalised, I forced a close-range winner with just nine minutes left. I was a relieved man. I thought it would make a difference to my season . . . I was right – I was dropped for the next game against Newcastle United!

I stormed up to see Howard in his Bellefield office and demanded the explanation that I felt I deserved. I got an explanation all right, but it knocked me for six. When I asked why I had been axed despite the fact that I had scored against Coventry, Howard replied, totally unexpectedly, that it 'wasn't a proper goal'. I asked him to expand on his bizarre remark. 'It came from a set-piece, so I don't consider it to be a proper goal,' he said.

I couldn't believe what I was hearing and we had a right argument about it. I felt that Howard wasn't being honest with me. I'd never ever heard him describe a goal from any sort of set-piece as not being 'proper' – this from the man who had encouraged me to take penalty kicks to increase my goal tally!

Andy had been out of the team with an injury, but he was now fit and to me it seemed as though Howard clearly wanted to bring him back in. Being dropped to make way for Andy was hard to take because, like everyone else, I wanted to play, but I would have accepted it more easily had Howard given me a legitimate reason: 'not a proper goal' was an insult to me. I left Howard's office in a blaze and vowed to hand in a transfer request. My semi-final exclusion was still fresh in my mind and I felt I was just being messed around.

Howard called Inchy, Andy and me together one afternoon and said that he was going to try a few permutations and play a certain two against certain teams. We told him that was unacceptable and that we needed to know where we all stood. The situation wasn't doing anybody any good – especially if Howard was going to continue to offer that kind of excuse whenever he wanted to make a change.

Up at Newcastle, Andy scored, along with Sheeds and Trevor Steven, and we won 3–2. I told Andy on the way back that my patience had snapped and that I was looking to get away. He tried to talk me out of it by explaining that being dropped from time to time was an occupational hazard and that I would bounce back in time, but my mind was made up. I'd lost a bit of respect for the manager and I felt that I could no longer work with him. I went home and wrote out a transfer request, which I took with me to Bellefield on the Monday morning.

I was a very angry young man, but I knew what I was doing: I didn't want to stay at Everton. I went to see Howard and informed him that it was my intention to ask for a transfer. I told him that I couldn't see myself playing for Everton again. He simply told me to leave the request in my jacket pocket. I did so, but I was still far from happy.

It was only Andy's misfortune that persuaded me to drop the

matter. Unbelievably he picked up an injury at Newcastle and Howard needed me to play in the very next match, which was against University College Dublin in Ireland in the European Cup-Winners' Cup. I didn't score in Dublin – none of us did – and we were held to a shock 0–0 draw by a group of part-timers. However, I did find the net in each of the four games after that, including the only goal of the second leg, and I was once again a regular feature of Howard's teamsheets. My season had been turned on its head practically overnight and it served to remind me just what a volatile profession I was working in.

Once again, rumours of my latest unrest had been leaked and Coventry City manager Bobby Gould was reportedly ready to make a £200,000 bid for me. Howard confirmed that they had made an enquiry but that he had told them I was not for sale. Improper goals from set-pieces were never mentioned again and the handwritten transfer request ended up in the dustbin.

But my relationship with Howard Kendall never fully recovered: the incident left a crack that couldn't be papered over. In truth, we had never seen eye to eye completely and when I analyse my Everton career I maintain that I would never have been given the opportunity to develop and progress had it not been for Colin Harvey.

I was never fully convinced that Howard rated me as a player but knew that Colin did and that he always defended my corner. Howard had every right not to rate me, if that was his honest opinion, but leaving me out of the team and giving me a flimsy reason, that, to me, was patently untrue, was unacceptable. I couldn't understand it because he proved time and again that he was perfectly capable of making big decisions. He recruited Pat Van Den Hauwe, for example, early in the season to replace John Bailey, who was exceptionally popular with teammates and fans alike. Bails was very disappointed, but Howard didn't hesitate because he felt a change was needed.

Andy didn't get back in after his injury and Howard stuck by Inchy and me as his first-choice strikers. Andy wasn't happy at not playing, as you can well imagine, but his reaction was different to mine because he had more experience. He looked upon his Everton swansong as a bonus, but even he didn't envisage the history and havoc we'd cause before the season's end.

He was still on the bench when we went to Anfield for the first derby of the season. It turned out to be an afternoon to savour and I go into that wonderful day in a bit more detail in a later chapter of this book. Suffice to say that it gave the team enormous self-belief and sent a message across the park that we were back as a leading First Division team.

Our 1–0 win left Liverpool, astonishingly, in 17th place in the table and moved us up to third. My goal came three minutes into the second half. I never tire of watching it! Ian Rush, who knows a thing or two about scoring, said that he'd be 'amazed if it [wasn't] the goal of the season'. But Ian Hargraves of the *Liverpool Echo*, who, for some reason, always seemed hesitant to give me due praise for anything I ever did, described me as 'erratic' in his report on the Monday. You can't please everyone, I suppose. After I had broken into the first team, I did one of those question-and-answer pages for *Shoot!* magazine and when I was asked to nominate something I didn't like about football I had replied, 'local newspaper match reports'. Maybe Hargraves had seen it and taken exception.

I remember one pre-season – I can't recall where we were – when he was covering the tour for the *Echo* and was travelling with the team. We were all aboard the airport bus and when Hargraves got on there was only one seat left and that was the one next to me. Rats knew that there was a bit of ill feeling between the two of us and so, at the top of his voice, invited him to come and sit next to me! I swung myself around, put my feet on the spare seat and Hargraves had to stand up.

If our 1–0 win at Liverpool suggested that we were a force to be reckoned with, then the match just seven days later confirmed it beyond a shadow of a doubt. I just loved playing against Manchester United. They were the biggest club in the country and although they hadn't won anything for a while they still always did things with the style and panache that you associate with massive football clubs. It was a top-of-the-table clash at Goodison, make no mistake about it. They had quality players like Bryan Robson, Gordon Strachan, Mark Hughes, Norman Whiteside and Frank Stapleton, but we overwhelmed them. We were on top from the very first kick and they had no answer. It finished 5–0, but it could have been a lot more.

After the match, the legendary Joe Mercer famously said, 'I have never seen an Everton team play as well as that. From the goalkeeper right through, they were tremendous.' That was some accolade, coming from a man who himself had played in fabulous Everton teams. Everything went right for us.

By this time, we really had the bit between our teeth. The punters could see that something was really starting to happen at Everton and this result alerted the rest of the country. The level of confidence in the side was something I'd never experienced before. We had complete faith in our own ability and we knew that we were going to win football matches. It's a terrific feeling.

Three days later, we had a League Cup tie . . . against Manchester United at Old Trafford. You can imagine how they felt and how much Ron Atkinson had them wound up to show us that the 5–0 game had been a one-off – but we went there, we battled very well and we won 2–1 after extra-time. I scored a penalty at the Stretford End, which is always nice, and John Gidman scored an own goal.

We were looking and feeling as though there was nobody who could beat us. The press loved it because we were the new kids on the block and, outside of Merseyside, we were largely an unknown group of players.

In all honesty, the possibility of winning the Championship was never mentioned within the confines of the dressing-room. We just carried on with the games and nobody, not one of us, ever stopped to say, 'Hey, we can win the League the way we are playing here.' That may sound unlikely, but it was well after Christmas before we started to consider that we could actually bring the title back to Goodison.

A distressing injury to Inchy gave Andy his turn in the starting eleven. Inchy and I were doing very well indeed and there was talk of him getting an England call-up, such was the quality of his own personal displays, and he was scoring some great goals. A horrible challenge from Sheffield Wednesday's Brian Marwood in December, however, brought his promising season to a premature end. Brian has since apologised and claimed that it was a complete accident, but at the time we were furious with him. Reidy was a close mate of Inchy's, and still is to this day, and he was gunning for Marwood – I believe one challenge left the Wednesday man with a snapped shin pad. Reidy wouldn't be denied, though, and eventually Marwood needed stretcher assistance to leave the field of play.

Inchy's campaign was over, but he impressed every single one of us with his determination to try and fight back. He kept his sense of humour at Bellefield, he came to every match and he worked so hard to try and contribute, but it was very tough for him.

Howard was rumoured to be looking for a centre-forward replacement when it was confirmed that Inchy would miss the rest of the season. I could understand the desire to strengthen the numbers in the squad, but it was still a bit unnerving to see players like Gary Lineker, Eric Gates and Peter Davenport linked with a move to Goodison. To be honest, there were always rumours because Everton were a big club and they would naturally be linked with players on a regular basis. I knew that if I ever went half a dozen or so games without a goal, the papers would suggest that Howard was in the market for a new striker.

The season was gathering such momentum that a 1–0 defeat to Second Division Grimsby Town in the League Cup at Goodison in November didn't really matter. We forced *eighteen* corners to their *none*, but they nicked it a minute before the end when Paul Wilkinson scored. Wilkie, of course, later joined us and, although he never forced his way into the team as a regular, he still played a part and scored some important goals. He's a really good lad and always makes an effort to turn up when we organise a reunion.

In the League, we were just about unstoppable and compiled some fantastic runs. The Liverpool and United wins were part of six on the spin and from Boxing Day right through to early May, we won 16 of our 18 League games. The other two were draws. We were a superb team, no doubt about it, but we could also mix it when we needed to.

One game that sticks in my mind is the goalless draw at Loftus Road against Queens Park Rangers that December. I hated playing there because of the 'plastic pitch'. It was a horrible place to go and, without question, it gave them an advantage. I don't care what anyone says: if you've got a surface that you train and play on every day, then it works very much in your favour when you play a team at home. It must do. It was like playing on concrete. QPR also played with a lighter ball, so the bounce was ridiculous.

The match itself was uneventful, but when Andy Gray made a tasty challenge on Terry Fenwick it all kicked off! Fenwick was perfectly capable of looking after himself, but his teammates piled in and of course we were right up for that. The only two players on the pitch not involved were Neville and Sheeds. Nev was too far away and couldn't be bothered and Sheeds was a pacifist who thought the fracas was disgraceful. He just stood by the touchline leaning against the dugout. Simon Stainrod got sent off for flattening Andy Gray and in the ensuing mêlée even the referee ended up on the ground. Pat Van Den Hauwe was frightened of missing out and ran half the length of the pitch to get involved: he arrived on the scene, didn't bother to ask questions and punched the nearest player in a blue-and-white hooped shirt – then got sent off.

The incident actually made the national nine o'clock news that night and my dad watched it in disbelief. Sure enough, even before the credits rolled at the end of the programme, the phone was ringing. 'What on earth went on there?' he asked.

For me, it merely summed up the fantastic team spirit that prevailed at that time. We looked out for each other on the field, as well as off it, and the camaraderie was second to none. We had absolute faith in one another's abilities to play good football and win matches, but we also had every confidence that, when the chips were down, every man amongst us would fight for each other.

We battered Nottingham Forest 5–0 at Goodison one afternoon and I got a public admonishment from Brian Clough. He wasn't overly enamoured at the way I was treating his defenders and after one crunching challenge on Gary Mills he jumped out of the Forest dugout and had a right go at me. I was always encouraged to close down the full-backs as quickly as possible if they received the ball from the goalkeeper and I did that when Mills got possession that day. My challenge wasn't the best, I must admit – it was a typical centre-forward tackle – but I caught Mills and unfortunately he broke his leg. It was a complete accident, but Clough was ranting and raving at me. My response was pure Glaswegian!

I thought he was being a bit hypocritical after some of the treatment I'd taken from his players, such as Larry Lloyd, Ian Bowyer and Kenny Burns. They could all leave their foot in, but Clough seemed to have forgotten while he was going apoplectic at the touchline.

There's actually a funny postscript to that incident. We played Forest at the City Ground when we only had four games of the season left. I was out of the team with a slight thigh strain and was sitting in the dugout before the game when Clough walked past us to take his seat. He stopped, wagged a finger at me and roared, 'I'm just sorry you're not playing. I won't forget what happened at Goodison Park.'

I was staggered by the outburst, but Clough carried on his rant. 'I told my son Nigel that even though he's got a broken toe, he had better give you a hard time and it is unfortunate that he won't get the chance.'

I just smiled at him and said, 'I've got more important things to worry about. I'm playing in a European final in four days' time.'

Clough thought for a moment and then he offered his hand. 'I know you are, young man, and all the very best for it.' He really was a complete one-off. Anyway, I didn't think his son Nigel could have pulled a sleeping cat off a polished table, so it didn't worry me too much!

Clough was the match summariser alongside Brian Moore in the commentary box when we won the European Cup-Winners' Cup final and he was very complimentary towards Everton.

As the season progressed, we began to establish a reputation as being the type of team you didn't take liberties with. We had a somewhat bruising encounter with Arsenal at Goodison. Steve Williams, in particular, seemed to have a bee in his bonnet and went around kicking everything that moved. He was always the same; in my opinion, he had an arrogance that his ability didn't merit. Andy and I scored in the 2–0 victory and Reidy and Brace had Williams in their pockets.

I also remember a game against Stoke City at the Victoria Ground, which we won 2–0, that was soured when a lad called Chris Maskery flattened Trevor and once again an unseemly fracas ensued. The 'all for one, one for all' attitude came right to the fore once more.

It was something that Howard actively encouraged. He'd tell us to swarm around the referee if we weren't happy with things and he ordered us to be right in there if a teammate was getting a rough time.

Although we were flying and winning matches, there was also a general feeling that we weren't quite getting the recognition we deserved. We were playing the best football in the country, scoring goals for fun and yet we had very few international caps between us. Bobby Robson named an England squad earlier in the January after we'd walloped Newcastle United 4–0 and there wasn't a single Everton player in it. Not Reidy, Trevor, Brace or Gary Stevens. Reidy, in particular, was in outstanding form. We were comfortably ahead of Liverpool in the table and yet virtually every member of their squad would be away during international breaks. Still, we had a laugh about it at Bellefield. Incidentally, after that big Newcastle match, Jack Charlton said he was happy his team had been beaten 4–0 because it could easily have been ten! And he was right.

We were just happy to be playing well for Everton – personally I couldn't have been more delighted at the way things were developing at club level. If international honours came along, then fine, though it was baffling that we were missing out on caps, as we were clearly the in-form players in the top division. I was irritated, rather than concerned, at being constantly overlooked by Scotland, but I didn't dwell on it.

Much was made of my partnership with Andy Gray in the media and we were invited to do some bizarre photo shoots. I've still got some of the pictures at home and I cringe when I look at them now. One shows me serving Andy his morning cup of tea while he sits up in bed reading the papers. In another one, it went even further: the photographer asked us to lie in the same bed to pose for a photograph. I can't imagine a couple of Premiership teammates doing the same thing today. When we were both being tipped for Scottish call-ups, a newspaper north of the border persuaded us to pose with a telephone receiver between us! The caption read: 'Waiting for a call'!

In those days, the lads posed for pictures from which modern footballers would run a mile. We didn't have press officers in our day, so the press boys would just bring a photographer down to Bellefield and ask us to do all these weird and wonderful things. I also have a picture of me and Sheeds at Bellefield with a fire extinguisher but have no recollection whatsoever why we posed for the photo. In another one, I am pretending to play a clarinet and Sheeds is strumming a banjo. I don't know what the story behind that was either.

Reidy, Rats, Sheeds and I posed on the Goodison Park pitch one afternoon with each one of us pushing a Flymo lawnmower. I didn't mind that, though, because they gave us a free Flymo. But I can't imagine Wayne Rooney doing a photo shoot purely on the premise that he got to keep some gardening equipment!

I was learning a lot from watching Andy Gray. He had mastered the art of jumping early for high balls and winning free-kicks against defenders who'd be all over him as he came back down again. He taught me how to be a bit more physical. He would say that we were 'going into battle' every time we went out onto the pitch and that was the way he approached every game. He was fantastic to play alongside and we had total belief in each other. We knew that we were both very good footballers and we also knew that we could never be intimidated out of matches.

He was playing out of his skin, but, although he was helping me enormously on and off the pitch, he went through a lengthy period when he just couldn't score goals himself. Before one match he was quoted as saying how proud he was of our 22-goal partnership and that the only downside was 'Sharpy has got 21 of them!'

When we went to Leicester City in February, Andy hadn't scored a League goal since September. I was injured, but he ended his drought with two great goals. I was listening to the game on the radio at home and was delighted that Andy was finally off the mark. He must have enjoyed the freedom of not having me alongside him! He even scored one with his right foot, which wasn't like him!

I missed out because I had been given some rough treatment by a non-League team in the FA Cup a week earlier. I go into more details about our Cup exploits in the next chapter but, suffice to say, a team of part-timers from Telford had taken their instructions to mark me a little too literally.

I missed four matches in total, including the next round of the Cup against Ipswich and I only returned for the replay at Portman Road. I'd scored twice there in the League earlier in the season and maybe Howard was hoping that it would be a lucky ground for me.

He was right! I scored the only goal to put us into the semi-final. I was back in the team, but I had lost the number 9 shirt – Andy had reclaimed it when I'd been injured and he didn't let me have it back. We both knew how important the Everton number 9 was and as soon as one of us dropped out of the team, the other reclaimed the shirt. He loved wearing it and so did I, but the unwritten rule was that whoever was in possession kept it until he missed a game.

By the time we went to White Hart Lane in the first week of April, we were starting to believe that the Championship could well come back to Goodison for the first time since 1970. Tottenham Hotspur were our closest rivals and the game, played on a Wednesday night, was justifiably billed as a title showdown. We won 2–1. It was a massive stride forward for us, but what a fight it was! Andy and me against Graham Roberts and Paul Miller wasn't a battle for the faint-hearted. Andy and Trevor scored the goals, but what Evertonians remember is the incredible save Neville made from an effort by Mark Falco. They had thrashed us 4–1 on the opening day of the season, but we had turned the tables. I think that was the night that the London press were forced to concede that we were the favourites to win the title.

Personally I hadn't dared to think that we might win it until we had beaten Sheffield Wednesday at Hillsborough in March. They were right up there with us in the leading pack and we knew that we were in for a right tough test. However, we beat them 1–0. Neville was absolutely outstanding yet again, but I always recall a rallying cry from Andy Gray before the game.

As the team bus pulled up outside Hillsborough and we shaped to get off, Andy made his way to the front and spoke to everyone. 'Listen to me,' he bawled, 'we have *not* come here to lose this match. We are not leaving here this afternoon with anything other than a win. We are good enough, we just need to show it. Come on, let's go.'

We were being touted as potential champions and Andy was making the point that games like Sheffield Wednesday away were the kind that champions needed to be winning. Needless to say, it was Andy who scored in our 1–0 win. All we needed to do now was beat QPR and the League would be ours.

That match took place two days later on a Bank Holiday Monday and there were over 50,000 fans crammed inside Goodison. We were confident that we were going to win it and, of course, we had the cushion of the remaining five League games if QPR shocked us. But they were never going to do that: they were just in the way on a day of total celebration. Derek Mountfield scored early on and I hit the post before I headed our second goal from a Pat Van Den Hauwe cross. Though I say it myself, I got a terrific head on it that gave the keeper no chance. It was at the Gwladys Street end and the place erupted. That was it. The Championship was officially ours and the atmosphere was incredible.

I didn't want the lap of honour at the end of the game to finish because you could see just how much it meant to the supporters. There were cheers, tears, singing, dancing: the lot. It was difficult to take it all in. I was just full of the feeling that I was the centre-forward in the team that could now, without argument from anyone, call itself the best in the country.

What a night I had afterwards! Andy and I went to the Casa Italia on Lord Street in Southport with a pal of mine, Dave Sheron, and a couple of other lads to celebrate in the time-honoured fashion. We'd had a few beers in the players' lounge at Goodison and had arranged for our wives to meet up with us in the restaurant. It was quite busy and everybody was eating and drinking quite happily – until the singing started! I think it was Dave who stood up and started chanting, 'Hand it over, hand it over . . . hand it over, Liverpool!' It was a popular song amongst our fans at the time and very quickly the five of us were belting it out at the top of our voices.

The restaurant cleared quite quickly, but the owner wasn't bothered because we'd stopped drinking wine and had started ordering champagne. We were stamping our feet, banging the tables and singing any old song that came to mind! Then the wives came in and joined in, too. It was a terrific night. We were the champions of England. All we had to do now was win the FA Cup and the European Cup-Winners' Cup and we would be making history.

SEVEN

EUROPEAN DREAM

Our defence of the FA Cup got under way in front of one of the most hostile crowds I have ever encountered in my life when we played Leeds United in the third round on a Friday evening in January 1985 in front of live television cameras. They were a Second Division club at the time and you could sense the hatred emanating from the packed terraces. I opened the scoring with a penalty and then Sheeds made it 2–0 to wrap things up, but the hostility in the crowd got worse and worse. I honestly thought that we were in serious danger. At one point, I was sure the punters were actually going to come onto the pitch and cause a riot. The mood was terrible.

As the final whistle approached, most of us Everton players had one eye on the tunnel. When the game finished, we didn't stop to shake hands with the Leeds players, we just sprinted back to the safety of the dressing-room. It was scary. Although at the time their supporters had a bit of a reputation, to this day I have no idea why they showed such animosity towards us that evening. Nevertheless it was a case of 'job done' at Elland Road because it was a tricky opening tie and the win gave us a fourth-round reward at home to Doncaster Rovers.

As I've already mentioned, we were never at our best against lower league opposition in the cup competitions, and Doncaster brought a lot of fans with them to Goodison hoping to see their team make some headlines.

I gather that Ian Snodin played for them that day! I say that because he claims that he never gave Andy Gray or me a kick all afternoon, but I can't even recall Snods being on the pitch! He remembers it vividly, but then he would because that was the biggest game of his life at the time! They were very defensive: I think Snods was playing sweeper behind the goalkeeper at one stage!

Gary Stevens and Trevor Steven scored our goals and we secured a comfortable 2–0 win. Fair play to Doncaster because they gave it a good go, but we were never in trouble.

The fifth round pitted us against Telford United and the press loved it. That was a real David and Goliath Cup tie and although nobody ever seriously contemplated a famous upset, we knew that they would have a game plan and wouldn't just roll over and enjoy the day out.

A newspaper reporter rang me to do an interview about the prospect of us playing against a lad called Kenny McKenna, who was a Telford player and a massive Evertonian. I initially agreed but as I spoke to the reporter it became clear that it was a comparison piece that wouldn't flatter Kenny. I was asked about my salary, my house, the car I drove and things like that, which I didn't like. I felt it was a bit disrespectful to Kenny and refused to carry on the conversation.

I knew of Kenny because he was a good non-League goalscorer. I later signed him when I was the manager of Bangor City. He was good for me because he was a great professional and as fit as a fiddle. I still see him around now because he is a manager in the League of Wales.

As soon as the referee's whistle blew, it was obvious that Telford's game plan was to boot everything in a blue shirt as regularly as possible! They got stuck right into us – their centre-half came through the back of me in the very first minute and caught me on the ankle. It hurt like hell, but I carried on until half-time. When I took off my boot in the dressing-room, my ankle swelled up like a balloon. There was no way I was going to get the boot back on and although the physio, John Clinkard, applied ice for ten minutes, it was clear that my involvement in the match was over.

But Howard wanted to me carry on. He urged me to squeeze on the boot and try to run off the injury, but I literally couldn't do it. I couldn't even walk on the ankle. Clinks backed me up and I played no further part.

Clinks was a great character and was as big a personality on Merseyside as the players! He looked like Tom Selleck, who played Magnum PI in the American television series, and he loved it. He got invited to open bars and clubs because of the resemblance. The Everton job was his first in football and he had come to us from a hospital in the Oxford area, where he was originally from. The whole atmosphere around the football club was new to him. It can be difficult for outsiders to adapt, at times, because of the banter. The humour can be vicious. It's very much a male environment and some people can't handle it – but Clinks could. He was a strong character with a smashing sense of humour of his own.

He even managed to put the frighteners on one of the toughest men ever employed by Everton Football Club! Dave Ashe, the caretaker at Bellefield, was a martial-arts expert. He was a kick-boxer who was really into his fitness and he worked as a bouncer in the city centre. He used to use the gymnasium when the lads had finished training. One day Inchy gave big Dave a bit of lip and so he lifted him off the ground and gave him a big bear hug. Dave was squeezing tighter and tighter and so Inchy gave Clinks a wink and then pretended to faint! He went limp and Dave dropped him to the ground. Clinks pretended to be in a blind panic and made moves to resuscitate Inchy while he lay on the ground.

'Jesus Christ,' he said to Dave, 'I think you've killed him.'

Dave went white. With his hands on his head, he started shouting, 'Do something, do something!' He was terrified. When Inchy sat up, smiling, Dave realised he'd been had. Inchy had to be up on his toes and out of the room otherwise Dave really would have killed him!

While Clinks was very much a part of the banter, he took his role extremely professionally and if he told you to do something, you had to do it. Before he arrived at the club, injured players had enjoyed the life of Riley. They'd come in for a bit of treatment, then have some tea and toast before going home. But Clinks changed all that when he started having injured players back in the afternoon. One day when I was coming back from injury, Clinks asked me to do a 12-minute run, at pace, around Bellefield. It was dancing down with rain and I genuinely didn't think I needed to do a run to prove my fitness, so I refused to do it. The ground was really heavy and it was the Thursday afternoon before a game on the Saturday that I hoped to play in. Clinks was getting more and more annoyed at my stance, but he could see that I wasn't going to budge.

'Right,' he said, 'I'm going to see the gaffer about this.'

He stormed upstairs to see Howard and I followed him up. Clinks raged that I was refusing to do the 12-minute run. Howard asked for my side of it and I reasoned that the ground was heavy and that there was just no need for it.

Howard thought for a moment. 'Sharpy's right,' he said. 'Now get out, both of you.'

Clinks was furious, but we laughed about it later when he reminded me of the day I undermined his authority.

I was still injured when Ipswich Town came to Goodison for the FA Cup quarter-final and so from my position in the Main Stand I had a good view of one of the most famous free-kick incidents of all time. Sheeds took the shot and curled the ball around the wall and into the net past the goalkeeper. We were all on our feet, but the cheers were silenced by the referee, when he spotted some sort of infringement and ordered a re-take. I recall thinking what a shame it was because Sheeds was denied a great goal. We all sat down again, Sheeds replaced the ball and then he promptly curled it into the opposite corner of the net! It was fantastic. We drew the game 2–2.

I was back for the replay at Portman Road. We knew it would be tough to reach the semi-finals because it was a difficult place to go to, but we won 1–0 and I scored the goal from a penalty. The decision was a bit harsh because a cross came over and the ball bounced awkwardly in front of a defender and struck his arm, but that wasn't my concern – I just thumped the penalty as hard as I could. The keeper got a hand to it, but it bounced into the roof of the net.

We were through to the last four again and with our progress in the European Cup-Winners' Cup it meant that, more often than not, we were playing twice a week. There was no issue about resting players, though. Everybody wanted to play and we more or less kept the same side all season. These days there is much more squad rotation – all we had back then was the first eleven plus a few who would come in from time to time. Kevin Richardson and Alan Harper were fabulous players and great lads and it was unfortunate they didn't get to play more games that season, but nobody wanted to rest regardless of the number of matches we had to play. It was incredibly hard for them because even when they came into the team and played well they would be on the sidelines again when the injured players returned. They didn't like the situation and complained to Howard, but it was only what the manager expected: he didn't want players around him who would be happy at missing out.

The semi-final was against Luton Town at Villa Park. For some reason, our matches against them often seemed to be bruising affairs. They had the likes of Steve Foster, Mick Harford, Mal Donaghy, Ashley Grimes and Mark Stein, who could all leave their foot in when required and they took the lead when we thought we should have been given a free-kick after Gary Stevens had been impeded. We were poor on the day and for a long time it looked as though it was going to be Luton that progressed through to the final.

Time was running out when we were awarded a free-kick outside the box. Sheeds had had a nightmare game – nothing had gone right for him all afternoon – and he didn't strike the free-kick as well as he could have done. It bobbled all the way through to the keeper, Les Sealey, and, to our surprise, ecstasy and relief, it squirmed past him and into the net. That gave us a huge lift and we were on top in extra-time. Derek Mountfield, who had taken a real battering from Harford, scored the winner with a fantastic header and we were back at Wembley.

We knew by now, of course, that we were within sight of becoming the first team in Everton history to win the much-coveted League and FA Cup double. There wasn't much talk of it in the dressing-room because the games were coming at us thick and fast and there wasn't time to discuss where we'd end up. In fact, there were so many games that the lads were too tired to even play golf on their rest days.

The training was great back then because it was structured just to keep us ticking over. Howard and Colin believed in retaining possession and we were encouraged to do it in training games. We'd have 'two-touch' and 'three-touch' matches with the objective of not giving the ball away. There were no proper formations and Rats could end up playing on the right wing or Reidy could be centre-forward. There was a lot of five-a-side and head tennis as well, but nothing that could cause any injury. It worked because we kept going right until the end of each and every one of the 63 games we played that season.

As well as the FA Cup, we were embarking on a fantastic European adventure. For most of us, it was a first taste of competition on the Continent and we were looking forward to playing in some weird and wonderful locations – so a first-round tie with UCD (University College Dublin) was something of an anticlimax. I'd never even heard of them! In fact when I was told that we'd been paired with UCD I thought they were from Romania or Bulgaria – I didn't realise what the letters stood for!

Ironically, they played their home games at a place called Belfield Park but because the capacity was only 4,500 the first leg was switched to Tolka Park, where Home Farm played.

I must admit that our approach to the tie was a bit lackadaisical because we fully expected them to cause us few problems and we looked at it as being as good as a bye.

The pitch over in Dublin was dreadful and we drew 0–0. I missed a few chances, but we weren't too worried about it because we knew we'd finish them off comfortably at Goodison. Or at least we thought we would.

They came over and shut up shop. They also gave us the fright of our lives when a lad called Joe Hanrahan hit the woodwork very late in the game. I scored to put us one ahead, but had they levelled just before the final whistle they'd have gone through on away goals and our European journey would have ended at the first hurdle. We took it as a wake-up call and it stood us in good stead.

The next round against Inter Bratislava was much more like a genuine European tie. They hadn't actually won the Czech Cup, but Sparta Prague had done the double so, as losing finalists, Inter were in. We'd had them watched and we knew that they were in poor league form and had only just scraped through the previous round against FC Lahti, a part-time team from Finland.

It was my first time behind the Iron Curtain and it was every bit as bleak as I expected it to be: it was grim and grey. We played in a massive stadium, but what I remember most is that the walk from the dressing-room seemed to last an age: it was underground and we must have travelled about a quarter of a mile before we reached the pitch. It was like a maze! It would have been very easy to get lost.

The food was poor in Bratislava and the hotel wasn't much better. We won 1–0 and it was a case of flying over there, getting the job done and then flying back home again. It wasn't the sort of place you'd like to linger in for longer than was necessary, although I would imagine that it's much nicer these days.

All credit to our supporters, too, because they made a great effort to get over there to back us. One of my closest friends, Joe Farley, caused a great scene at Bratislava airport when he was stretchered on board the aircraft. He'd contracted food poisoning and was in such discomfort that he couldn't walk. Joe is a great character. He was one of the main men around Liverpool when I first came to live in the city. He owned a bar in Seel Street in the city centre and was a pal of Dave Sheron's. Joe has always been a massive Evertonian and he used to go to all the matches, home and away.

We won easily against Bratislava back at Goodison and I scored one of the goals in a 3–0 win. We were in great form at the time and were far superior to them.

The first leg of the quarter-final is remembered as Andy Gray's night. We got Fortuna Sittard and, just as in the first round, they were a team that I'd never heard of. I was injured for the game, a legacy of our bruising encounter with Telford United, so I watched from the stands as Andy threw himself all over the place. He murdered the Dutch defence and helped himself to a magnificent hat-trick. We won the game 3–0 and we knew that we were as good as through to the semi-final. The second leg was always going to be nothing more than a formality and I scored in the 2–0 win with Reidy getting the other.

It was Andy's turn to be injured for the second leg in Sittard, but he still wanted to be a part of it so he travelled over there with the rest of the squad. The night before the game, Andy and Inchy went for a few beers in the local area and in one bar they met up with Howard and Jim Greenwood. They all had a few more drinks and the night was going fine by all accounts until Howard suddenly told Andy to stop drinking.

'Why?' asked Andy.

'Because I might need you tomorrow,' was the unexpected reply.

'But boss, I'm injured, I can't play even if I wanted to,' Andy replied.

'You'll have to go on the bench because I've just done a count and we haven't brought enough players,' said Howard.

It was astonishing, but the extended number of substitutes in European ties had caught us on the hop. So Andy, who was injured and had been on the ale the night before, took his place on the substitute's bench.

The Sittard ground was near the Dutch border with Germany and when we ran out that night we were amazed at just how many English supporters there were. We knew that we'd have a decent number across from Liverpool, but the crowd was swelled by the presence of hundreds of British soldiers serving in Germany. They wanted a good night out and gave us their full vocal support as we won 1–0.

That win gave us another semi-final to prepare for and this time we knew all about our opponents. For my money, Everton versus Bayern Munich was *the* final that season. The winners of the tie would have every chance to go on and win the cup. The Germans were the team that we wanted to avoid at the semi-final stage because we were aware of how many quality players they had within their ranks.

I remember sitting in the superb dressing-room at the Olympic Stadium in Munich thinking that this was really what European football was all about. We'd been to the ground the night before and it was a magnificent setting for a football match. We trained on the pitch and it was just about the best playing surface I had ever seen. It was superb, just like a billiard table.

We had a patched-up team that night with Alan Harper and Kev Richo in the starting eleven. I was a lone striker and we did very well to get a 0–0 draw. It was a great result for us because they had internationals like Lother Matthaus, Soren Lerby, Klaus Augenthaler, Jean-Marie Pfaff and Dieter Hoeness.

Joe Farley made another scene at Munich airport on the way home! After the game, while we were in the hotel bar having a few beers because we weren't flying back until the following morning, we noticed a guy in a pilot's uniform who was really,

really drunk. At the airport the next day who should stride across the tarmac towards the plane but the very same pilot! Joe clocked him and refused point-blank to board the aircraft. 'He was pissed last night!' he said to the bemused airport staff, who were trying to persuade him to get on the plane. 'He was in a right state.'

Back on Merseyside, we had every confidence that we could become the first Everton team to contest a major European final. We were right in the middle of an incredible ten-game winning run in the League and we believed we would win every time we played.

I have written about the night of 24 April 1985 in the preface and, suffice to say, it is popularly recalled as the greatest game in the history of Everton Football Club. It was the night that the team bus took an age to make its usual journey. It was the night that Andy Gray and I took on the might of a German defence and battered them into submission. It was the night that Howard Kendall, his backroom staff and a host of Everton substitutes had responded to some criticism from the highly regarded Bayern coach, Udo Lattek, by shouting, as one, 'Fuck off!' As I have said, it was no ordinary night!

We considered the showdown with Bayern to be the virtual final because we rated them as far more imposing an opposition than the Austrians of Rapid Vienna. Rapid had actually been beaten in an earlier round by Celtic, but UEFA ordered a re-match after the Austrians claimed that they had been affected by a Scottish fan who had run onto the pitch and attacked one of their players. The replay was at Old Trafford, so Andy, Inchy, Reidy and I went along to watch it. I thought that Celtic were the stronger of the two sides, but from where we were sitting there was nothing from either team that would give us too much to worry about.

Incredibly, we had four League matches to play in the month of May before we contested the European Cup-Winners' Cup final in Rotterdam on the 15th. That's a schedule that simply wouldn't be tolerated these days. We even played three more League matches after the two finals.

My mum and dad went over to Rotterdam on a bus that had been organised by Joe Farley. Mum is quite reserved by nature, so travelling abroad with Joe and his pals was certainly a new experience for her. She says to this day that the trip to Rotterdam 'opened her eyes'! She couldn't believe some of the stuff that was going on. But they had a fantastic time and Joe made sure they were well looked after. Ann Marie travelled over on a separate flight with all the wives and the Everton staff.

It was all fairly low-key and Howard tried to keep the preparations as normal as possible. 'Why change anything now?' was his philosophy and it was the right one to adopt. We stayed in a hotel right on the river in Rotterdam and the pre-match routine was virtually the same as it would have been for any other match.

On the night, Rapid held out for the opening 45 minutes. Andy did force the ball into their net six minutes before half-time, but the referee called offside.

We always felt that the breakthrough was merely a matter of time and on 57 minutes I intercepted a sloppy back pass, took the ball around the goalkeeper and pulled it back across the face of the goal for Andy to lash into the back of the net. If ever there was a player for the big occasion, then it was Andy. During his career, he'd already scored in the finals of both the League and FA Cups and now he had a European final goal for his collection. We scored again in the 72nd minute, when Sheeds swung over a corner kick that eluded everyone bar Trevor Steven, who knocked the ball into the net.

Rapid gave us a bit of a scare when Hans Krankl pulled a goal back, but we attacked them again straight from the restart and Sheeds scored a great goal to restore the two-goal cushion. That was always going to be enough and the second leg of an unprecedented treble was safely in the bag. The presentation ceremony left a bit to be desired but that didn't dampen the enthusiasm of the 25,000 Evertonians inside the stadium that night.

After the game, we had a few beers in the players' lounge and then boarded the bus that would take us to the airport. We had some corporate passengers who had paid extra to travel with the team and they gave us a rousing reception when we got on the plane with the trophy. We had a couple more drinks during the flight because it was still only Wednesday night and we knew we had plenty of time to recover before the FA Cup final against Manchester United at Wembley on the Saturday.

People have since suggested that we should have abstained from alcohol completely, but, goodness me, we'd just created Everton history. Nobody went overboard with their celebrations and we were fit young men who had plenty of time to recover before the next game.

When we landed at Liverpool, we met up with our wives, who had flown back a bit earlier. Ann Marie and I jumped into the car with Andy and Jan and we went back to his house in Formby to watch the match. Their babysitter had taped the game for him. We sat down and watched it right through, before Ann Marie and I got a taxi home. That was the extent of our celebrations after a momentous achievement and I was up early on Thursday to pack all my gear for Wembley.

It was a shame in some ways that we couldn't have a proper party because, as I say, we were the first Everton team to win a European trophy. It was all down to circumstances, though. If we were in the same situation now, then I'm sure the FA would put the Cup final back 24 hours to give us a bit of recovery time, but, back then, after winning in Rotterdam on the Wednesday night, we were due in London to take on Manchester United less than 72 hours later. We stayed at the hotel we'd used ahead of the '84 final, the Bellhouse in Beaconsfield, and Howard kept to the same routine.

It was a hot day at Wembley and I remember Howard being a bit disappointed at that because he'd been hoping, against the odds, for a drop of rain. He knew he had a group of players who had given their all for the entire season and he was aware that we didn't have too much left in the tank: a blazing hot day was the last thing we wanted.

I made a run after just ten minutes and I was knackered. I had a feeling in my legs that I didn't like one bit: they felt very heavy. I knew I was in for a long afternoon. I had no zip and no power and I told Andy that I had gone. I hoped that the feeling would pass and that I could shake myself back into condition, but I just couldn't do it. I felt really lethargic and it was awful.

I didn't like the atmosphere that day either. Against Watford the year before, there had been a typical carnival-like atmosphere inside Wembley, but against Manchester United it was sinister. The mood wasn't helped at all by the sending off of Kevin Moran with 12 minutes of normal time left. Their fans were furious. I felt there and then that there would be trouble if we had gone on to win the match. Kevin Ratcliffe agreed with me when we spoke about it later.

I've seen Kevin Moran's sending off hundreds of times since and I have to confess that it looks a harsh decision. I blame Reidy! If he'd have bothered to look up he would have seen Andy and I both making good forward runs and he could have slipped the ball to either of us, but he took an extra touch and that's when Moran went through him with the tackle. The way I was feeling, I probably wouldn't have got anywhere near it, and Andy wasn't the quickest at the best of times, but at least United would still have had 11 players on the pitch. I believe the sending off galvanised them.

We'd beaten Manchester United 5–0 at Goodison earlier in the season and we were the favourites ahead of the game, but we went down 1–0 after extra-time. We lost because we were shattered. It was purely and simply one game too far in a long, long season. The whole campaign, and the emotions that had come with it, had finally caught up with us. I still maintain that if the final had been played two days later then we would have won it without a problem. But we lost when it mattered and it was a bitter pill to swallow – even if the winning goal was superbly tucked away by Norman Whiteside.

I was actually a bit critical of Neville at the time because he covered his near post a bit too much which gave Norman the opportunity to curl the ball past him, but I do admit that it was a great finish. It might sound churlish to blame Neville, but maybe on reflection he would say the same. One thing for certain is that he had no need whatsoever to apologise to the lads after the game because he had kept us in so many matches that year with his sheer brilliance. He had helped us to win through to the final and he had earned us dozens of points in the League. Big Nev was the best in the world and he was, quite rightly, voted the Football Writer's Association Footballer of the Year for 1984–85.

Our Cup final banquet was obviously nothing like the previous year's. We were very down when we arrived at the hotel for the dinner and the only thing in my mind was to get drunk, but as time went on, the mood relaxed a bit and the people around us, our family and friends, reminded us of how well we'd done that season and I began to think, 'Yeah, we haven't done too bad here.' We'd come a long way together as a team and we'd achieved more than I ever could have dreamed of. We were as close off the pitch as we were on it and that's what made us a special team.

When we returned to Merseyside, the homecoming was unbelievable. More than a quarter of a million fans lined the streets to welcome us back – the memory of it still makes the hairs on the back of my neck stand on end. One banner that proclaimed 'Two will do, we thank you' summed it up.

We've since been labelled the greatest Everton team of all time and I wouldn't offer an argument to that. The next challenge was to prove ourselves in the biggest club competition of them all: the European Cup.

We had all the credentials to win it and the fans, I think, fully expected us to, but this most memorable of seasons was to have a tragic and far-reaching postscript.

On 29 May 1985, I had been out to see a friend and when I got home I was surprised to switch on the television and see that the European Cup final between Liverpool and Juventus at the Heysel Stadium in Brussels had not kicked off. You could tell straight away that the delay had something to do with crowd trouble and, as the night wore on, the horrific details became clear.

Football went to the back of my mind and I couldn't believe it when they announced that they were going to get the match started. Before the game, I had wanted Liverpool to lose but, when it kicked off, I really didn't care one way or the other. The football was completely secondary.

The English game didn't enjoy the best of reputations at the time and I feared that there would be repercussions, but I honestly didn't think that Everton would be punished. In fact, it didn't cross my mind that the dramatic and awful pictures unfolding that night would mean that I had kicked my last ball in a European competition. And I wasn't the only one: Rats, Reidy, Andy, Sheeds, Derek, Pat and Brace never got another chance. It was cruel and I felt it was unnecessary.

In my opinion, the two clubs involved should have been punished severely. There was no need for all of the English clubs to suffer. Liverpool and Juventus were to blame, as was the organisation that made the decision to stage the final at such an inadequate venue.

The ruling, which banned English clubs from competing in Europe until further notice, was very harsh indeed and there is no doubt that it had a huge effect on our team. Every one of us was disappointed because we wanted to play in the European Cup. It seemed so unfair because we had just had a wonderful European campaign that had taken us all over the Continent without a hint of trouble. I recall some of our fans having an impromptu game of football with the Dutch police in Rotterdam when Everton had been roundly praised for our supporters' behaviour. Then, all of a sudden, a golden opportunity was snatched away from us. All of us: players, staff and supporters were denied something that the whole club had waited so long for and had worked so hard to get. Things were never quite the same again . . .

EIGHT

DOUBLE DISAPPOINTMENT

I was really looking forward to the 1985–86 season. I was a regular in the team that had won the Championship and there was a World Cup to aim for at the end of the campaign. I didn't think anything could ruin my optimism as I enjoyed the summer break. Not for the first time, and certainly not the last, I received a sharp reminder that you can take nothing for granted in this wonderful game of ours.

When I took a Sunday morning phone call from Andy Gray asking me to meet him for a lunchtime drink, I thought nothing of it. He'd just bought and moved into a new house in Formby and we often used to get together for a few beers, but when we met up that day, the conversation left me speechless. 'I've had the gaffer round to my house,' said Andy. 'He's bringing in Gary Lineker and he's told me I can go.'

I couldn't believe my ears. If Andy hadn't looked so hurt, I would have assumed it was another of his pranks. 'After the season we've had?' I said. 'I can't believe it.'

Howard had explained to Andy that he would be the odd man out between himself, Lineker and me and that a deal had been negotiated with Aston Villa. It was all done and dusted. The partnership that had terrorised England and Europe in equal measure was no more.

Andy wasn't the type to sit around and be used whenever the manager deemed it appropriate; he wanted to play in every game and he felt that he still had plenty to give in the top flight.

So he signed for Aston Villa and left me feeling devastated. I honestly couldn't believe what was happening. Andy wasn't just my striking partner, he was a great friend and it took the shine off everything.

It was a real bolt from the blue and it was hardly the most positive way to kick off our defence of the title: we weren't just losing an excellent footballer, we were losing a massive character from our dressing-room. Andy was the leader and he helped mould everything together. Of course we were professional footballers, accustomed to comings and goings, and once the football started up again, the team spirit was still very good, but weekends were never the same again.

The rest of the lads were just as shocked and the punters weren't best pleased either. The *Echo* got sackloads of letters and the radio stations were inundated with phone calls from angry fans demanding to know what was going on. Poor Andy and Jan hadn't even taken most of their stuff out of the boxes after moving into their new house.

Howard's reasoning behind it all was that he wanted more pace in his side and, as everyone knew, Lineker had that in abundance. Even so, given the way we had finished the previous campaign, it was a stunning decision to let Andy go. In hindsight, it might have been the wrong decision because we didn't win a thing that season.

Links came in and scored lots of goals, but we changed as a team because of his phenomenal pace. We'd won the title playing some magnificent football, but with Links in the team we relied a lot more on the 'route one' method. I'd win plenty of balls in the air and Links would get on the end of them. He did well and finished as the country's leading scorer, but Everton finished empty-handed.

Once the shock of Andy's departure had abated, we had no choice other than to get on with things, as professionals do. It was important for Links to get off to a good start because, even as we kicked off the season, the supporters were still not wholly convinced. If I recall correctly, he didn't get the greatest of receptions when his name was read out before his Goodison debut. That must have been a bit daunting for him, but he soon won the fans over. It was tough for him, to be fair, because he knew the situation and he knew just how popular Andy was with everyone.

The first thing that struck me about Links was the size of his thighs. He had sprinter's thighs, which gave him tremendous pace off the mark. At the time, he wasn't a great footballer blessed with a good touch, nor could he link the play awfully well, but he was up there with the likes of Ian Rush when it came to putting the ball into the net. He had the priceless knack of being in the right place at the right time inside the penalty box. In fact the only goal I recall him scoring from outside the box was in an FA Cup replay against Luton Town.

Ironically his Everton debut was against the club he'd just left – Leicester City – at Filbert Street. They battered us, with Mark Bright scoring twice. We missed Andy more than they missed Links!

I opened my account for the season at home to Coventry in our third match. But I was rewarded with the axe: Howard played Inchy and Links in the next game at Tottenham and I was furious. We were only three games into a new season, for goodness sake. I felt that this was becoming a very unsettling pattern with Howard. His explanation on this occasion was that he'd mix and match the three of us depending on the opposition.

Clearly, he had no intention of leaving his record signing on the sidelines, so that meant that neither Inchy nor I would get a settled run in the team. I wasn't having that and not only did I tell Howard as much, I also told the press. That wasn't my style, but I was just so annoyed at being dropped after three games. The papers made a big issue out of it and Manchester United were rumoured to be interested, as were several Italian clubs.

At the time, Serie A clubs couldn't buy foreigners but those in Serie B could. Perugia were linked with me in the papers, though I never heard anything from them.

Aston Villa were also sniffing around for the umpteenth time in my career. Graham Turner had signed Andy in the summer and he was obviously keen to resurrect our partnership at Villa Park. It would have been tempting, such was my state of mind. I thought the way Howard treated me was grossly unfair. Links and I had been doing quite well and as a partnership we were always going to take a little while to develop, but Howard still saw fit to leave me out. As I've said previously, Howard and I didn't always see eye to eye; ours was an uneasy relationship at times.

Links found his scoring touch early on and he kept in the groove all season, but those opening weeks were unsettling for Inchy and for me. Nevertheless we all enjoyed a splendid win over Sheffield Wednesday at Hillsborough.

Mick Lyons was in the Wednesday team that night and we wound him up throughout the match about comments he had made one lunchtime during the summer when a group of us had been enjoying a few cold beers in a local pub near Bellefield. Big Lyonsy had come in on his way home from training after we'd been there an hour or so. He was full of himself after putting in another tough session under Howard Wilkinson. 'We'll be the fittest team in the division this season,' he said. 'All our training has been carefully planned and we will be right up there in the League. What have you lads done today?'

'A bit of ball work, a bit of five-a-side, nothing too strenuous,' I replied.

Lyonsy scoffed and suggested that fitness could be the crucial difference as the forthcoming season wore on. It was our sixth match of the new season against Wednesday and we hammered them 5–1.

We gave Lyonsy dog's abuse that night. 'Fitness is the key,

isn't it, Lyonsy?' we laughed. He was really losing his rag as the goals flew in.

I was back in the team again but after I'd played in Scotland's 1–1 draw with Wales that confirmed our World Cup qualification (see Chapter Nine), I was shocked and hurt to be dropped by Howard yet again. I was on the bench for our home match with Luton Town and although I came on to score our second goal in a 2–0 win, I was far from happy. In fact, I was at the end of my tether and the row between Howard and me got a bit more public. Even Inchy joined in, saying that a decision needed to be made. 'It's not good for me, Graeme or Gary, who must be wishing he had a settled partner,' he told Howard. I said that I was fed up being mucked about and that he had had enough time to sort out who and what his strike force should be.

As for Howard, he merely said, 'It looks as though players want to pick the team, but I will decide it.'

The last thing we wanted was a stand-off, so we went to see Howard and put our case forward. To be fair to him, he listened then made his decision: it was to be me alongside Links for the foreseeable future. It was disappointing for Inchy and I felt for him because it could so easily have been me, but we needed to know: putting us in the team in fits and starts was no good for anyone.

I had also suffered some personal heartache around this time. One day an urgent call came through to me at Bellefield from one of our neighbours telling me that Ann Marie had been rushed into hospital. She had had a miscarriage. It was a devastating blow because we had tried to make sure that she did everything right during her pregnancy. We were really looking forward to the arrival of our first child and we were getting quite excited at the prospect of starting a family. It was sadly just one of those things that can happen, but it was very upsetting for both of us.

I actually could have moved to Manchester United at this

time. Their physiotherapist, Jim McGregor, was an old pal of mine from his Everton days and he contacted me to say that Ron Atkinson was very keen to take me to Old Trafford. I must admit that going there appealed to me. But Everton were a far better side than United and I knew I had a better chance of winning things at Goodison than at Old Trafford, so I told Jim thanks, but no thanks.

With the striking problem resolved, Links and I set about making ourselves the most productive partnership in the First Division, with Inchy slotting into a midfield role.

We played Arsenal at Goodison one afternoon in November and we brushed them aside. We beat them 6–1 and it could have been more. They had an experienced back four of Viv Anderson, Tommy Caton, David O'Leary and Kenny Sansom but we were irresistible. Links and Inchy got two each, while Trevor Steven and I got the others. Mine was the all-important sixth goal that just about finished them off!

The Arsenal game was Neil Pointon's Everton debut. Howard had signed him from Scunthorpe United and none of us had ever heard of him when he was introduced on the Thursday before the Arsenal match. He walked into the dressing-room on the day of the game wearing this absolutely horrendous woollen, checked crossover bolero-style jacket with a shirt and tie! Neil's dress sense has never been the best, but that gear was something else. He got slaughtered for it, but he was a smashing lad who took the stick on the chin, gave a bit back and very quickly settled down. He needed to be a big character to make the step up from Scunthorpe to Everton in the space of 48 hours.

Neil played brilliantly against Arsenal and it was an unbelievable debut for him. He did very well for Everton and I was interested to read recently that Gary Naysmith, a current Everton left-back, said that Neil had a great influence on him when they were at Hearts together.

As the 1985–86 season progressed, Links and I just kept

scoring goals. We didn't specifically work at our partnership: it developed naturally. We couldn't work at it anyway because he hardly ever trained! He used to tell the physio that his hamstrings had tightened during the game and so all he'd do on the Monday was relax in the bath to soften his muscles. We'd all be trotting out in the wind and the rain for another session and Links would be wallowing in a hot bath!

Inchy, unsurprisingly, wasn't happy about the little set-up one bit. He'd be working his socks off in training whilst the most strenuous work Links did during the week was to try and turn the taps on and off with his toes! By Friday, he would have upped his output to include a bit of head tennis and he'd be named in the team. In fairness he'd then usually score a couple of goals on the Saturday, so nobody could argue with either his record or his inclusion.

Off the field, Links and I got on well together and he fitted in with the lads. He was no Andy Gray, but he always joined in whenever there was a social gathering. He bought a barn out in Tarleton, past Southport, close to where Trevor Steven lived, so they were quite close.

We were going well in the League when we went to Newcastle United on New Year's Day 1986 for a game that will always be remembered as the one that stalled the blossoming career of Paul Bracewell.

It was a dreadful day on Tyneside. The match was played in blizzard conditions and they had a beast of a centre-forward called Billy Whitehurst. He put a tackle in on Brace that ended his season on the spot and put his career on hold for a very long time. I firmly believe that Brace would have been in the England squad that went to Mexico for the World Cup had he not suffered that injury. The game finished 2–2 and I scored our equaliser from the penalty spot, but we knew that Brace had done himself a really bad injury. He fought back bravely after about 18 months on the sidelines, but he was never the same player again.

Whitehurst later joined Oxford and the next time he played against Everton was at the Manor Ground the following season. We were all lined up in the tunnel before the start of the game waiting to go out onto the pitch when Whitehurst came out of the Oxford dressing-room and shouted over at us.

'You lot, listen up,' he roared. 'We know what happened with Bracewell last year and if any of you want to have a go back at me, let's do it now. Don't wait until we're on the pitch, get it over with now because I'm fucking ready for it if any of you are.'

There were no takers.

The week after I'd scored that penalty at Newcastle – given, incidentally, for a foul by Glenn Roeder on me – I converted another one at Goodison against Queens Park Rangers in a 4–3 win. Once again I was the victim of an illegal challenge inside the box, this time from Steve Wicks. It was a big moment because we were two goals down at the time.

After the match, Wicks was fuming. 'It's the most abused trick in the game when a forward backs into the centre-half and Sharp is a past master at it,' he moaned. 'Glenn Roeder at Newcastle warned me this would happen because Sharp had done the same to him a week ago.'

Andy Gray had always encouraged me to jump early for the ball. If you waited, there was every possibility that the centre-half would be all over you with his arms and there would be no way you could get any sort of height. The easiest way to combat that was to leave the ground early and back into the defender at the same time. It was a trick of the trade and, anyway, centre-halves had no qualms about going through the centre-forwards from the back. It was considered to be part and parcel of the game. I won a lot of free-kicks with my style, but I would prefer to call it gamesmanship. Not for a moment would I compare it to the modern-day problem of players diving to win free-kicks and penalties.

In late February of that season, I was delighted to put pen to paper on a new four-year contract with the club. I was enjoying my football, Ann Marie and I were settled in our house in Ainsdale and the problems with Howard seemed to have been smoothed out. I had never had an agent, so I just did the negotiations myself with Howard and Jim Greenwood. The club made me an offer and I simply took it away to talk it over with Ann Marie. It was a good deal, which offered me some security for the next four years, and I was happy to sign it.

Ann Marie had found it tough when she first came down from Scotland. I had struggled as well, of course, but at least I had my football as a major distraction, whereas she had a lot of time to kill. It was, therefore, important that she was happy for me to sign the contract. If she hadn't been, then I would have thought about it again.

I actually put my signature on the forms on the morning of a game against Aston Villa at Goodison Park in March and it was announced over the tannoy before the kick-off. I was relieved that the fans received the news very well indeed. I got a great reception from them.

We beat Villa 2–0, with Links and me getting the goals. After the match, Allan Evans, their big centre-half, said, 'If Sharp and Lineker are going to be together for the next four years, then Everton are going to be winning things for the next four years.'

Even Links got a bit carried away after that game. 'I'm delighted Graeme is staying and I reckon we are going to get even better over the next few years,' he enthused.

We'll never know . . .

What I do know is that after that win – which Andy missed, by the way, because he was suspended and thereby denied a hero's return – we were eight points clear of third-placed Liverpool with eleven games to go. Manchester United were six points behind us, but we still considered Liverpool to be our main rival for the title. The feeling amongst the lads, though, was that we'd definitely be top of the pile at the end of the season.

Our philosophy hadn't changed, we still took each game as it came, but that Villa success was our ninth from ten matches, the other being a draw. We were in great shape and we were many pundits' tip for the title.

However, Liverpool then had an incredible run of results. They had not lost after we'd beaten them at Anfield, when Rats had scored his wonder goal from forty yards, but by late April we were still in the driving seat and knew that three wins from our last three games would give us the title again. Liverpool were two points clear at the top, but they only had two games to play.

Oxford United were fifth from bottom of the table and we didn't expect much trouble when we went there on the balmy Wednesday evening of 30 April. It was an astonishing night. We comfortably outplayed them, but Links, for just about the first time that season, was missing chance after chance. He reckoned that the apprentice who looked after his boots had packed the wrong pair and that's why he fluffed so many opportunities, but that was a load of nonsense: he should have scored. So should I and so should one or two of the others, but we didn't. They beat us 1–0 and we lost the title.

We should have beaten Oxford; Everton should have won the League. Simple as that.

Liverpool beat Leicester City that same night, which put them in pole position. It was too late to recover and they won the title at Chelsea the following Saturday.

We knew in the dressing-room at Oxford that we had blown it. We should have put five or six past them, but we had failed to score even one. It wasn't Links's fault: it was a collective responsibility.

Typically we then scored nine in our last two matches against Southampton and West Ham at Goodison. We walloped Southampton 6–1, with Links scoring a hat-trick, but I remember it for being my first introduction to a young defender called Jon Gittens. He was obviously out to impress somebody because he was kicking lumps out of me from the start. I had a word with him at one point, saying that I knew it was a big game for him at Goodison but that he'd better calm it down a bit. He took no notice, so I gave him a final warning. I had a World Cup to look forward to, after all.

He just carried on whacking me whenever I had the ball, so in the end I caught him with my elbow and he was down and out for the count. He walked into the players' lounge afterwards with his head swathed in bandages. I apologised but reminded him that I'd warned him enough times to behave himself.

I'd been annoyed on the pitch that day anyway because at one point I'd heard shouts from the crowd that Liverpool were losing at Chelsea, which, of course, they weren't.

Losing our Championship crown was a bitter blow. We'd had every bit as good a chance to do the double that year as we had done 12 months previously.

Our march to a third successive FA Cup final had been solid yet unspectacular. The current Everton physiotherapist, Mick Rathbone, a great character, played against us for Blackburn Rovers in the fourth round at Goodison and we had a great win at Tottenham, but the tie that sticks out the most is our quarter-final with Luton Town. They were out for revenge after their semi-final defeat in 1985 and they had home advantage on their awful plastic pitch.

They were 2–0 up at one stage and we looked down and out until I scored with a great header to pull one back. When the ball hit the net, about five or six of us all ran after it to get it back to the centre spot again. Some of the papers the next day credited the effort as an own goal but that was wrong. It was definitely my goal . . . and a good one too! We then levelled when Inchy netted an equaliser for us.

We always fancied ourselves in the replay at Goodison, but it was another close-run affair. Luton had a very good team in the mid-'80s and all our games against them were tough. It was 0–0 when I knocked a long ball forward and Links showed electric pace to overtake Steve Foster and Mal Donaghy and then lash one past the keeper. That put us into yet another FA Cup semi-final, this time against Sheffield Wednesday at Villa Park. It was a venue at which I always enjoyed playing, but Wednesday were a real handful.

Carl Shutt scored the opening goal and they had their tails up. But Alan Harper scored for us with a superb lob and we were right back in it. I had a great chance to clinch it just before the end, when I was clean through, but I missed the target completely. That took us into a period of extra-time, but I was still confident that it would be our day and I worked desperately hard to get another chance so I could make up for my miss.

My moment arrived when I got on the end of a cross from the right and managed to volley it past Martin Hodge and into the net. It was my first-ever FA Cup semi-final goal and to get it in front of the Evertonians who were packed into the Holt End at Villa Park was an incredible feeling.

We were back at Wembley again, but the celebrations just weren't the same without Andy. Of course, we partied well that night because we'd reached another Cup final, but, for me, there was a vital ingredient missing: Andy was always the life and soul of the celebratory nights out.

Thankfully we did still have some big characters in the dressing-room. Pat Van Den Hauwe for instance! Paddy lived in the same close as me in Ainsdale and his wife, Sue, was very friendly with Ann Marie.

Pat was a mad man! We'd be out having a quiet drink somewhere – he'd never been one for too much conversation, much preferring to listen – and his eyes would be everywhere, scanning the pub or the restaurant we were in. He'd then often make his mind up that someone was looking at him and he'd tell us that he was going to 'sort him out'. We'd have to calm him down and reassure him that anybody catching his eye would just be looking over because he was a famous footballer. We'd be on pins then for the rest of the night!

Paddy and I would often get a lift from Sheeds into training because he lived close by and Sue would spend the mornings at our house having a coffee with Ann Marie to kill the time while we were at Bellefield. One day after training we were getting back into Sheeds's car when Paddy decided that he'd prefer to have a few beers rather than go straight home. 'Tell Sue I'm having a bit of treatment,' he said to me, knowing that his wife would be at mine when I got home.

So when Sheeds dropped me off, I explained to Sue that he was having some ice applied to an injury and would be home later on. He was away for three days! I'd no idea where he was spending his evenings, nor did I want to know, but he was still in for training and Sue would come around in the afternoon asking me where her husband was. I could only say that I honestly didn't know. Paddy had put me in a terrible position.

I have to say, though, that I got on great with him. A lot of people didn't like him, but he and I were fine. I'd tell him things straight and he liked that. Because of his strong London accent, for a while I called him Reggie after the gangster Reggie Kray.

It was funny when he got a Welsh international call-up because his nickname then became Taffy. He'd never even been to Wales until he played football for the national team!

It was actually a Welsh international in March 1986 that could have wrecked our chances of achieving anything that season. Wales were in Dublin to take on the Republic of Ireland in a midweek game and on landing after jumping to catch the ball Neville Southall twisted his ankle. He left Landsdowne Road on crutches and that was his season finished.

It was a major setback because Big Nev was the best goalkeeper in the world. Luckily for us we had Bobby Mimms to deputise. He was fantastic. He kept six consecutive clean sheets in the League after getting his chance. He didn't let anybody down as we chased the League and Cup double. I saw Mimmsy in May 2006 when we played for Everton at Anfield in a charity match for Marina Dalglish and he looked better then than he did 20 years earlier!

Back in the FA Cup, there was unprecedented hype ahead of the final because our opponents were Liverpool. It was the first-ever all-Merseyside FA Cup final with the added spice that they had pipped us to the title the week before we met at Wembley.

The clamour for tickets was unbelievable. I was never going to be able to satisfy everyone, so I just made sure that my closest friends and family were all right and then tried to refuse every other subsequent request.

One afternoon both teams got together for a combined team picture. It was taken at Bellefield on a very windy and blustery day. Liverpool were far from happy about it because they wanted the picture taken at their Melwood training ground. They had to squeeze into the away dressing-room, which we saw as a little preliminary victory for us. In fairness, I thought it was a bit of a daft idea and I don't think it would happen today.

On the day of the final itself, we were by far the better team for about an hour. We were all over them and at half-time should have been ahead by more than just Gary Lineker's 40th goal of the season. Bruce Grobbelaar also made a terrific save to deny me and we should have been home and dry before we allowed them back into it.

Kenny Dalglish admitted afterwards that he told his team at half-time that they should have been out of it but that if they kept working they may get a chance. That came when Gary Stevens gave the ball away on the right and, within a flash, Rushie had the ball in the back of our net. They took over from then, and Craig Johnston and Rushie – again – gave the final score a somewhat flattering look about it.

It was heartbreaking for us. To come second to Liverpool in both the League and the FA Cup was a cruel way to finish what had been a great season for us.

Unbelievably both clubs had agreed to a joint open-top bus

homecoming on the Sunday, which meant we also had to share the flight back from London to Merseyside. It was little short of torture for the Everton lads.

In fact Reidy refused to get on the plane. 'I'm not going back with them,' he said. 'I'm not going back at all. I'm staying here.'

He got into a bit of trouble with Howard over that and was linked in the press with a move to FC Cologne, but Reidy was right on that occasion. It was a preposterous idea and, given my time again, I wouldn't have gone back either.

Just picture the scene. The Liverpool boys are drinking away, singing and celebrating, passing the FA Cup to one another, while we are sitting in a different area of the plane having to look at them doing it. I'm not sure who agreed to the idea in the first place, but whoever it was gave no thought whatsoever for the feelings of the players.

It got no better when we landed either because Liverpool were in the first bus with the Championship trophy and the FA Cup and we were in the one behind it with nothing. A few of the lads just stayed downstairs on the bus and had a few drinks.

In fact by the time the bus reached Queens Drive, we'd had quite a few and a number of us needed the toilet. Someone provided a bucket on the top deck, but there was no way I was going to use that. Instead I persuaded the driver to stop at a random house where half a dozen of us filed off and I knocked at the door. A lady answered and when I explained our predicament she very kindly allowed us to use the upstairs loo. I was first in and the others, led by Pat Van Den Hauwe, queued in an orderly fashion on the stairs. I had just got to the bottom of the stairs after my turn when an elderly gentleman rushed out of the living room, demanding to know what was going on. He was watching the homecoming on the television and was astonished to see that the Everton bus had stopped outside his house. He was also a Liverpool supporter and threw the rest of the lads out of the door!

We'd reached the final of another tournament that year, but

it was held over until the following season, which just about summed up how seriously everyone took the Screen Sport Super Cup, which the Football Association introduced as an initiative to raise money for the clubs who were missing out on European football. It was a complete farce and many players couldn't stand it. Nor could the supporters, judging from the sparse attendances at matches. If it was meant to soften the blow of there being no European football, it certainly didn't work.

The fact that 1986 saw one of the worst European Cup finals ever just made the ban on English clubs even worse in my opinion. It was a dreadful game between Barcelona and Steau Bucharest and, although there is no guarantee that we would have won the cup that year, we knew that we would have had a very good chance. We had loved our experience in the European Cup-Winners' Cup but to know that we wouldn't be getting a crack at the European Cup was heartbreaking.

In conclusion – and I hate to sound repetitive – I genuinely believe that things would have been different that season had Andy Gray stayed around. The camaraderie wasn't the same after he left and when you look at some of the games we didn't win, I feel sure he could have made a difference. He would have shaken things up at Oxford on the night we blew it, that's for sure. He didn't want to be a bit-part player and we had to respect him for that, but we missed our driving force.

Links did terrifically well, but he didn't stay long. His goals at Everton earned him a mind-boggling financial move to Barcelona. Nobody could blame him for that and I think his spell in Spain made him a better footballer. The training under Johan Cruyff at Barcelona probably helped and his technique improved. Cruyff played Links on the right wing at times and so he had no choice but to make himself a better linking player and improve his passing of the ball. I used to tell Links that I earned that move for him with the number of goals I set up for him!

SHARPY

At the end of the 1985–86 season, however, all we were both thinking about was the World Cup. We were both off to Mexico for the greatest football show on earth . . . but what a contrast in fortunes when we got there. He finished as the first-ever Englishman to top a World Cup goalscoring chart. I returned a very bitter, frustrated and confused young man.

NINE

FLOWER OF SCOTLAND

Playing for Scotland in the final stages of a World Cup tournament should have been the pinnacle of my career. Instead it was one of the biggest disappointments.

I knew that Scotland had a reputation for being the nearly men ahead of the 1986 World Cup finals in Mexico. We had a decent record with regard to actually qualifying for the tournaments, but we had still never progressed beyond the first phase.

After a roller-coaster qualification process, we eventually confirmed our place for the finals, where, following the untimely death of Jock Stein, we were under the stewardship of Alex Ferguson. I was fairly confident that I would be included in the final squad – the fact that Alex had tried to sign me earlier in my career, I was sure, would work in my favour. He also knew my family quite well because he had signed my brother, Richard, when he had been the manager at St Mirren.

I was duly named in the squad, but Alex left out Alan Hansen after 'Jocky' had just won the double with Liverpool. Kenny Dalglish then pulled out with an injury and some people claimed that those two incidents were directly related, but I don't think they were.

Alex took five strikers to Mexico – Charlie Nicholas, Frank McAvennie, Paul Sturrock, Steve Archibald and me. We were a good set to select from and as I had just completed another very good season with Everton I felt that I had every chance of making an impact on the biggest stage of them all.

I was obviously looking forward to the whole experience immensely. The only niggling doubt in my mind concerned Ann Marie. She was pregnant at the time and had decided to stay in Scotland with her family for the duration of the competition – we were taking no chances after the miscarriage she had suffered a year earlier.

The team left Scotland full of confidence, even though we'd been handed a really tough group with Denmark, West Germany and Uruguay.

To help us acclimatise, we flew to Los Angeles a couple of weeks before the tournament kicked off and then moved on to Santa Fe before arriving in Mexico. When we first arrived in LA, we were delighted to receive an invitation from Rod Stewart to join him at his mansion for a pre-World Cup party. I've always been a Rod Stewart fan and was excited at the prospect, but when the Scottish press found out about the get-together we weren't allowed to go.

We worked hard every day in training, in extreme heat, and so one night Graeme Souness, who was the captain, asked Alex if the lads could have a bit of a night out just to break the monotony of the hotel surroundings. Alex was fine with the suggestion, but we were under instructions to be back by half-past eleven. Graeme Souness, Steve Archibald, Frank McAvennie, Charlie Nicholas, Alan Rough and me went to a really nice bar in Beverly Hills that Graeme had heard of. It was decorated in blue tartan and, although we didn't know it at the time, it was Rod Stewart's local. Unbeknown to us, Graeme had tipped him off about our presence. The next minute a limousine pulled up outside and Rod got out! He took us to a top restaurant in Beverly Hills where we ate the most fabulous food. I was just in awe of him. It was a memorable night, but we were back somewhat later than our half-eleven curfew!

When we moved to Santa Fe, there was little chance of anything similar occurring because we were right in the middle of the desert. It was really hot and at times it was tediously boring, but we knew that it had to be done to prepare correctly for Mexico. While we were there, we had an 11-a-side kickabout with the Northern Ireland team, who were staying close by in Albuquerque. There were no goalposts, so we made piles of tracksuits and got on with it.

Our base when we finally arrived for the finals was just outside Mexico City. There had been a major earthquake in the area not long before and in some places we could clearly see the devastating effects. It was certainly a bit of an eye-opener. Our hotel was in the middle of nowhere and little Gordon Strachan immediately likened it to a prison. We were all in single rooms and struggled to get to sleep at night because the armed guards would walk their dogs on the flat roof of the hotel.

The excitement grew as our first game against Denmark approached. The lads were all speculating about who would play and I must admit I was surprised that I wasn't even on the bench when Alex named the line-up. Charlie and Paul Sturrock started up front and it was hard to take because I felt like a spare part around the hotel on the day of the game. We lost 1–0. The same thing happened for the West Germany game. I had travelled all that way with the squad and had worked as hard as anyone, I looked sharp in training and I was full of confidence after a good season with Everton, yet here I was in Mexico for the biggest event of my life and I wasn't even getting a look-in. I was hurt and baffled. What had I done wrong? Steve Archibald played against the Germans, but we lost again.

I thought I must surely figure in the third must-win match against Uruguay and, sure enough, I was straight in from the start alongside Sturrock. I was pleased to be making my World Cup debut in a fixture that we had to win, but Alex had dropped a bombshell by leaving his captain out of the team. There was no place for Graeme Souness against Uruguay, which we all thought was madness given that the South Americans had a global reputation for the toughness of their approach. When the team was read out, the lads were stunned that Graeme hadn't been included. Personally I thought it was an ideal game for someone like Souness. He was missed in a match that was often violent and at times brutal. Within the first 30 seconds of the game, for example, they had a man sent off.

Not including Graeme was a big mistake by the manager. Alex Ferguson was a bit critical of me in his autobiography, claiming that I should have been more physical during this match, but some of the things that went on were unbelievable. Their behaviour was disgraceful. They were animals – spitting, pulling hair, shoving their fingers in places they shouldn't have done – and it was difficult not to react. In the end, we drew 0–0 and were out.

The whole experience was a disappointment. I think managing Scotland in a World Cup came too soon for Alex. His achievements at Aberdeen spoke for themselves, but it was possibly a bit early for him to be dealing with bigger-name players with more experience. I feel certain things should have been done differently.

After the Uruguay game, we still had one night left in Mexico and I, for one, after all my frustration, was determined to make the most of it. Along with Alan Rough and Andy Goram, I decided to have a night out. Nobody else fancied it, so the three of us boarded the official SFA team bus and a police escort accompanied us through the streets into Mexico City.

The trip ended with a good night out and I am honoured to have represented my country in the World Cup, but I was bitter that it had panned out the way it did. In some ways, it was symptomatic of my international career. I never felt that I ever got a fair crack of the whip with Scotland. It always seemed as though I was on trial when I joined up. I was really successful with Everton, scoring goals and winning trophies, but I always felt that I had to prove myself all over again every time I put on a Scotland shirt. I'd get half a game here and half a game there, which I didn't think was fair.

Of course, I understand that there was an abundance of

quality Scottish strikers during my time, but I think I deserved a run of games to try and establish myself as a regular in the team. Even during Everton's greatest-ever season, when I was top scorer with 30 goals, I didn't win a single cap. Everton were winning virtually every week, domestically and in Europe, but it seemed as though Scotland were going to try every other striker before they turned to me.

I honestly believe that not playing my club football in Scotland counted against me. There was definitely a bias towards the players who were plying their trade in the Scottish Premier League. Consider Alan Hansen, who surely should have won far more than 27 Scotland caps, and Gary Gillespie, who should have tallied up more than 13. To be playing for an English club and be a regular for Scotland took some doing and if that sounds like sour grapes, it's too bad. That is how I viewed the situation and, I can promise you, I was not alone in thinking this.

When I did finally break through, I never got the feeling that I would be given a reasonable chance to prove myself and, if I'm being perfectly honest, it quickly got to the stage where I wasn't even enjoying being away with my country. I was really envious of Neville Southall and Kevin Ratcliffe, who both loved being with the Welsh international team because there was such a wonderful spirit amongst the players.

The press always had too much sway when it came to the selection of the Scottish squads and under certain managers I always thought that the media actually picked the team. Like I have said, they certainly knew the team before anybody else. People suggest that the media has a big influence on the England team these days, but back then the Scottish press were much worse.

When I was a young boy growing up in Glasgow, I used to watch as many Scotland games at Hampden Park as I could. I loved going to watch us play England. I remember my dad taking me to watch Scotland beat them 2–0 in 1974 in the Home Internationals. Jimmy Johnstone was playing, as were Billy

Bremner, Joe Jordan and Kenny Dalglish, and there were almost 95,000 supporters inside the ground – mostly Scottish, I hasten to add! We were also there when England thumped Scotland 5–0 in the Scottish FA Centenary Celebration match at Hampden the previous year. That was a terrible night, but happily I can recall little else other than the shocking scoreline, though I do remember that the weather was awful. It was an icy and bitterly cold February night. At one stage, they didn't think the match would go ahead.

In those days, you could just walk up to the Scottish FA headquarters in Park Garden in Glasgow and buy tickets for the games. They were relatively easy to get hold of – although with Hampden Park then having a capacity of 100,000, there were more tickets to go round, I suppose.

I didn't get any national recognition when I was at school and I was never invited for trials for the Scottish Schoolboys team. In all honesty, though, I wasn't overly concerned about it. It's amazing the number of young players who did play in Schoolboy internationals who then never got anywhere near making it as a professional footballer. I was more concerned with furthering my football education with Eastercraigs and then Dumbarton.

When I started knocking in a few goals for Dumbarton, of course, I eventually got my Scotland call-up for the Under-18 squad, but the smashed cheekbone I had received at Clydebank put paid to my chances of playing. It was a big disappointment to miss out through injury, but I couldn't do anything about it other than to keep working hard and hope that another chance would come my way. I was focused on getting back to fitness for my club team.

I didn't get another shout for Scotland until I had moved to Everton when I was included in the Under-21 squad that took on England at Maine Road in the spring of 1982. It was a massive thrill for me. I've still got the call-up letter informing me that English-based players were required to meet at the Post House Hotel on Merseyside before travelling by coach to Manchester.

That was easy enough for me! But my family had to hire a minibus to ferry everyone down from Glasgow for the game.

We drew 1–1 and I scored our goal. Ironically Adrian Heath scored for England. Steve Nicol, Frank McAvennie, Jim Bett, Tommy Burns and Roy Aitken were in our team while Sammy Lee, Justin Fashanu, Gary Shaw, Terry Fenwick and Steve McKenzie played for England. I did well, but it was the second leg of the European Under-21 championships and, as England had won the first game at Hampden, we went out. I was a bit down because we'd gone out on aggregate, but I was consoled by the fact that I felt I had done well.

My dad had always said that when I first represented my country, he would like to have my shirt and, sure enough, he was waiting outside the dressing-room when I came out after the game.

Scotland's elimination meant the end of my Under-21 career. By the time the next squad was announced, I was too old to be considered, so the next step for me was a full call-up. I just concentrated on establishing myself at Everton in the First Division. Everton weren't the most successful team in the early '80s, which probably counted against me, but I considered myself to be as good as any of the other Scottish strikers around at the time. It was frustrating, but I bided my time.

I had to wait until the end of the 1984–85 season before I was selected for the Home International match against England at Hampden. Jock Stein came to Goodison to watch me play against Bayern Munich in the second leg of our European Cup-Winners' Cup semi-final – that was certainly a good one to pick! – and I was absolutely thrilled to bits when my place was announced. Scotland against England is every schoolboy's dream and I was joining up with the squad having just won the League with Everton. Unfortunately for me another kick in the teeth was lying in wait.

Everton still had one League match left against Coventry City at Highfield Road. As Coventry were still involved in a relegation fight, the other clubs near the bottom of the table protested that our side would be weakened by the absence of international players. The England match was on the Saturday and the Everton match was 24 hours later. Howard had already given us full permission to play in the international; indeed he had even allowed Andy and me to miss the Merseyside derby against Liverpool at Goodison during the week.

Jock Stein had already told me that I would be playing against England, so I was really looking forward to it, especially as Andy was my likely striking partner. To be selected by such a great man was the ultimate for me. He was a legend and he had shown faith in my ability to do a job for Scotland, which meant an awful lot.

I was unaware of the controversy in Merseyside until Jock called me to his room at our Gleneagles Hotel base. He told me that there was a problem and that Coventry's rivals were concerned about them playing a weakened Everton. Had Luton Town defeated Coventry the night before, then we'd have been OK because the relegation issue would have been sorted, but Coventry won and Andy and I were under instructions to return to Everton with immediate effect.

The SFA secretary, Ernie Walker, protested to the Football League and even threatened to involve UEFA, but it was all to no avail. The Football League had ruled that Everton were obliged to field their strongest possible team. To say I was gutted was an understatement. I said at the time that I felt like 'the guy who has got a winning pools coupon and forgot to post it'. I was devastated because my whole family had tickets for the game. You can imagine my state of mind when I played for Everton at Coventry. They beat us 4–1 and so stayed up anyway, although I wasn't the slightest bit bothered one way or the other. I don't think Howard was either. He had labelled the decision to bring us back a 'disgrace'.

Scotland, meanwhile, had beaten England 1–0, thanks to a Richard Gough goal and the party then flew out to Reykjavik for a World Cup qualifier straight after the game. Andy and I had to make our own way to Iceland, so after our game the Coventry chairman, Brian Richardson, gave us a lift to the airport to catch a flight.

I remember sitting down to lunch on our first day in Iceland. Jock Stein was at a table with the staff but he had an uncanny knack of being able to keep a close eye on every single person in the room. The waitress came around the dining room with the lunch menu and, as I was a touch nervous, I kept my order simple, ordering soup and steak. Andy decided to be a bit more flamboyant. He looked hard at the menu before opting for a prawn cocktail, but before he could order his main course there was a loud bellow from the staff table. It was Jock.

'Prawn cocktail?' he roared. 'Gray, you are from Drumchapel, you don't even know what a prawn cocktail is. Soup! You'll have soup and you'll like it!'

Andy was a star of the team, but he knew his place and sheepishly changed his order.

One other memory from the Iceland trip again involves Rod Stewart. We were training the day before the game, using the sparse facilities, when we were distracted by a limousine with blacked-out windows that pulled up alongside the pitch. We wondered what was going on and were surprised to see Rod step out of the vehicle with Kelly Emberg on his arm! He had flown out for the game and had come to watch us train. On an ordinary day Kelly Emberg could have been something of a distraction, but this was my international bow and Rod could have been with Bella Emberg for all I cared!

On 28 May 1985, I could legitimately call myself a Scottish international footballer and it was an extremely proud day for my family and me. The team was Jim Leighton, Maurice Malpas, Richard Gough, Roy Aitken, Alex McLeish, Willie Miller, Graeme Souness, Gordon Strachan, Andy Gray, Jim Bett and Graeme Sharp. It was a dream come true for me and to partner Andy Gray up front made it that bit more special.

Although it wasn't much of a spectacle, we won the game 1–0 to keep our qualification hopes alive. We left it very late, though: there were only four minutes to go when Jim Bett scored the winning goal. There were 15,000 fans inside the National Stadium in Reykjavik that night and it was an inauspicious place for an international debut but that didn't concern me.

The win against Iceland got us back on track in the World Cup. We had lost at home to Wales earlier in the tournament when Ian Rush scored the only goal of the game and had been in danger of missing out on qualifying for Mexico '86.

I will always be grateful to Jock for giving me my Scottish debut and, like everybody else connected with the national team, I was extremely distressed when he passed away in September 1985 on the night we secured qualification for the World Cup finals in Mexico. We were up against Wales at Ninian Park, Cardiff, and we needed to avoid defeat to qualify for the play-offs.

It was a strange game for me because I was playing against Kevin Ratcliffe, Pat Van Den Hauwe and Neville Southall. Rats and Pat were the centre-halves. I'd never played against them before other than in training.

Wales scored first on the night and it looked as though we were on our way out until David Speedie crossed the ball into the penalty area in the 81st minute. It hit a defender's hand and Davie Cooper kept his nerve to score from the penalty spot past Big Nev.

It was a fabulous result for us, considering that we'd had to substitute our goalkeeper at half-time. Jim Leighton had lost a contact lens and, unbelievably, he didn't have a spare set. We were in the dressing-room at half-time during the biggest Scotland match for years and the goalie had to tell the manager he couldn't carry on because he couldn't see properly! It could only have happened to us. We were fortunate to have a replacement as experienced as Alan Rough.

When the final whistle sounded, we were all ecstatic and the thousands of Scottish supporters who had travelled to South

Wales celebrated with us. We had only qualified for the play-offs at this stage, but we knew we only had to beat Australia over two legs to reach the finals and, with all due respect, they were nothing like the team they are now. There was a party atmosphere, but then nobody knew anything of the tragedy that was only moments away.

After celebrating on the pitch, we headed for the dressing-room to pop some champagne, but we were stopped by an SFA official who urged us to go back out again. It soon became apparent that Jock had suffered a heart attack. That took the wind out of our sails straight away, but not for a moment did we consider that the Big Man wouldn't be all right. When we were finally allowed into the dressing-room it was very quiet and sombre as we waited for news.

When we were told that Jock hadn't managed to pull through, we were completely flattened. Nobody could believe it.

Jimmy Steele, a lovely old man who was the team masseur and who had been very close to Jock, was very upset. Indeed there were a few tears shed in that dressing-room. It was just a case of getting showered and changed and getting away from it. I was travelling to Birmingham because I was staying with Andy. We had planned a night out, but, needless to say, we simply went back, had a glass of wine, remembered the great Jock Stein and went to bed. Quite rightly, the result and the consequences of World Cup qualification didn't matter in the press the following day.

It was left to Alex Ferguson, who had been Jock's assistant, to guide us through the play-off matches against the Aussies. I was a substitute for the first game at Hampden – I came on for the last 20 minutes to replace Dalglish – and we won 2–0 with goals from McAvennie and Cooper. We could, and should, have got more goals, but we were fully confident that Australia weren't going to put three past us Down Under.

The journey for the second leg was horrendous. It took so long to get there and we didn't have much time to acclimatise before the game at the Olympic Stadium in Melbourne. It was December 1985 and so I had to miss a couple of Everton games whilst we were away, but it was worth it because we drew 0–0 to qualify.

As I have explained, the '86 World Cup was a source of huge disappointment to me and afterwards, under Andy Roxburgh, things didn't get too much better. Andy was a smashing man, who was a very good coach, but I don't think he was an international manager. He faced the intensity of the Scottish football press and he often seemed worried what sort of reaction he would get from the media. The press tried to bully Andy and I felt he was a bit too easy to manipulate. I have to say that he was always straight and honest with me, which I appreciated, but I was still never a regular in the team.

Ironically my last game for Scotland saw me score my one and only international goal. We played Malta in the Ta'Qali Stadium in Valletta. Ally McCoist and Alan McInally were on the scene by then, so there was still fierce competition for places.

It wasn't a particularly memorable game, but I managed to score our goal with a header and I remember giving my shirt to referee George Courtney after the match. I wasn't one for keeping my shirts and recall attempting to swap with Kevin Sheedy at the end of a match in Dublin against the Republic of Ireland when an Irish supporter snatched his off me and ran away! Sheeds had my shirt, so I had to sprint after the fan, weaving my way through the crowds, until I finally caught up with him and grabbed it back!

I didn't realise that the Malta game was my Scotland swansong, but I had been getting more and more disillusioned with the whole scenario of travelling around the world and not playing, or just getting a brief run-out as a substitute. And I had a young family by then.

When I wasn't picked for the 16-man squad for a friendly at Hampden, I phoned my dad from the Gleneagles Hotel and told him to come and get me. He calmed me down, told me not to be daft and suggested we talk after the match. I went to Hampden, watched the game and then when I got home I decided that enough was enough.

I explained my feelings to Andy Roxburgh at Ayresome Park after Everton had played Middlesbrough one night. I was coming back from injury and Andy came to see how I was progressing. He came down to the dressing-room area and I told him that I no longer wanted to be considered. I gave him my reasons and said that I would help him out if ever he felt he needed me, but that I wanted to concentrate on my career with Everton.

'OK, but don't tell the press!' he said.

In fairness, he was great about it because he is a genuine man, but, of course, the emergency call to help my country never came.

I should have won more than 12 caps, I know that. Had I played for Celtic or Rangers I would have done. But, of those 12 matches, I am proud to record that my country never lost a single one.

TEN
CHAMPIONS AGAIN

Everton may have lost Gary Lineker, but I spent large parts of the summer celebrating a new arrival. My son, Christopher, was born in June 1986 just after I had returned from World Cup duty in Mexico. Compared to the disappointment of that tournament, the birth of my first child was a hugely uplifting event.

Ann Marie went into labour while we were sitting at home and I telephoned her parents as soon as the girl from over the road had driven her to Oxford Street Women's Hospital in Liverpool. A gynaecologist called Mrs Francis delivered the baby and I'll never forget her. She had been wonderful throughout the pregnancy and had looked after Ann Marie very well indeed. I was present during the birth and once Christopher had been safely delivered I was officially in celebration mode.

Ann Marie's mum and dad had made it from Glasgow in time and were sitting outside the ward when Chris was born. They popped in to see Ann Marie and then I instructed John to drop me off at the Weld Blundell in Formby. I had a really good night wetting the baby's head with Pat Van Den Hauwe, Sheeds and a couple of the other lads.

The next day I was back in the Weld Blundell nice and early and had a few more before John came to pick me up and take me to see Ann Marie and Chris. I made sure my new family was doing OK then was promptly delivered to the door of the Weld again. This pattern went on for four days and it was marvellous!

Howard always used to say that the season after the birth of a baby was usually a struggle for a player and in my case he was right. Although we went on to win the title, I missed a lot of games with injuries and didn't contribute as much as I would have liked. Chris was a good baby, but my sleep pattern had obviously changed and maybe that affected me more than I realised at the time. Ann Marie will have a wry smile reading this because every time Chris cried in the night or needed feeding, she'd be the one to get out of bed and see to it. She lost far more sleep than I ever did.

At Everton in those days, if a new father was having a bit of trouble sleeping at night Howard would encourage him to spend a couple of nights in a hotel to catch up on his rest. It was a decent idea in principle, but I must admit it wasn't something that I took advantage of. I preferred to take my chances in my own bed.

As I reflect on the birth of our first child, it is as good a time as any to give Ann Marie her due praise for the way she has helped my career over the years. A professional footballer needs a really strong woman behind him and I consider myself to have been very fortunate on that front. The rewards of the life are crystal clear, but players spend a lot of time away from home and the divorce rate is quite high. Whenever the lads from the mid-'80s get together, Rats always jokes about me and him sitting at the married table. A lot of the players from our time are no longer with the wives or partners they had in the '80s.

The women have to put up with a lot. Football is very much a male-orientated industry: like it or not, it is a man's world. The womenfolk do suffer because of it on occasions.

The annual end-of-season trips were a shining example. The wives all knew and understood that there would be a pre-season tour at the end of every summer. That's just part and parcel of the job and it always will be. But the end-of-season tours were a real bone of contention with some of them. In reality, the players had no choice but to go to Magaluf or Marbella or wherever, but some needed a bit of help to smooth things over at home.

Some of the players were under pressure from their wives not to go on these trips, however Howard would get a letter typed up at Bellefield informing the lads that the tour was not optional. The letter stated that we had to go away and that there would be a friendly fixture somewhere along the line. We rarely played games on these tours, but some players needed the letter to clinch it with their wives.

It would be funny when we were sitting in a bar in sunny Spain listening to someone phoning home and discussing an imaginary football match with his wife. Sometimes the lads would get the details wrong and when the wives met up back home they would discover that they'd been given different stories.

It was not always easy being a footballer's wife, but Ann Marie was always there for me and although as a typical male I don't often let her know, she has been magnificent and I couldn't have done it without her.

One small thing that I most certainly did *not* get away with was the time I gave her a Christmas card and inside it I had written: 'To Ann Marie, Best wishes, Graeme Sharp.' I was so used to signing autographs that I went into autopilot when I got a pen in my hand. We laugh about it now, but she wasn't amused at the time.

Getting back to football, losing Gary Lineker was a blow for us, there is no question about that, but once he started scoring goals for fun in the World Cup it was inevitable that the biggest clubs in the world would come knocking at Everton's door. We'd lost Andy after winning the title and now we were losing Links, a proven quality goalscorer, after having him for just one year. I didn't blame Links for going, but it was a shame that we couldn't develop our partnership.

In all honesty I wasn't as disappointed when Links left as I was when Andy was transferred because we had changed our style

Above: Fourteen months old and I don't look too sure of myself on that wooden horse! Richard is on the left of the picture and Andrew on the right.

Left: Aged eight, a pupil at Stepps Primary School in Glasgow.

Above: The Coatbridge team, 1975. I'm second from the left in the front row. (Glasgow *Herald*)

Right: Creating an opening for Dumbarton against Hamilton Academical . . .

Below: . . . and then smashing the ball into the net.

Chasing the ball for the Scotland Under-21s against England in 1982.
(George Ashton)

Andy Gray and I celebrate our 1984 FA Cup win with our wives.
(*Daily Express*)

Celebrating the 1984 FA Cup win with my mum and dad
at the post-match party.

The glory of Rotterdam: celebrating our 1985 European Cup-Winners' Cup
success with Kevin Sheedy, Trevor Steven and Andy Gray. (Bob Thomas)

With Scotland as the team prepare to leave for the 1986 World Cup in Mexico. I'm in the middle row, third from right.

Champions again! Adrian Heath and I toast our 1987 title success.
(Terry Mealey)

My only goal for Scotland, against Malta.

Walking out with Emma and Chris ahead of my testimonial match.
(Terry Mealey)

A pre-season picture during my Oldham Athletic days.

My first day as manager of Bangor City, collecting my sponsored car from chairman Ken Jones and two other club officials. (*Liverpool Daily Post*)

The family: Ann Marie, me, Emma and Chris on holiday in Portugal, 2006.

of play quite dramatically to accommodate Lineker. His move to Barcelona also gave Inchy and me the chance to work together up front again. I had shared a great understanding with Inchy in the past and I knew we could be successful again. He'd fought back from that dreadful injury and although it was suggested in some quarters that he'd lost a yard or so of pace and a bit of his sharpness, it didn't matter too much because he was such an intelligent footballer.

Howard also made some excellent signings during the summer. Bringing in Paul Power was one of the best bits of business that Everton ever did. When I heard that the manager was planning to bring Paul in from Manchester City, my first thought had been 'Why?' I'd seen him playing on a few occasions and I thought that he was possibly too old to have much of an impact. Pat was likely to be missing for a long time with an injury and so we were short in the left-back department, but it still seemed to be a strange one from Howard. I thought Paul would be a squad member at best.

But Howard's judgement once again was absolutely spot on. Paul proved to be a fabulous buy and he brought some valuable experience to the dressing-room. He was a smashing professional and worked the left flanks extremely well.

Another great signing, and much more of a safe bet, was Dave Watson. The club paid big money for the centre-half, but Waggy was full value. It was another brave decision by Howard to bring in Waggy and leave Derek Mountfield on the sidelines and the punters gave the new man a bit of a rough time. He soon won them over though and went on to become a Goodison legend.

I knew what we were getting because I'd played against Waggy a few times and I didn't like it. He was an old-fashioned centre-half who didn't lose many headers inside his own penalty area and he had more aggression than Derek Mountfield.

Kevin Langley's recruitment was also inspired. We didn't know anything about him when he arrived from Wigan Athletic, but he was a great player and made a good impression on us.

SHARPY

The lads christened him 'Jack' because we reckoned he looked like the film star Jack Palance. He didn't have an abundance of pace, but he was good on the ball and he played very well after being thrown in at the deep end. He gave a masterly display early on when we took Manchester United apart at Goodison and beat them 3–1. He had to make quite an adjustment when he left lowly Wigan for the top division and although he put in some great performances, the gulf in levels soon became apparent and after 16 games he lost his place in the side and never got it back. He drifted off the first-team scene as quickly as he had arrived.

The 1986–87 season offered us our first experience of Wimbledon's 'Crazy Gang'. After an incredible journey through the leagues, the club had made it to the top flight less than 20 years after being promoted into the Football League from the old Southern Division. It was an amazing real-life story and it didn't stop at promotion to the First Division either because when we played them at Plough Lane that September it was billed as a 'top of the table' clash after they made a terrific start.

Plough Lane was a horrible place to go to and Wimbledon were a dreadful team to play against. You knew exactly what they would do in every game: the goalkeeper would roll the ball to the full-backs and they would launch it forward as quickly as they could. You expected a tough physical battle every time and you had to match them and stand up to them.

Some of their tricks and tactics were pure non-League. They'd take the light bulbs out in the dressing-room, or they'd leave the windows open so that it was freezing cold when you were getting changed. They'd turn the heating off, too. The bath water was always cold. You'd hear them playing their loud music on a huge ghetto blaster. It was an intimidating ground and Wimbledon thrived on it. Fair play to them, though, because it worked and they achieved a level of success they could never have imagined.

I never had too much trouble from the most infamous Crazy Gang member, Vinnie Jones. I remember Rats and I tucked him up beautifully once at Goodison and he got sent off. He tackled me and I went down as though I'd been shot, then Rats tumbled over when Vinnie lightly brushed his head against him. Vinnie stormed into the players' lounge after the match shouting, 'Who fucking wants some? Who wants some?' The guests in there were rather startled by him, to say the least! Nobody took him on, that's for sure.

Sheeds and I scored at Plough Lane where we beat Wimbledon 2–1, but it was a poor game. It was difficult for forwards playing against them because they pushed out so quickly and so regularly that you were always running after their defenders, trying to stay onside in case we won possession. Howard actually encouraged us to stay offside at times rather than use up energy trying to get back onside.

As it progressed, 1986–87 turned out to be a strange season in many ways. Howard was unable to select many settled line-ups yet we kept churning out good results. The football was nowhere near as entertaining as it had been in 1985, but the results were great. For me personally, it was a bit frustrating because I missed chunks of the campaign through injury, as did a few of the lads: Big Nev sat out the first dozen games and Pat was out for a long time, as were Reidy and Gary Stevens.

One particularly good result was our first-ever win on Queens Park Rangers' plastic pitch. We went there early in January and I scored a fine solo goal (though I say so myself!) to give us a 1–0 win. I beat three defenders – with skill rather than pace, I hasten to add – and then curled my shot around David Seaman and into the net. It was one of only five goals I scored in the League that season, although my contribution in cup games at least carried me into double figures. I was much more of a goal provider that season.

The year before, Links, Inchy and I scored 78 goals between us, which is an amazing statistic. In 1986–87, they were spread around more evenly: Inchy, Trevor, Wilkie, Sheeds and I all ended up with double-figure goal tallies at the end of the season.

When I played in the 1986–87 season I was reasonably pleased with my form but obviously would have liked to have been involved a lot more often.

When it became clear that I was going to be out for quite a while, Howard made yet another shrewd move in the transfer market. He brought in Wayne Clarke from Wolves, and he did a great job for the team. Clarkey had been around a bit without ever looking like an outstanding prospect. Perhaps throughout his career he suffered in comparison to his brother, Allan. They were very similar players in fairness – I used to think that they even walked and ran the same way. Clarkey was quite a reserved character, but he had a very dry sense of humour and he settled in well with the lads.

As did Ian Snodin, who joined us from Leeds United. I knew of him because he'd made a few headlines at Leeds and at one stage it looked like he was going to sign for Kenny at Liverpool. But he chose Everton and we were glad that he did. He had a great engine and was a classic box-to-box midfield player. He loved getting stuck in and he could move the ball well, although when it came to finishing there was room for improvement in my opinion. He could get into the positions, but when the ball came his way he had little composure in front of goal and he should have scored a lot more.

He was an archetypal Yorkshire lad. He didn't complicate things and in all the years we played in the same team I only ever saw him order soup and a steak at restaurants. Soup and steak was even his pre-match meal and he never varied it! I tried to persuade him to order some smoked fish once and his response was entirely typical. 'Smoked fish? I'm not eating any of that crap!'

He took to the dressing-room banter straight away. He was a class midfielder, but he was an even better right-back later in his Everton career. Had he stayed clear of injury he would certainly have won some England caps because there was no one better than him in that position in the country. He was also a very good sweeper because he could read the game so well. Picking up his injuries when he did was a crying shame. I considered Snods to be technically a better footballer than Gary Stevens and he would have been an England regular.

When Snods first signed for us, he still lived in Doncaster and would drive himself across the Pennines every day. When we were out one afternoon, I had a right go at him about it. 'You need to live over here,' I snapped at him. 'It's not good for team spirit if you don't even live in the area. Get over here and your game might even improve.' It became a really heated exchange of opinions, but to be fair, Snods listened to me and took it on board and eventually did move into the local area. Our little fallout was rare because we got on great together – I signed him for Oldham when I was manager there.

It was also Snods who nearly caused Howard to drown during an end-of-season tour to Spain. Snods was swimming in the sea and Howard was watching him, whilst sipping champagne and puffing on a big cigar.

'Come in, gaffer,' shouted Snods. 'The water's lovely. I can stand up in it, so you'll be OK.'

Howard needed some convincing because he couldn't swim, but he thought that if Snods was standing up then it would be fine to have a paddle around. Howard made a great show of carrying his bottle of champagne over to the side of the boat in readiness for an elaborate jump into the sea. What he didn't realise was that Snods was standing on a sandbank! Howard duly jumped in and disappeared beneath the waves. The champagne bottle shot into the air and one of the crew members had to dive in and pull him out! He was part frightened, part angry and gave Snods a right verbal volley when he calmed down a bit!

Back to 1986–87 and as we kept getting positive results, we began to consider that we might actually win the title again.

I recall the match that really hammered the message home for me. It was the end of March and we were at Highbury to play Arsenal. They were right up there with us, but we won 1–0 thanks to a wonder goal from Clarkey. That result, more than any other, really gave us the self-belief to go on and push for the title again.

That big win came a week after we'd beaten Charlton Athletic 2–1 at Goodison in a game I recall for a show of petulance from Ian Snodin. He had a running feud with Andy Peake and he ended up getting himself sent off. Snods exploded and when he left the field he stormed up the tunnel and tried to kick his way into the Charlton dressing-room. I don't know what he would have done had he got in because it was empty – perhaps he was going to put all their clothes in the big bath!

The following month, we lost 3–1 at Anfield, where Sheeds gave the Kop the V-sign, but we were clear at the top by then and although any defeat against Liverpool hurt us, it didn't matter too much with regard to the wider picture. That was our only defeat in the last 12 games of the season. The week before the derby, Clarkey bagged a hat-trick in a 3–0 win against Newcastle, but I was watching from the Main Stand by then because of an ankle injury.

I was back in the team by the time we went to Carrow Road in May to play Norwich City and by then we knew that a win would be sufficient to give us the Championship again.

Norwich was a great place for us to seal it. Pat scored his only goal of the season early in the match and the journey home to Merseyside was fabulous. Normally it was not a journey to relish because of the distance, but that day we didn't want it to end. Terry Darracott organised a karaoke session at the front of the bus and there was wine and beer for everyone.

Jimmy Martin, the kit manager at Everton these days, was the coach driver in the '80s and we were shouting at him to slow down as we moved along the motorway. Every time he drove at over 40 mph, we would remind to him to take his foot off the gas.

We wanted to enjoy the journey for as long as possible. It was great seeing carloads and busloads of delighted Evertonians pulling alongside us en route home.

We had been on the bus for over six hours and we were all the worse for wear by the time it pulled into Bellefield that night! Ian Snodin had fallen fast asleep at one point and a couple of us made a right mess of his brand-new suit with a pair of scissors. When he stepped off the bus with his new gear slashed to pieces, his wife's face was a picture.

Of course, we still had two matches to play, but they were meaningless.

Or so we thought.

When Luton Town came to Goodison five days after we'd won the title, they treated the game like a cup final. They kicked lumps out of us and we were really surprised by their attitude. While we had turned up to enjoy a celebratory atmosphere and parade the trophy, Luton seemed intent on being party-poopers. We weren't going to stand for it and it became an unnecessarily bruising affair. I caught their goalkeeper, Les Sealey, on the back of the head and he suffered a bit of concussion. It wasn't deliberate. It was a high ball that I had every justification to challenge, but the Luton players reacted.

As we were leaving the pitch at half-time and making our way down the tunnel, Ashley Grimes, who was on the substitute's bench, whacked me with a kit bag. I turned around and caught him flush in the face with a great right hook.

One nice thing about that night was that we at least got to show the Evertonians the proper League Championship trophy. When we'd won it in '85, it was the Canon-sponsored trophy and that just wasn't the same. I thought it looked like a gold skittle.

Winning the title was a tremendous achievement that season – perhaps even more so than winning it two years previously, given the number of injuries we'd had to contend with – but I didn't enjoy it as much. I have to feel that I have really contributed to something before I can enjoy the rewards. Not being involved regularly in the team and only scoring five League goals in 1986–87 as opposed to twenty-one in 1984–85 dented my personal satisfaction at an excellent team achievement.

In some respects, I felt like a substitute in a cup final. I was delighted to receive another winners' medal, but I knew that I hadn't done a great deal to get it. Even today, most Evertonians can reel off the team that won the Championship in 1985, but if you ask them to name the team that repeated the feat two years later, then they'd struggle. That's because there was no definitive team that season. We used 24 different players to win the crown.

The first Championship was won by a team, the second was won by a squad. The team spirit was still good, but it wasn't the same. Obviously Andy Gray was a big factor in that, but, although we still had our good days out, there just wasn't the social togetherness that had bonded us so strongly in 1985.

Howard did his best to foster that unique spirit by using 'fine' monies to pay for nights out. If we were late for training or got booked for dissent, Howard would fine us and keep the money aside to cover the cost of a night out at a Chinese restaurant for the whole squad. He was always a great believer that we worked hard and we played hard and the camaraderie in the camp was still excellent, but we all knew that the crop of '85 had been special. Attempting to recreate that magnificent atmosphere was always going to be difficult.

Having said that, the end-of-season trip after clinching our second title was the stuff of dreams. We flew to New Zealand and Australia via Los Angeles. We were the champions and we were going to party.

We downed a lot of champagne, wine and beer on the flight from Manchester to Los Angeles, including some alcohol that we'd bought from the duty-free shop. There were some high jinks and tomfoolery but nothing that would cause offence or trouble.

When we landed at Los Angeles airport, I was one of the last through security and I stopped in my tracks when I saw all of our lads lined up against a wall being marshalled by a couple of armed guards. I was asked if I was a member of the party and when I confirmed that I was I got shunted towards the wall as well.

The security chief was not a happy man. 'You are a disgrace,' he scolded us. 'We've had complaints from several passengers about your behaviour on the flight.'

I thought it was all a little bit over the top. One of the directors, Keith Tamlin, was doing his utmost to smooth things over before it degenerated into a national incident. At one point, the authorities weren't going to let us proceed on our journey and we faced the very real prospect of having to fly right back home again.

During the flight from Manchester, Howard had dropped off to sleep and we'd removed the laces from his shoes and prized a few buttons off his shirt. It was a moment of pure comic farce when the security chief demanded to know who was in charge of the squad. We all turned around and saw Howard walking towards security with the tongues of his lace-less shoes flapping around his ankles and half the buttons missing from his shirt.

Puffing on a big cigar, he approached the security chief and said, 'What's the problem here, lad?'

In the end we were allowed to board the connecting flight on the proviso that we didn't consume any more alcohol. We were perfectly happy to comply with this request because we all needed some sleep anyway. Just to make sure, the cabin crew were officially informed not to serve anything stronger than mineral water to anyone from Everton Football Club.

We later discovered that Pat Van Den Hauwe had been walking around the aircraft in his underpants, but we all still thought the reaction was way too heavy handed.

When we finally landed in New Zealand, there was a message

for Sheeds to contact home. His wife had given birth! That was all the excuse we needed and we spent our first night in New Zealand wetting the baby's head.

New Zealand were hosting the 1987 Rugby World Cup during our trip. I remember in one dingy bar the match between New Zealand and Fiji was being shown on television. It looked as though we were the only people in the place because nobody appeared to be watching it and one of the lads shouted, 'Get that rubbish off!'

As a hand reached up to change the channel, a deep local-sounding voice bellowed from a dark corner of the bar: 'Leave that alone!' Two massive Fijian rugby fans emerged from the shadows and we went nowhere near the television set again.

From New Zealand, we went to Australia and then finally to Hawaii, which was brilliant. We stayed in the Hilton hotel by Waikiki beach.

It was whilst sitting in the bar with Reidy that I first tasted a Mai Thai. It is a ridiculously strong cocktail that comes in a big glass that looks more like a goldfish bowl. Not only was it strong, it was also dangerously tasty. Sheeds had one and refused to have another, but Inchy, Rats, Reidy and I stayed on them. It was quite a way back to our hotel and en route we had to walk right around a huge lagoon, but Rats and I figured that we'd save time if we swam across it! We just about managed it – and it was a process we repeated every day, even though we were shattered by the time we reached the other side. It was only on our last day that we discovered the water in the lagoon was no more than three feet deep. We could have waded across it instead of nearly killing ourselves swimming!

It was a fantastic trip and we all thoroughly enjoyed it. While we were in Hawaii, Neil Pointon took the opportunity to visit Pearl Harbor. He was somewhat surprised that nobody else fancied going with him, but the rest of us opted to stay in the bar. Looking back, I wish I'd gone with him: it was an opportunity that was unlikely to come along again. He was full of himself when he got back, telling us that we'd missed the chance to see something highly significant in the history of the world. He told us that he'd taken dozens of pictures and that they would be the closest the rest of us would ever get to the famous Pearl Harbor.

He dashed off to get them developed and couldn't wait to show us his snaps. When he got them out of the packet, Rats grabbed them, ripped them up and threw them into the sea! The old spirit raised itself up from time to time, but I could sense that there was a wind of change beginning to blow through Goodison Park.

ELEVEN

A NEW ERA

It was during that end-of-season trip to Hawaii that Howard first started to indicate that he was seriously considering leaving Everton. Inchy and I were sharing a room at the hotel and one day Howard popped in for a chat. We were discussing football in general when the approach from Barcelona for Howard entered the conversation. It was common knowledge that they had been interested in his services at one point, but nothing had ever come of it.

'What would you think if I left the club?' said Howard, looking at Inchy and me.

There wasn't much we could say. Of course we had no idea that at the time Athletico Bilbao were poised to offer him a lucrative deal. It wasn't until we returned home that the story broke.

I must admit I was a bit surprised by the move. Nobody would have blamed him if he'd gone to Barcelona, who were, and still are, one of the biggest clubs in the world – but Bilbao? I thought that was a strange one, but Howard wanted to try his luck abroad and Bilbao offered him the opportunity to do that.

Once the shock had subsided, talk amongst the lads inevitably turned to the matter of his successor. There were a few names bandied about because we were the League champions – the manager's job at Everton was one of the biggest in the country – but the board of directors made a great choice when they opted to keep it in the family and appoint Colin Harvey. Everyone at the club, and I really mean everyone, had the utmost respect for

Colin and although he had no top-level managerial experience, he did seem to be the logical choice because he'd had such an influence on the success that we'd enjoyed under Howard. Colin knew exactly how that success had been attained and he knew all the attributes of the players, so we didn't have to prove ourselves all over again to an outsider.

For me personally, it was a great appointment. I had grown up at Everton with Colin and I had already benefited enormously from his expertise and experience.

The transition was a smooth one, although it did take the lads a few weeks to get out of the habit of calling him 'Col'. That's how he'd always been known and it wasn't easy to remember to refer to him as 'Boss' or 'Gaffer'.

Colin had been a major cog in the club's success and so he knew he wouldn't have to tinker with the systems too much. He made a couple of alterations to the coaching staff and they, too, were very popular with the lads. He gave Reidy some coaching responsibility, he got Terry Darracott more involved and he brought Mick Lyons back to the club. Three tremendous fellows and each with a really genuine feel for Everton.

Reidy may have been handed a more senior role within the club, but it didn't stop him getting some unmerciful stick when he turned up at Bellefield with jet-black hair! He'd been going grey since his late teens and it was obviously of some concern to him and he had decided to do something about it. I'm not too sure what effect he was after, but it looked as though he had gone ducking for apples in a large bucket of tar! When he ran out for the first time with his new look, the Everton supporters thought we'd signed a new player!

I was mindful of not giving him too much stick because every now and then a picture of me with my permed hair would surface, but I still managed to rib him about it a few times. He deserved it!

The only player that Colin had signed before the start of the season was a goalkeeper called Alec Chamberlain from Colchester United. He was a nice, quiet lad who lived in

Southport. He had also got married that summer, so it was some close season for him. Although we could see that he was a competent goalkeeper, he wasn't going to replace Neville as the first choice and he never played a senior first-team game for the club.

We had a good pre-season in Spain, where we stayed in the beautiful city of Santander on the coast. While we were there, we played Benfica and Sporting de Gijon, though we didn't win either match.

Colin's first game was at Wembley against Coventry City in the 1987 Charity Shield and we beat them 1–0, thanks to a Wayne Clarke goal. I was becoming a bit blasé about playing at Wembley now, and the Charity Shield was no more than a glorified friendly, but I was delighted for Colin that he got the chance to lead his beloved team out under the Twin Towers and then guide them to victory. It was our fourth consecutive Charity Shield appearance – we'd won three and drawn the other.

Colin's first game at Goodison went well, too: we beat Norwich 1–0. I recall that, for some reason, I spent a lot of the game playing on the right wing. I even supplied a textbook cross from a wide position that Paul Power headed home for the game's only goal! But we only won one of our next six League matches and, for the reigning champions, that wasn't good enough, especially as Liverpool had started the season in rampant form.

Colin made an early foray into the transfer market when he brought Ian Wilson to the club. I wasn't overly enthused by that one. Willo was a great lad and I had the pleasure of playing alongside him for Scotland, but he wasn't a signing that was ever going to change our season. To be fair, every new player would struggle to live up to the standards of the all-conquering team of a few years earlier. Willo operated on the left side of midfield and, although he was neat and tidy, it was felt that he couldn't hold a candle to Sheeds. I thought we could perhaps have set our sights higher and that Everton players should have been more than 'neat and tidy'. But there were worse signings than Willo to come in the following seasons.

The pressure was really on Colin in so many ways. Not only did he take over a team that had just won the Championship, but he also took over from someone who had done exceptionally well in the transfer market. The likes of Pat Van Den Hauwe, Paul Bracewell, Wayne Clarke and Paul Power had been brilliant signings by Howard, but, by bringing in Willo, Colin didn't get off to the best of starts on that front. But in the League, we were doing OK.

I had a real red-letter day at Southampton at the end of September. The Dell was always a difficult place to play, but we went there and beat them 4–0, and I scored all four goals. I had an amazing day and, in actual fact, I could, and should, have scored six or seven because I missed a few good chances as well.

I had scored three goals for Everton the year before in the Full Members Cup against Newcastle, but this was my first real senior hat-trick. I was already reasonably pleased with my form, but I was even happier that I could add a few goals to my tally.

I was playing with plenty of confidence and, not for the first time in my Everton career, a lot of that was down to Colin Harvey. I knew that he rated me highly as a player and I knew that I wouldn't have to constantly try to prove myself to him.

After that four-goal haul, however, I noticed another difference between Colin and Howard: on the long journey back from Southampton, Howard would have instructed the coach driver to call in at the first off-licence by The Dell so that we could celebrate in a highly appropriate manner on the way home. But Colin was looking at the way footballers behaved with respect to what they put into their bodies: he believed that drinking beer and champagne all the way home from away matches was old school. I still enjoyed the trip back from Southampton, but it was a lot more reserved than it would have been under Howard.

To be fair to Colin, he was working very hard to prove that he was his own man and that he could achieve things his way and it was inevitable that he would make some changes.

We played a friendly challenge match against Israeli champions Betar Jerusalem before Christmas in the national stadium. We drew 1–1, but the only thing I can remember from the match is that, for some reason, Bobby Mimms played in goal for them!

Back in the League, I scored two more in the very next game against Chelsea at Goodison. We thrashed them 4–1 and Inchy and I scored two apiece. I was particularly pleased with my contribution because Howard was back to watch his first game since leaving for Spain. He'd often said that I struggled to score 'poacher's' goals from in and around the six-yard box, but against Chelsea that's precisely what I did twice.

I scored a memorable goal at Portsmouth the following month. It was lashing down with rain and our supporters were in the uncovered end at Fratton Park getting soaking wet through. The away end is still the same now, which is incredible in this day and age. How supporters can be expected to pay good money to watch a Premiership football match but get drenched if it rains is beyond me.

Even though the weather was atrocious that day, I was glad to be able to cheer our fans up a bit when I thumped an unstoppable shot into the top corner from about 30 yards. The Evertonians were right behind the goal, so they got a perfect view of it.

It was the type of goal that I'd scored when I first burst onto the scene at Everton. My dad had always encouraged me to shoot from distance when I had the ball at my feet and I'd netted some spectacular efforts as a youngster, but my role changed as I got older: I became more of a target man and a linking player. I got a lot of satisfaction from setting up goals for others, so it was nice to turn the clock back a bit and score a stunner of my own.

My dad was still coming down to watch me play whenever he could. His trips were less frequent now that I was married with a young child, but he still enjoyed coming to the games from time to time. He'd have loved watching me play for Everton against Rangers that December . . . but the match was played in Dubai! It was the unofficial British Championship and it was another smashing trip, although it got off to an inauspicious start at the airport hotel at Heathrow the night before we were due to leave.

A Scottish journalist called Gerry McNee had written a preview for the game in which he questioned the sanity of Rangers travelling all the way to Dubai to play a match against a 'second-rate English team'. I was outraged when I read his piece. I thought 'You cheeky bastard!' I took the paper to show the lads and there was anger at what McNee had written.

We played Charlton on the Saturday then stayed at the airport hotel before the flight the next day. A group of Scottish reporters were in the hotel, too, having travelled down from Glasgow to catch the same flight. I knew some of the boys and, with Reidy and Colin, was having a chat at the bar when, lo and behold, McNee walked in. I pointed him out to Reidy, who put down his drink and marched right over to confront him.

'What's your name?' he asked, prodding McNee in the chest.

McNee was a bit flustered, but told Reidy who he was.

'You're the one calling us a second-rate team, aren't you?' said Reidy. 'What's your fucking game? Who do you think you are?'

The rest of the Scottish press lads cowered away to the other side of the bar whilst we gave McNee a really hard time.

On the flight the following morning, we were sitting with some of the decent Glasgow reporters and they asked me about Graeme Souness and the Rangers revolution. They suggested that a transfer to Rangers would be a good move. I confessed to being a boyhood fan but assured them that I was happy at Everton, so they asked Inchy the same question. Now Inchy had been substituted at Charlton and he wasn't happy about it, so he informed the Scottish press that he'd love a move to Rangers. It was all over the papers north of the border the next day.

The game itself was a good one. We were all over them and

were leading 2–0 when Souness brought himself on. He changed the game completely and, with Souness in complete control, they got it back to 2–2 and eventually beat us on penalties. Snods missed our crucial kick!

In those days, Dubai boasted just one decent hotel, which was located by the airport. I had a few drinks in there with Ally McCoist and Ian Durrant and ended up sitting in their room chatting the night away with a few bottles of wine. I knew both lads, of course, from the Scotland set-up and, as usual, they were terrific company. We had a really good laugh together.

Once we got back home, I missed a game for the most bizarre reason of my career. It was the New Year period and we'd played Sheffield Wednesday on 1 January. I had a golden retriever called Max at the time and he was a really lively sort. When I got home from the match, I was rolling about on the floor with him, messing about, and I remember Ann Marie warning me that one day he would bite me. Well, this was the day because, as I was teasing Max, he sunk his teeth right into my hand. There was blood everywhere and I needed seven stitches that night. I had to contact John Clinkard and tell him that there was no way I would be able to play against Nottingham Forest on 3 January. My hand swelled up to twice its normal size. We kept it from the press before the game, but I had to confess afterwards. The headline writers had a field day, especially as my replacement, Wayne Clarke, scored the only goal of the game.

Liverpool were storming to the title that season. They had the likes of Peter Beardsley, John Barnes, John Aldridge and Ray Houghton all playing very well for them and they seemed unstoppable. We had beaten them in the League Cup at Anfield in September, when Gary Stevens scored, which was nice, and we ended their unbeaten record in the League when Wayne Clarke scored at Goodison in March, but they fully deserved the title. We were never contenders and, even if we had been, I'm sure our cup schedule would have been our undoing.

We played eight FA Cup ties in 1987–88 but still only reached the fifth round – it had only taken us eight games to win it in 1984! In the third round, we played Sheffield Wednesday and drew 1–1 at Hillsborough. The replay ended with the same scoreline when I added another cracking goal to my collection. It was a volley from 12 yards that flashed past my old teammate Martin Hodge. The second replay, also at Goodison, ended 0–0 and so it was back up to Yorkshire to try for a fourth time.

The first three games had been really tight; you couldn't separate the two teams. So it was bizarre that in the third replay we were five goals ahead by half-time. A lot of Evertonians had encountered problems travelling across the Pennines and they refused to believe that we were 5–0 up at the break. We were controlling the game so well that even Snods scored a one-on-one, which was never his strong point. I was fortunate to score a classic hat-trick – one with my head, one with my left and one with my right – and Inchy got the other. With the game won, Colin took the opportunity to bring Brace on during the second half for his first game in about 18 months.

The tie had taken so long to settle that we only had three days to prepare for a fourth-round tie against Middlesbrough at Goodison, which we drew 1–1. The replay was an amazing game. We thought that we were going out of the competition at 2–1 down before Trevor Steven scored a headed equaliser in the 97th minute! That meant yet another replay at Goodison.

I remember that game because it was so windy. I had never played football in such a gale. Players had to put their finger on the ball to stop it rolling away in set-piece situations. It was a really difficult match, but we came through 2–1.

Our eighth tie of the season, the fifth round, was against Liverpool at Goodison. They beat us 1–0.

We had also been making progress in the League Cup, though we eventually lost against Arsenal in the semi-final.

At one stage early in the year, we'd played ten matches and only one of them had been a League game. We finished in fourth place in the table, but we were twenty points behind Liverpool.

Colin worked hard during the summer of 1988 to try and redress the balance. He spent a lot of money on recruitment, but, in my opinion, he didn't spend it very wisely. Tony Cottee came for a club record from West Ham, Pat Nevin joined from Chelsea, Neil McDonald from Newcastle and Stuart McCall from Bradford City.

Colin was attempting to put his mark on the squad and trying to rebuild, but I never considered these new signings to be 'Everton' players. Not one of them would have been anywhere near the 1985 team, which is how I assessed new players. That might sound unfair, but they were the standards that we had set for the football club and it frustrated me when I felt that those standards weren't being adhered to.

Cottee got off to an unbelievable start by scoring a hat-trick on his debut against Newcastle, but straight away I realised that this was going to be a new type of striking partnership for me. I had been used to sharing the workload with my partners, but I could tell that this was going to be different. Cottee was a penalty-box striker – working hard to close down defenders and put them under pressure didn't appear to be one of his remits. Scoring goals was the be all and end all for him. I used to get very angry when we lost games in which he'd scored because I used to think he would consider it 'job done', whereas I was more concerned with the final result.

Pat Nevin was a skilful enough footballer, but I didn't think that we'd ever win anything with him in the side. He was a luxury player and they rarely win trophies. He was never going to mix awfully well in the dressing-room either because he was a complex individual. Just after he'd signed for the club, he used to come to training wearing a full-length trench coat that he must have bought 15 years earlier. He was a lovely guy, but, like Cottee, he wasn't seen as the type to roll up his sleeves and battle for the team when the chips were down. Things were certainly changing at Everton, but, in my opinion, not for the better.

Cottee later claimed that he had never been accepted by the senior Everton players, myself included, but that was complete nonsense. We tried to include all new players in everything we did, but this particular group didn't want to know. It got to the stage when they did their thing and another group of us did ours. But that wasn't the Everton way. There had never been factions within the camp, but there was now and it was only going to get worse.

I will say that Stuart McCall at least tried to join in, but he was caught between the two groups within the dressing-room. He knew the value of a good team spirit, but he also felt some loyalty to the other lads who had joined the club at the same time as him.

We'd actually had a very good pre-season together in southern Ireland, where we were based in Drogheda. It was just after the 1988 European Championship in which Ireland had done terrifically well. When we arrived in Drogheda, Sheeds was treated like a god. The Irish hadn't had a national team to brag about for decades and they worshipped Sheeds. The locals put on a do for us in a typical Irish pub on Drogheda High Street. It was a fantastic day and night.

Colin had to attend a function in the evening, so he left Terry Darracott in charge, which was the signal for the party to just get livelier and livelier – Pat Nevin showed straight away that he wasn't going to be a social asset to the dressing-room by snubbing the party to have a walk around Drogheda, looking at the local architecture.

We stayed up through most of the night, drinking, singing and dancing with the local people. It was like a blast from the past and should have been an ideal way for the new lads to integrate and show a willingness to join in with the rest of the squad. But the spirit of '85 was dead and gone, and the players were slowly leaving, too.

Derek Mountfield went to Aston Villa in June, although that wasn't too much of a setback because he was never going to dislodge either Rats or Waggy at the heart of the defence. Gary Stevens went to Glasgow Rangers, his reason being that he wanted to play in European competition again – English clubs were still barred, don't forget – but I believe that money was a key issue. Rangers could pay him more than Everton and, as an England international, there was no way Gary was going to Scotland purely for the football, though I didn't begrudge him that. If Rangers were going to treble his salary, then good luck to him. The same thing happened for Trevor Steven 12 months later when he joined Rangers. I firmly believe that both lads went for the money rather than any desire to play in the SPL.

When these players left, it put pressure on their replacements because they had been so successful and they'd been so popular with the punters. Good players moving on is part and parcel of the game, but it disappointed me that we weren't replacing like for like.

One of the old stalwarts, Mark Higgins, made an emotional return to Goodison Park for a League Cup tie with his new club, Bury. We all thought that Higgy's career was over when he quit Everton, but it was a measure of the man that he paid back every penny of his insurance settlement to enable him to re-register as a player and he got a marvellous reception from the fans when he walked onto the pitch.

We beat Bury comfortably, but we couldn't quite find any sort of consistency in the League. This wasn't helped when Colin had to take off some time for a hip operation. He always wanted to join in the five-a-side matches in training, but it was getting harder and harder for him and an operation was the only way to sort things out. Terry Darracott temporarily took charge and, although he was always more like one of the lads, we treated him with every respect while Colin was away.

By the end of December we were sixth from bottom in the table and we were struggling. It was very difficult for me to take because I'd not so long since been part of an Everton side that knew full well it was going to win games. Now it seemed as though we didn't have the backbone for a fight. There were times when I'd leave the field feeling extremely frustrated because my efforts during the 90 minutes hadn't been matched by my striking partner.

Another good pal had had enough by Christmas. Inchy left the club to join Spanish side Espanyol. They weren't the biggest club in Spain, but they were based in Barcelona, which was a lovely place and the lifestyle obviously attracted Inchy. It was a blow for me from both a personal and a professional perspective. Inchy was one of my closest friends and he was also a very good footballer, who had worked his socks off time and again for the Everton cause.

Inchy and I were together when I had signed one of my first-ever boot sponsorship deals with Le Coq Sportif who designed the Everton team kit in the early and mid-'80s. The first three players they signed up were Inchy, me and, for some reason, Garth Crooks. They were big on the tennis circuit, but they were looking to break into football and the financial package was very good. Inchy and I stayed with them until Jim Pearson, a former Everton striker, came along and dangled a Nike deal under our noses.

Jim was a representative for the company and he took Inchy and me to the Nike warehouse one afternoon to get some free gear. We were stopping over in a hotel and Jim's role was to make sure Inchy and I didn't abuse the privilege. We had a few drinks in the hotel and by the time we got to the Nike place, Jim had had one too many. We ran riot! Inchy and I clawed as much gear as we could carry – boots, tracksuits, trainers, the lot. Jim woke up the next morning with tennis rackets and cricket bats in his hotel bedroom!

So I was sad to see Inchy leave Everton, but not long after I had an offer to move abroad myself when I was approached by the well-known agent Dennis Roach, who told me that French club Monaco were interested in taking me over there. I didn't have an agent of my own and I'd never met Dennis, but I must admit that it sounded like a tempting offer.

I still don't know to this day how he obtained my phone number, but he rang me out of the blue and after introducing himself we had a cordial chat about holiday destinations, amongst other subjects, before he told me that Monaco had asked about my availability. I confirmed that I would be interested in hearing a bit more about it, but he had thought that my contract at Everton was about to expire when in actual fact I had another year to go. That was a deal-buster, as far as he was concerned. He thanked me for my time, wished me all the best and I never heard from him again. In fact, I've still never met him.

The fact that I had even considered a move showed how dissatisfied I was with the way things were going at Everton. I was pleased enough with my own contribution to the games because I didn't know any other way than to give 100 per cent every time I wore the blue jersey.

I also had a further off-the-field reason for not uprooting and moving away: Ann Marie and I had a second child by now. Emma was born the day after we'd beaten Newcastle in the opening match of the season. I was overjoyed that we had a little daughter to complete our family. Emma's arrival was the signal for a few more visits to the Weld Blundell!

As Chris was only two years of age, I decided that it would be the best all round if I made plans to elongate my Everton career and give my young family a solid base, so, just before Christmas I put pen to paper on a new four-year deal with the club. It was a busy old time for secretary Jim Greenwood because Rats and Waggy also signed four-year deals and Neville signed a contract for seven years. We didn't have agents so an insurance broker called Neil Ramsey sorted things out for us. He was a friend of Reidy's and we were happy for him to negotiate new deals on our behalves. We didn't even have to pay him because he made good money from the commission from the pensions that we took out with him. A four-year deal was great for me. I was settled in the Merseyside area and we had recently upgraded our property from the house in Formby to a nice place in Birkdale, near Southport.

I had never really given too much thought to my future, but I was always a great believer in putting as much money into my pension scheme as I could. All my bonuses were pumped into that – other lads bought big, flashy cars, but as I still couldn't drive that was never an option for me. The house in Birkdale was a lovely three-bedroom place, but it was no mansion (though I made a tidy profit on it when I later sold it to move to North Wales).

When I first joined Everton from Dumbarton all those years ago, Asa Hartford advised me to put at least £10 a week from my wages into my pension. It was good, sound advice and I followed it throughout my career, although the payments went up a bit as my career developed.

During that 1988–89 season, I began to struggle more and more with a groin injury and it soon became evident that I would need surgery to correct the problem. I was one of the first players to wear cycling shorts in matches just to give myself a little bit of extra protection, but the stiffness in my groin after games was getting worse. At the beginning of December, we played Tottenham at Goodison and as I stretched for the ball I felt an excruciating pain shoot right through my groin. That was it.

The physio knew that I would need to see a specialist and he arranged for me to travel to Harley Street in London to see a Dr Gilmore. I went down on the train to Euston and caught a taxi to Harley Street. Dr Gilmore had a look at me and asked if I had an overnight toilet bag. Before I could answer, he explained that I was going to be whisked across to the Princess Alexandra Hospital for an operation.

'I'll come over in the morning and perform the operation,' he explained.

I was a bit shocked at the speed of things.

I got another cab to the Princess Alexandra, which was as

plush as a five-star hotel, and settled myself down in my own private room. Sure enough, first thing in the morning a nurse came to de-fuzz my nether regions and Dr Gilmore popped his head around the door to say he would see me in theatre.

When I came out of the anaesthetic, I was in agony. I had never experienced pain like it. My moaning and groaning attracted the attentions of one of the nurses and she explained that Dr Gilmore had performed a hernia operation and had also made another small incision so that the muscles around my groin could be stretched to prevent the problem occurring again.

The pain and discomfort were horrendous, but the nurse was having no sympathy. She instructed me to get out of bed to use the toilet.

'Get out of bed! I can't even move,' I complained.

She merely pulled back the blankets, grabbed my two legs and swung me around so that I was sitting upright on the edge of the bed.

'Come on, Mr Sharp, you'll be all right once we get you moving,' she smiled.

It took me about 20 minutes to shuffle to the bathroom, but gradually I managed a bit more each day and before long I was able to slip out of the hospital into the pub next door! Terry Connor, a big centre-forward with Portsmouth, was in for an operation at the same time and we would nip down the staircase and out through the fire exit into the street so that we could have a couple of beers in the pub.

I rested in hospital for a bit longer than I needed to because Everton were playing Queens Park Rangers in London at the end of the week – I just stayed where I was until the day of the game and then travelled back to Merseyside on the team bus.

My comeback game, after missing 12 matches, was an FA Cup fourth-round tie at Plymouth Argyle at the end of January, which we drew 1–1. I became embroiled in a controversial incident during the replay three days later when I went to challenge for the ball with Kevin Summerfield and unfortunately he ended up breaking his leg. I was closing him down and he kicked my foot, so it was a complete accident, but a lad called Tommy Tynan made some unnecessary comments about it afterwards.

Another era ended for me when Reidy left the club that February to join QPR. He didn't always see eye to eye with Colin, and Stuart McCall had clearly been introduced as his midfield replacement. We played QPR at Goodison at the beginning of April and Reidy got a hero's welcome from the crowd. He then played a sloppy back pass straight to Wayne Clarke, who scored. I said to Reidy afterwards that it was the best pass he'd played at Goodison for years!

Later that month, I played in the most forgotten FA Cup semi-final ever. We beat Norwich City 1–0 at Villa Park on 15 April 1989, but it was a black day for football. Our game had been poor and, even before we became aware of the tragedy unfolding in Sheffield, our celebrations had been subdued because we had fully expected to win our match. It was only in the dressing-room that we heard that there had been some trouble at Hillsborough. We thought it was crowd disturbance at first, but as more and more terrible news filtered through our dressing-room fell silent.

It was a very flat group of players that boarded the bus for Liverpool. A few of us decided that we'd have a few beers to unwind before we went home. We were in The Grapes in Formby having a couple of pints when someone approached me and called me a disgrace for being out in a public house after what had happened. I was taken aback and asked the fellow what he was doing out in that case. He couldn't answer. 'I'm doing the same as you,' I said.

I was as devastated as everybody else, but there was nothing we could do. Perhaps the fact that we were Everton players had riled him. We were talking about the tragedy but we certainly were not celebrating our own semi-final win in any way, shape or form.

The following day, Father Brian, who was always around the

football club, asked Sheeds and me to go to the Catholic cathedral for a memorial Mass. We went, of course, but they were very trying times for everyone. It was hard to know what to do at times. It was awful for everybody and I went to a few memorial services around the city. The Everton lads did everything that was asked of us, but obviously the Liverpool players had it far tougher because they were a lot more involved.

I thought that Kenny and all their lads deserved credit for the way in which they conducted themselves in the aftermath of Hillsborough. They were always at the end of the phone and were ready to help anyone who needed them. Liverpool Football Club did incredibly well because it couldn't have been easy.

I remember when I went to Anfield to lay a wreath and the sight that greeted me was unbelievable. The people of Merseyside really pulled together and helped each other. So many people were affected, but you couldn't help but be impressed by the spirit of togetherness.

It all made for a very strange atmosphere for the FA Cup final when we met just over a month later at Wembley. There was obviously a very emotional atmosphere and it felt a bit surreal. The fans were sitting on the edge of the pitch and they swarmed on when the goals went in.

People suggested that it was Liverpool's destiny to have won the final in the end, but it was a game that I desperately wanted to win. It was an FA Cup final against our local rivals, so of course I wanted to win. But that wasn't an attitude shared by my teammates and I was absolutely furious after the match.

I thought that too many of our players had accepted our 3–2 defeat too easily. It was never ever going to be just another FA Cup final, but we didn't give a good account of ourselves. I sensed that defeat at Wembley didn't hurt enough Everton players. A few of them were at Wembley just to enjoy the occasion, regardless of the result, just the way that Watford had been against us five years earlier.

The likes of Tony Cottee and Neil McDonald hadn't

experienced a Cup final before and they were both poor on the day. In my opinion, they didn't seem willing to go the extra mile . . . and I wasn't alone in thinking that.

They quickly recovered from the defeat to concentrate on enjoying the night out after the game, but I didn't. I stormed straight up to my hotel room and didn't even give an explanation to Ann Marie. I just took off my tie, told her she could meet me in the bar and headed straight back down again! She protested that she wasn't ready, but I was in no mood to be sitting around waiting and she knew it.

Terry Darracott came over because he knew that I was in a foul mood and I told him exactly what I thought. 'I'm not happy, Tex,' I said. 'Some of them didn't care whether we won or lost. They were there for the day out and I can't handle that.'

He didn't argue.

Liverpool's win didn't earn them another double because they lost out on the title in the last minute of their last match against Arsenal at Anfield. We were in Magaluf that night and we settled down to watch the game in a bar that had a television. Just as the match kicked off, the television conked out. We could hear the commentary, but we couldn't see the pictures, so all we could do was sit there and listen intently to Brian Moore. When Michael Thomas netted his injury-time winner, there was pandemonium in the bar and we had a rather enjoyable evening, I can tell you.

The Sharp family had also squandered a unique double that season because my brother Richard played for Strathclyde Police against West Midlands in the British Police Cup final. They won 3–1, at Ibrox of all places, to become the first Scottish team to win the tournament for 35 years – so it was my derby FA Cup final defeat that let the family down.

But I have got some pleasant Merseyside derby memories too . . .

TWELVE

DERBY MEMORIES

I was brought up with the Rangers and Celtic rivalry and although people on Merseyside used to tell me that their derby was comparable to Glasgow's, I had my doubts. Nevertheless the whole build-up to my first match against Liverpool in March 1982 was unbelievable.

Despite the warnings from the local lads, the demand for tickets took me completely by surprise. People turned up at the training ground claiming to know me or telling the receptionist that they were relatives of mine in order to get hold of tickets. It was incredible! I had no family anywhere near Merseyside. There was one well-known villain who, despite being a Liverpool supporter, thought nothing of waiting outside Bellefield to demand tickets from young Everton players. He had a reputation and could be a very intimidating character – I used to hide, then sneak out in the back of someone else's car. The expectation was massive and it was all anybody would talk about all week.

I was one of six derby debutants in our starting eleven – Neville Southall, Brian Borrows, Kevin Richardson, Adrian Heath and Alan Irvine were the others. I recall sitting in the dressing-room at Goodison feeling nice and relaxed and looking forward to my first taste of it, but as we walked up the tunnel and out onto the pitch, the noise that reverberated around the stadium nearly knocked me off my feet. It was absolutely incredible.

We'd had 16,000 fans for the previous home match against Middlesbrough and suddenly we were playing in front of a

51,000 sell-out against Liverpool. Attendance had increased by 35,000! No wonder the noise shook me up a bit.

That was by far the biggest gate I had played in front of in my life and, for the first ten minutes or so, I literally could not hear any of the other players such was the volume from the terraces. I didn't see much of the ball either such was the pace of the early play.

We lost 3–1, but at least I had the not inconsiderable consolation of scoring our goal. We had a corner at the Park End and I went up with Bruce Grobbelaar when the cross came over. Bruce dropped it and I managed to swivel sharply enough to drive the loose ball into the net. What a noise there was when the net bulged!

I enjoyed the experience and thought I did well enough against Phil Thompson and Mark Lawrenson. I was gutted to have lost because I was aware of how much the occasion meant to the Evertonians, but, as I found out later in my career, the fans never forget anyone who finds the net against Liverpool.

That afternoon a couple of Evertonians ran onto the pitch dressed as jesters to have a go at Bruce Grobbelaar, though he had the last laugh when he saved my volley in the second half, which looked for all the world as though it was going in.

I was gratified to read Graeme Souness's comments after the game. He said that he was 'particularly impressed with Everton's number 9, Graeme Sharp' and that I looked 'very dangerous'. Coming from a respected Scottish international, it was a most welcome pat on the back.

My first actual match against Liverpool had been at reserve level. The mini-derby, as it is known, was a fairly big occasion and we had some big crowds at both Goodison and Anfield. I played against the likes of Kevin Sheedy, Ronnie Whelan, Alan Harper and Steve Foley – all good players – and we had some close encounters . . . though that is most certainly *not* how I would describe my second derby as a first-team player the following season.

SHARPY

We were going steadily in the First Division after 12 games and we'd had some very good results, so there was absolutely no indication of the footballing disaster that was about to hit us when we welcomed Liverpool to Goodison on 6 November 1982 – a date no Evertonian will ever forget. It was a truly horrendous occasion.

For some reason, and I still have no idea why, Howard brought in a player on loan from Blackburn Rovers called Glenn Keeley. It was such a late decision that Glenn's first training session with his new teammates was on the Friday before the game. We were surprised to see him at Bellefield and we were gobsmacked when Howard named the team and Glenn was in it instead of Mark Higgins. The lads just looked at one another, wondering what the heck was going on.

The poor lad had a complete nightmare! He got sent off early in the game for pulling down Kenny and that left us really up against it. Rushie ran riot, scoring four of the goals in a 5–0 win for them. We were all shell-shocked – no one more so than Neville Southall, even though none of the goals had been his fault. It was a crushing blow. Jim Arnold was restored to the line-up for the next game while Big Nev was sent to Port Vale to rebuild his shattered confidence.

Not one of us could even lift our heads up in the dressing-room afterwards. We just wanted to hide away. There were supporters saying that they couldn't go to work for a week after that. I think I had our only effort on goal in the entire 90 minutes. One of the Scottish journalists commented in his match report that I'd had 'as much support up front as an English Nationalist candidate would have in a Lanarkshire by-election'!

Bringing Glenn in for such a big game was a major mistake by Howard, but he was learning his trade at the time and he did what he thought was best. I considered the recruitment of Alan Harper, however, as a masterstroke when he saved my bacon in a Goodison derby in March 1984.

Liverpool had whacked us again earlier in the season at

Anfield, where the scoreline was 3–0. Everybody had billed the return as the Milk Cup dress rehearsal because we were due to meet at Wembley at the end of the month. We were 1–0 down when we were awarded a penalty at the Gwladys Street end. I had scored twice in a remarkable 4–4 draw with Watford the week before so I was full of confidence and I offered to take it. It was a poor tame kick and Bruce saved it quite comfortably. I put the shot to his left, which was most unlike me because I much preferred to aim for the right-hand side, coming across the ball with my left foot. When Bruce kept it out, I was mortified. My first thought was, 'Oh no, I'm going to cost us the derby.'

There were 52,000 fans inside Goodison and I just wanted to walk off the pitch. I really thought I'd blown it for the lads. Andy Gray told me to forget all about it and get on with my game, but I couldn't. It was too big a moment and too big a miss and the game passed me by for a while as I struggled to come to terms with it all.

And that was when good old Alan Harper, on as a substitute for Trevor Steven, scored his first-ever goal for the club. And what a relief it was!

Being at home, most people inside the ground were going berserk, and there was no one more delighted about it than me! I grabbed Harpo around the neck and was screaming, 'You've saved me, you've saved me!' in his ear. I think I was more pleased than he was. From then on, if I had the opportunity to take a penalty in a big game or at a crucial stage, I would just put it on the spot and blast it as hard as I could.

I always enjoyed playing in derby matches. If you didn't enjoy them, you were in the wrong job. That was always my opinion. You can name as many local derby clashes as you like – London, Manchester, Sheffield, Birmingham, wherever – none of them can say that that they played them at Wembley as many times as we did. Make no mistake about it, Merseyside football ruled the roost in the '80s.

I obviously include Charity Shield matches here and,

regardless of its importance, it was still a Wembley showdown. The 1984 Charity Shield match will always go down as the day Bruce Grobbelaar scored the winning goal – but even now I still think I could have claimed it!

We were flying at the time, having just won the FA Cup, and we went to Wembley thinking that we could not only win the game but also put a marker down for the new season. Liverpool had just won the European Cup, but we firmly believed that the Mersey tide was there for the turning and the pre-season showpiece was the very place for us to show the rest of the country that we meant business.

We beat them 1–0, but the goal was a bit messy, I must admit. At Wembley that day, I only had Bruce in front of me and if I'm being honest, I never enjoyed those situations for the simple reason that I was never the best at them. Some strikers can stroll through and stick the ball past the keeper without thinking but that was never my forte. I have every respect for players like Thierry Henry who just know that they are going to score when they only have the keeper to beat, but I really didn't like having too much time in the box. I was always a more instinctive goalscorer. If the ball dropped to me, I could make a split-second decision and either place it in the net or smash it, but my record when I was through on goal with all the time in the world wasn't very good. And that's not something you can coach: you are either very good in that type of situation or you're not, and I fell into the latter category.

So, I was in a one-on-one with the keeper and I didn't get the cleanest connection on the ball. Grobbelaar saved it with his legs, it cannoned into Jocky Hansen, hit Bruce again and ended up in the net! Like I say, I still think it was my goal!

The important thing was that we beat them. No professional footballer – or manager, for that matter – really puts much importance on the Charity Shield, but the fact that we had put one over on Liverpool gave us a lift and I think it served notice to them that we were about to become a force to be reckoned with. We had beaten Liverpool at Wembley and had every chance to take the Merseyside supremacy from them: it was a big psychological boost for a young Everton side. The fans thought so, too. There were so many positives to take from that day . . . but the press just wouldn't give me the goal! I tried to claim it in my post-match interviews, but Bruce got the credit.

There wasn't much of a celebration afterwards, but then there never was after Charity Shield games. There was no pouring of champagne in the bath because we knew it was merely the first blow in a much longer battle. At the end of the day, it was just another pre-season friendly.

The match at Anfield on 20 October 1984, however, was an entirely different matter. The champers flowed like tap water that night! I get asked about that day more than any other in my entire career. Of course, Evertonians like to discuss my goal, but I look back on that afternoon as the day that we said to Liverpool, 'Move over, we are the top dogs now.'

We had won the FA Cup, we were third in the league table and Liverpool were struggling at the wrong end, but we still knew that they were the team to beat. If we were ever going to achieve anything, we knew we had to finish ahead of Liverpool and that was the day that we really knew we were capable of doing exactly that.

Beating them at Anfield gave us so much self-belief. We were already a confident bunch of footballers and we knew we were contenders, but that day stamped it on us.

All week at Bellefield, we just couldn't wait for that game to come. The week before, we had beaten Aston Villa 2–1 at Goodison and I had scored my customary goal against them (I really must add up my Villa total!). Although we hadn't won at Anfield since the days of Harvey, Ball and Kendall, we knew that we had a fantastic chance. And the goal will live with me for ever.

Gary Stevens played it forward. My first touch was good and I knew straight away that I had two options: either I could push it forward and run or have a pop. Well, I knew that I was always going to be the second favourite in a sprint with Mark Lawrenson, so I had a quick glance and then smacked it.

In those days, Liverpool were the only team who played with Tango footballs. It wasn't like it is now, with the Premier League negotiating deals with football suppliers to have some uniformity. Home teams could use whatever ball they wanted. All week at Bellefield we had been using Tango balls that Howard bought and they were terrific. He got a job lot and that was all we kicked that week. I loved them. They skidded off the turf perfectly and if you struck them right, they could swerve and move in the air.

At Anfield, the Tango sat up beautifully for me after my first touch. I caught it just right and it flew in. I didn't really know where to run when it hit the net.

When I looked at the celebration pictures during the following week, I could actually see some people I knew in the crowd. Eddie Don, the butcher who delivered meat to Bellefield, and still does, if I'm not mistaken, was in there, jumping up and down, but I didn't see him at the time because I was swamped by teammates and fans. Everyone remembers the boy with the red hair and glasses who lost it completely and ran onto the pitch waving his arms aimlessly in the air.

I actually met the boy many years later and he was highly embarrassed about his moment of fame. We had moved house from the Southport area to North Wales and my new window cleaner said that he knew the boy. I thought little of it until I met the window cleaner at a function one night in Liverpool. He came up to me and told me that the fan who'd run onto the pitch was in the room. 'The derby lunatic wants to say hello,' were his exact words! I would never have recognised him because he looked a lot more refined than he did when he went bonkers at Anfield.

It's 20-odd years since that game, but I still sign pictures of that goal regularly. People come up to me in the strangest places and tell me that my goal at Anfield is their computer screen saver. I'd like to think I am remembered for more than that shot, but I know how thrilled the fans were about it. They never tire of talking about it. Andy King gets the same thing. He scored a spectacular winner against Liverpool and the fans have not forgotten it either. Lee Carsley will doubtless experience the same in years to come.

The only slight on the whole day for me was that my dad couldn't get down from Glasgow for the game. He made his usual phone call that night and went through his 50 questions, but when he asked me about the goal I simply said, 'Wait until you see it!'

He wasn't a bit of good until he'd watched *Match of the Day*. 'Aye, it wasn't bad,' he said when he rang the following morning. He wasn't one for going overboard with praise! And he didn't need to: I knew when he was pleased, I didn't need him to tell me.

I still have a box full of scrapbooks that my dad compiled during my career. They are great to look back on, but it was a bloody nuisance at the time. I had to buy all the newspapers and sit in the kitchen with a pair of scissors to cut out anything that mentioned my name. If I was featured in *Shoot!* magazine, I had to go and buy it so I could post it back to Glasgow for my dad to look at. I'm sure the woman in the local paper shop thought I was an egomaniac.

The dressing-room at the end of that Anfield game was fantastic. It wasn't just the fact that we had beaten Liverpool at Anfield, it was the significance of it. The Mersey balance of power had just swung our way and the rest of the country now knew it. It sounds bashful, but although I knew I'd make the headlines because of the goal, I was more pleased for the whole team, for the whole club.

Evertonians hadn't had the bragging rights in the city for years and now they could go to work and go to the pub with their chests out and their heads held high. I never underestimated the privilege of making that sort of difference to people's lives and that's why victories over Liverpool were so special.

The following week's training was a different class. We were on cloud nine, and rightly so. There were more autograph-hunters at the gate, more reporters wanting to speak to us, and Bellefield was buzzing.

If that was 'my' day at Anfield, then 22 February 1986 belonged to Kevin Ratcliffe. He is still dining out on it now! Straight away I will say that I considered Rats to be the best defender in the world – and he is also one of my closest friends – but he was no goalscorer! Even in training he never scored goals. He took the odd free-kick from outside the box, but his attitude was to hit the ball as hard as he could and he never troubled the goalkeeper. We had two left-footed players who wanted to take free-kicks: one was Kevin Sheedy and the other was Kevin Ratcliffe. No prizes for guessing which one we preferred! But cometh the hour, cometh the man and in February 1986, Rats was 'the man'.

I couldn't quite believe it when he aimed to shoot from 40 yards at the Kop end. Links and I had scored eighteen goals between us in the previous eight League games and we both peeled off waiting for Rats to slip the ball forward. But the skipper had other ideas and I wasn't best pleased when he pulled his left peg back and belted the ball towards the goal. The rest is history. The ball bobbled towards the goal before, inexplicably finding its way past Bruce Grobbelaar and into the net!

Rats spent the whole of the next week in training shooting from everywhere. It had gone to his head. Normal service was rapidly resumed, though, and his efforts on goal were more of a problem to the residents of Sandforth Road than they were to Neville Southall. Not many players can look back over their career and say that half of the goals they scored were Merseyside derby winners – but Rats can. His other one was against Norwich City!

Links scored as well that day at Anfield and we were full value for a 2–0 win that should have been the springboard for a title-winning run-in. But Liverpool went on an incredible run after that and pipped us to the Championship.

The first derby of that season in September 1985 hadn't gone quite as well. Kenny Dalglish scored after about 30 seconds and before we knew it we were 3–0 down. We were the champions, we were at home and we were being well and truly spanked. I remember wanting the game to end at 3–0 because I thought it was going to be 1982 all over again: I thought we were going to get beaten 5–0.

At one stage, it could have been any score they wanted because we just weren't in it. But then I crashed one in off the crossbar from about eight yards at the Gwladys Street end just after half-time and the whole mood changed. Links scored as well and the momentum was with us, but they were a very good side then and they held on.

I mention the fact that I scored at the Gwladys Street end because we always liked to attack that part of the ground in the second half. If Rats won the toss, he would always opt to play towards the Park End in the first half. In those days that was where the away fans were congregated and there were times when we needed the Gwladys Street to help pull us across the finishing line.

I always enjoyed the derby matches because I knew that Alan Hansen and Mark Lawrenson hated them. They were two outstanding footballers, but they never fancied the rough and tumble of the derby, which just made it better for me.

If we tried to pass our way through a derby, they would pick us off because they were great players, but if we launched it, then it was an entirely different proposition. Howard would tell Andy Gray and me to get amongst the defenders. 'They don't fancy it one bit,' he'd say.

Jocky Hansen will admit that derbies were the worst games of his career. At his peak, there wasn't a better defensive player in the country, but when Andy and I were in his face he couldn't stand it.

In contrast, Steve McMahon certainly fancied it. He was a good pal of mine when I first joined Everton and we spent a lot of time together, but by the time he arrived at Liverpool, via Aston Villa, there seemed to me to be an edge to him. The Everton and Liverpool players would socialise in those days because a lot of us lived in the same area, but Steve seemed to have changed as a person. I felt he carried a vendetta into derby matches.

We had a mutual friend, Dave Sheron, and for some reason Steve fell out with him and tried to take it out on me. He had a go at me during one game and it snowballed from there. Our disrespect for each other seemed to develop from nowhere just because Steve had a problem with Dave. Steve, Paul Lodge, Dave and I were good pals, but once this rift appeared things got a bit silly.

I hated Liverpool at the best of times and the grudge with Steve McMahon just added spice. I wasn't bothered on a personal front because I knew I could give as good as I got, but it was all a bit unnecessary. During one derby at Anfield, Steve walked up to me when play was at the other end and poked me in the eyes with two fingers. Later in the game, I gave him a whack to even the score and our relationship hit rock bottom. From being close pals as youngsters, we were now sworn enemies.

When he signed for Liverpool, Steve appeared to become what players refer to as 'Billy Big Time'. He had a swagger about him and I felt that he looked down on Everton. He tried to tackle John Ebbrell in one game and he came off worse: Steve made a challenge but ended up being stretchered off. There was enough aggression and passion during a Merseyside derby without carrying personal feuds onto the pitch.

Steve even managed to wind up the mild-mannered Kevin Sheedy. Sheeds was never an aggressive footballer, but he dived in with both feet at Steve during one game and that, more than anything, displayed the depth of feeling at the time.

It really was a shame because Jocky, Kenny, Gary Gillespie and Ronnie Whelan were great pals of mine and, although we never went on many prearranged nights out together, we would always have a beer and a chat in the Fisherman's Rest, a really quiet, discreet, homely place in Birkdale. We'd also send drinks across if we were ever in the same restaurant. That was the way it was. Steve and I get on fine now, I'm glad to say, and we can laugh about the old days, but it did get a bit tasty in the '80s.

Even Ronnie Whelan has had a go at me about a derby incident. Ronnie and I were next-door neighbours. We always got on fine, but he reckons that I went right through him in a tackle when we were youngsters during a reserve derby. He says that I left a big gash right down the side of his leg, though I can't remember it. But it's probably true because every derby match was fiercely competitive in those days. It didn't matter that you weren't a local boy, you quickly picked up the passion and played every derby as if your life depended on it.

I loved winning them and hated losing them, which is why I'll never forgive Ian Rush. Not many people got the better of Kevin Ratcliffe or Neville Southall, but Rushie certainly did. Nev was the best in the business at dealing with one-on-ones, but Rushie was a natural-born goalscorer and was never fazed by Nev. I think Rats will admit that he dreaded facing Rushie. They were best pals but that counted for nothing when they were on opposing sides. Rushie was a smashing guy away from the pitch and we would regularly have a beer in the Holiday Inn on Paradise Street in the city centre.

Rushie did Derek Mountfield like a kipper in one of Derek's first derby matches in 1983. Liverpool were defending a corner and Rushie engaged Derek in conversation. He said that he was wearing new boots and that the laces wouldn't tie properly. He bent down to fiddle with them and Derek was taken in by it. Liverpool promptly cleared the ball forward and, as Derek was looking down at the 'lace-fiddling', Rushie jumped up, spun away and found himself in acres of space to receive the ball. I think Derek was still chatting about the merits of good laces when Rushie took a shot at goal!

I remember two derby matches that didn't matter a jot to anyone. Both were during 1986–87 – the season we won the League title – as part of the Full Members Cup. It wasn't a popular tournament. Liverpool beat us 3–1 at Anfield and then 4–1 in the second leg at Goodison, but nobody really cared.

I remember we played Norwich in the competition at Goodison one night. There were a group of senior players, including me, who weren't involved, and we sat in one of the executive boxes and laughed at the lads who were out there on the pitch! We were gesturing to them and they were giving a bit back – that summed up the whole competition. It was a Mickey Mouse tournament and the fans never took to it. All I recall about them is that a young centre-half called Peter Billinge played for us. He took the very rare route from non-League football to the First Division, having joined us from South Liverpool. Howard signed him and pitched him straight into training with us at Bellefield without introducing him to the lads. We played an 11-a-side match inside the big gym and Billo was clearly out to make an impression. He kicked everything that moved! It was no more than a Monday morning loosener, but Billo was treating it like a cup final. He threw himself into every challenge. We were all thinking, 'Who the bloody hell is this?' Howard stood there laughing his head off.

Billo was a really nice lad and he quickly settled down. He never made it at Everton, but he had a good career with Crewe and Coventry City.

If Rats and I had our Anfield derby days to remember in 1984 and 1986, then 1987 belonged exclusively to Sheeds. We were on the way to winning the League and, for once, the result at Anfield didn't really matter too much, as far as points on the board were concerned. Liverpool beat us 3–1, but Sheeds scored an absolute belter for us with a direct free-kick at the Kop end. That was memorable enough, but it was his subsequent celebration that made the headlines.

He found the top corner of the net with a trademark left-foot shot and then ran towards a packed Kop to give them a two-fingered salute. Sheeds was pulled up by the FA and tried to come up with every excuse under the sun – he even suggested that he had done a 3-2-1, like Ted Rogers' sign-off at the end of his television show. But the FA didn't buy it and Sheeds was hauled to London for a tribunal.

Another controversial derby incident that same Championship-winning season centred on a challenge by Gary Stevens on Jim Beglin. We were going well in the League Cup and had scored a lot of goals to reach the fifth round, where we were paired with Liverpool at Goodison. There were over 53,000 fans inside the ground that night and I would imagine that the majority of them winced when Gary Stevens launched at Jim in the first half. I was very close to the incident and it was a horrific injury. I ran across to see how badly hurt Beglin was and I was sickened by the sight of his shin bone sticking through his sock.

Although we lost the game 1–0 – Rush again! – the night is remembered for Jim's injury. It killed the game a bit, although anyone who knows Gary will back me when I say that there is no way he would have intentionally tried to hurt an opponent. He just wasn't that type of player. Poor Jim never fully recovered from it, which was a shame because he's a nice lad. He was never an aggressive type and perhaps if it had been Reidy and McMahon going for that loose ball, it would have been different because they did know how to tackle.

My record against Liverpool in the latter stages of my Everton career was poor and the only other time I was involved in a winning team against them was the epic FA Cup tie in 1991. Yet again we were drawn out of the hat for the fifth round of the FA Cup at Anfield. There was nothing in the first game, which ended 0–0, that would have given any hint of the unique drama that was to follow.

In actual fact we should have won that game because Pat Nevin was brought down for a blatant penalty that Neil Midgeley waved away. He knew after seeing the incident on television that it was a stonewall penalty – at least he was honest enough to hold his hands up afterwards and admit that he'd made an error – but we were furious at the time because we were the better side on the day.

Neil is sadly no longer with us, but he was a lovely man. I used to see him from time to time after I'd finished playing and he would always remind me that if it hadn't been for him, then one of the greatest derby matches ever would not have been played. It's a strange logic to apply, but he's probably right.

I had a lot of time for Neil. The standard of refereeing was no better in the '70s and '80s than it is now, but I firmly believe that the referees were better men. They were much easier to get along with and I had respect for the likes of Neil, George Courtney, Joe Worrall and Roger Milford because they knew that players had to be competitive and you could speak to them on the level during matches. There was never any shortage of banter – if players were doing badly, the referees wouldn't hesitate to let them know! There was far more give and take and there was a better atmosphere between players and officials than exists today. I get the feeling that some of the modern referees think the fans have come to see them and not the players.

But back to 1991. Not one single person privileged enough to be at the derby replay will ever forget it. It was an astonishing night and certainly one of the most dramatic matches that I've ever been involved in. Martin Tyler and Andy Gray were covering it for Sky and they couldn't quite believe what they were watching.

Four times we fell behind and four times we pulled ourselves level. It was breathless stuff of the highest calibre. It had everything, even though some of the Liverpool defending left a lot to be desired. Each of their goals was very well executed indeed – Peter Beardsley got two, John Barnes made a terrific shot from distance and Rushie weighed in with his usual.

I scored our first two equalisers. The first was a header at the far post from an Andy Hinchcliffe cross, although I didn't get the power I would have liked and Bruce should have kept it out. My second came after a horrendous mix-up between Bruce and Steve Nicol and I reacted quickly enough to slide in and poke the ball into the net. Tony Cottee equalised for us right on full-time and then he did it again in extra-time. It finished 4–4, but it could have been 7–7. We showed unbelievable character to bounce back so many times and they were deflated after the final whistle.

They must have flicked a coin after the end of extra-time because by the time we got to the dressing-room we knew that the second replay was going to be at Goodison.

I saw Kenny outside the players' lounge and he had a playful go at me because I'd scored two goals. He was naturally gutted at seeing his team squander the advantage on four occasions, but it was still a massive shock when he announced his resignation the following day. He gave no inkling on the night: I think that he'd just had one night of heart-thumping drama too many. It was a remarkable end to his Liverpool career and that match had served as a reminder to the watching world that the Merseyside derby is up there with the best of them.

The second replay was never going to match it – I don't think any game has done since – but we won, thanks to a goal from Dave Watson.

Those two goals in the 4–4 game were my last in a Merseyside derby though it was nice for the team to finish the job off in the third game. I was up against Glenn Hysen, a Swedish international, in those matches. I always enjoyed playing against him because I knew I would get the better of him.

Tackles would fly in all over the park in those games, which wasn't Hysen's cup of tea. I don't think the modern derbies are as tough or as competitive as they were in my day: the punters expected blood and guts and they usually got them.

Away from the cauldron of the pitch, I used to get on fine with the Liverpool players. I hadn't been at Everton long when I had a night out in the Moat House Hotel in the city centre. I was hardly a recognisable face at the time, but Graeme Souness came over to me and introduced himself. He knew I was a young lad from Scotland and he told me that if there was anything he could do to help me settle in, then I only needed to ask. I thought that was a terrific gesture and I never forgot it.

The spirit and camaraderie that existed between the two camps in the '80s came right back to the fore in May 2006 when we all got together to raise money for a very worthy cause. Marina Dalglish, Kenny's wife, established a charity in her name after she made a successful recovery from cancer in 2004 and the players from the 1986 FA Cup final between Everton and Liverpool were invited to re-enact the event at Anfield to raise money. It was a terrific idea, but getting all the lads back together was a difficult task!

For some reason or other, and I still can't recall why, the onus of assembling the Everton squad fell on me. I had a series of meetings with Kenny at Goodison to discuss the finer points of such a huge project and we set about trying to gather together as many of the original squad members as possible from that '86 final.

From our starting eleven, I knew that Gary Stevens, Derek Mountfield and Kevin Sheedy wouldn't be able to play because of various injuries and operations they'd had. I also knew that Pat Van Den Hauwe couldn't come over from South Africa. That left me with a bare nucleus and so I had some ringing round to do. Ian Snodin, Barry Horne, Paul Wilkinson, Neil Pointon, Ian Atkins and Alan Irvine were all drafted in.

The only player from the 1986 Everton squad whose attitude

disappointed me was Neville Southall. He said he couldn't make it because it was too short notice, but I think he knew that Bobby Mimms had been asked to play. Bobby was the keeper in the '86 final so it was only right to give him a game, but Neville knew full well he would have got to take part at some point.

Snods asked if Mike Newell could come along and play, but Kenny was against the idea. He felt that Newelly was a bit too far from the '86 era to qualify, although I suspect that Kenny was probably a bit worried that he still had enough pace to worry Messrs Hansen and Lawrenson.

The day of the game, the May Day Bank Holiday, was truly memorable. We all met up at the Sir Thomas Hotel in Liverpool and we enjoyed a fine pre-match meal with plenty of banter. It was great to see Gary Lineker again. He'd been the subject of some unpleasant newspaper revelations regarding his marriage just the day before, but he put that behind him to see the lads and support a very good cause. I thought that was big of him and I know Kenny really appreciated it.

All the lads were smartly attired in suits, shirts and ties . . . apart from Snods! He looked as though he was going to a rave in his native Doncaster with his faded jeans, beige boots and baggy jumper. He protested that nobody had informed him of the dress code, but his whole demeanour reminded us of how he used to dress when he was a player. That sparked more banter and Snods had a go at Neil Pointon.

'You could pay £500 for a suit, but you'd still look like a Guy Fawkes!' he said.

Sitting in the area reserved for the players was Meg Mathews, the ex-wife of Oasis singer Noel Gallagher. I don't really know why she was there, but she probably *had* paid £500 for her suit . . . at least!

The official Everton team bus collected us from the Sir Thomas and ferried us to Anfield and it was just like old times. Howard stood at the front and read out the team and Bails complained loudly that he wanted a transfer because he wasn't in the starting eleven. Bails was at it again as we got changed at Anfield. Unbeknown to the rest of the lads, he'd stuffed tissue paper into each shoulder of his jersey and then walked around the dressing-room geeing everyone up. He looked like an uneven body builder and, not for the first time, he had the lads in stitches.

The game was played at a far slower tempo than the '86 match and I only stayed on for 45 minutes, which is what I had originally planned. Links lasted 45 seconds! To be fair, he couldn't play because of an injury, but he agreed to put on a strip and kick the game off with me in the centre circle.

Bails made a late cameo appearance as a substitute and had us falling about again when he went to head the ball but jumped a bit too early. The ball caught him in his midriff and knocked him over.

Liverpool won with a last-minute goal from John Durnin. He had made two League Cup appearances for Liverpool but is a regular in their six-a-side Masters team so they churned him out again. I think Kenny was stretching the unwritten eligibility ruling with that one. But the main thing was that over 32,000 supporters backed the event and they raised a terrific amount of money for Marina's charity.

THIRTEEN

THE LAST EVERTON YEARS

Having lamented the distinct lack of backbone in the Everton team in the 1989 FA Cup final, I was gratified to see Colin sign a couple of players who were more than capable of looking after themselves: Martin Keown and Norman Whiteside were very welcome additions to the squad. Colin also brought in Mike Newell, Ray Atteveld and Stefan Rehn.

Martin, Norman and Newelly were winners, but we didn't know a great deal about the other two. It became apparent that Stefan Rehn was a strange cookie who wore moulded-stud boots for every match, regardless of the weather or the conditions. Colin wasn't happy about it, but Rehn carried on. Atteveld thought the world of himself, but he wasn't a bad player and at least he had a bit of character about him.

Trevor Steven left the club, having been lured by the Scottish pound. You can dress his move to Rangers any way you want, but it was a stonewall fact that the English First Division was far superior in quality to the Scottish Premier League. Everton couldn't compete with Rangers in the wages stakes, though, and Trevor travelled north to team up with his close pal Gary Stevens. Trevor was a big loss to our squad, but I'm sure he'll be the first to admit that the standard of his individual performances had slipped a bit. Maybe he was feeling a bit stale, but it was more likely that he was now playing alongside teammates who just weren't on the same wavelength as himself.

Once again, I'll go back to the crop of '85. Would we have beaten Bayern Munich after going a goal behind if we'd had Stefan Rehn, Ray Atteveld and Ian Wilson in the team? Never in a million years.

I hate to sound disrespectful of fellow professionals, but I believe that every player from the international stage down to parks and gardens amateur football always finds his level and some of the Everton players under Colin Harvey were operating out of their depth. That's why Norman Whiteside did so well for us. He was a big-club player and he knew the value of team spirit. He came in and ingratiated himself straight away. The lads loved him; he was one of the old school. He could battle away on the pitch and leave his foot in when he felt it was required and he would be right in amongst it when we socialised together away from the pitch.

Before the 1989–90 season kicked off, we travelled to the Far East for a two-week tour taking in Japan, Thailand and Malaysia. Everton's main sponsor at the time was NEC and they arranged for us to play Manchester United in the Japanese city of Kobe. We beat them 3–1. Norman scored one of our goals against the team he'd only just left. We had a night out after the game, though we didn't go berserk because we knew we had to be up early the following morning to catch the bullet train from Tokyo to Hiroshima. The plan was that the players who were up first in the morning would make sure all the others were up, too. That way we could all check out in time and nobody would miss the train.

But the plan went awry. The telephone in my room rang to wake me but it was Terry Darracott informing me that I had two minutes to get up, pack my gear and check out. I was sharing with Brace, so I roused him straight away, but we were falling over each other trying to pack our bags. We had absolutely no chance of catching the team bus to the railway station.

'The bastards! The bastards!' we kept muttering, as we threw our gear together.

We dashed down to reception, ordered a taxi and instructed the driver to take us to the main Tokyo station as quickly as he could. The city boasts one of the biggest railway stations in the world. We didn't have a clue where the lads were and we were charging around the place frantically looking for someone we recognised. It was pure good fortune that we spotted the team in their Everton tracksuits. They took great delight at the sight of Brace and me sweating profusely, dragging our bags along the platform.

But we weren't the last to arrive. Snods, Pointon, Rats and Sheeds had all been left to lie in. Snods and Points came galloping along just before the train arrived and then Rats and Sheeds came after them with, literally, seconds to spare.

Colin's face was like thunder.

After Hiroshima, it was off to Bangkok. As we arrived at our hotel at midnight, Colin instructed us all to go straight to bed. My reaction was one of incredulity.

'We're in the middle of Bangkok at midnight and he wants us to go to bed? He's having a laugh,' I said to Rats.

I did a quick poll of the lads and it transpired that seven of us were up for a night out. We knew that Colin would be sitting in the main reception, so we had no choice other than to walk down the back staircase, down 15 flights of stairs, and leave the hotel via a fire door. When we got there, we found the fire door closed and alarmed.

We were debating about what our next move should be when one of the lads, I think it was Snods, said, 'Sod this,' and booted the door open.

The alarm went off immediately and we had to run out and jump into the nearest two tuk-tuks. 'Take us to Patpong,' I shouted. 'And be quick about it.'

Unfortunately for us the Thai driver steered his little tuk-tuk right around the side of the hotel and straight past the main reception area. Colin was sitting there sipping tea when seven of his players shot past all perilously clinging on to two tuk-tuks.

He hammered us for it in the morning, and his mood had improved little when it was time to leave Thailand for Malaysia.

When we got to the airport, there was a hurricane battering Bangkok. When I saw some palm trees bent double with the force of the gale, I declared that there was no way I was even contemplating getting on an aeroplane. Thankfully an announcement confirmed that there would be no flights from Bangkok airport until the hurricane had passed. They estimated the delay at seven hours and we were all given vouchers to spend in the airport.

Snods and I used ours in the bar and eventually all the lads joined us. The seven-hour delay began to pass quite pleasantly. Colin was sitting quietly, reading a book, and when he looked up all the lads had gone. He sent Terry Darracott to round us all up, but when Tex found us in the bar he threw his vouchers into the kitty and joined us.

Colin got his own back when we finally landed in Malaysia and he ordered us to check into the hotel in Kuala Lumpur and then report immediately for training. He arranged for a tough running session and, in the heat of Malaysia, it was a really testing session – so much so that Neil Pointon collapsed. It was all too much for him. But Colin wouldn't let us stop.

'Keep going,' he screamed at us, 'keep going!'

We had to keep jumping over Neil or running around him as he lay poleaxed on the grass!

That was some tour and when we got back to Merseyside, Colin had arranged a friendly match with Oldham Athletic at Bellefield behind closed doors. They were 'nothing' matches, but on this particular day their centre-half kept coming right through the back of me and he was a real nuisance. Time and again, he put hefty challenges in on me. Finally I turned around and snapped at him, 'Are you all there, you idiot?'

He just fixed me with a piercing stare and offered to sort things out around the back of the gymnasium. That was my first introduction to Andy Holden, now the coach of the Everton reserve team and a very good friend of mine!

Once the season started, Newelly scored goals for fun and even got himself called up to the England squad. He was a wholehearted centre-forward and he made a really good impression during the opening couple of months of the campaign.

I picked up a nasty injury against Southampton in only the third game when I was 'done' by Jimmy Case. I'd nutmegged a Saints player and as I moved around him to pick up the ball, I saw Case coming at me. I didn't have time to get out of the way. His tackle was well over the top and I needed six stitches, which kept me out of the next game. When we played Southampton at The Dell in the return fixture, I tried to get Case back, but I couldn't get near him because he was far too crafty and clever.

At the start of November, Paul Bracewell left the club and Colin signed Peter Beagrie. For me, that just summed up how far Everton Football Club had slipped. I always remember Kenny Dalglish ringing me at home to tell me that he'd booked me in for an operation. I didn't have a clue what he was talking about, but he repeated that he'd sorted me out a private clinic for a cartilage operation. I was really confused by now and told him that there was nothing wrong with my cartilage.

'There will be, Sharpy, there will be,' he said. 'You've just signed Beagrie and so you'll be in the box, out the box, in the box, out the box.'

He wasn't wrong. Peter Beagrie infuriated me. In my opinion, he was never an 'Everton player'. He had ability and he could take on defenders, but he had a terrible habit of going back to try and beat them again. And again. It was almost impossible to play centre-forward when he was in the team.

I recall one trip abroad when Rats, Snods and I were having a quiet drink in a hotel room. Suddenly there was an awful banging on the door and when I looked through the spyhole it was Beagrie and Cottee. We didn't want to let them in, but they persevered with the banging so eventually I opened the door. I asked them to behave themselves because they were representing the football club, but they'd had a few beers themselves and were getting decidedly mouthy.

The conversation turned to the atmosphere at the club and the fact that new players were accusing the existing squad members of not making them feel welcome, which was total rubbish.

'I've had enough of this,' Snods said eventually. He got up from his bed, grabbed Beagrie by the scruff of the neck and lamped him straight on the nose before throwing him out of the room. Beagrie's eyes had blackened by the morning, but nothing was ever mentioned about the incident.

Beagrie made his Everton debut against Aston Villa when we lost 6–2. I started the game on the substitute's bench and it was a total embarrassment. I'd never played in an Everton side that had conceded six goals and there didn't seem to be any desire to stop them going in. Again, defeat was accepted too casually. It was summed up by Cottee scoring two goals when we were already 6–0 down. He came off content that he'd done his job by netting twice. The team spirit was as low as I had ever known it.

This was also the year of the infamous Kevin Sheedy–Martin Keown incident. We were in a Chinese restaurant in Southport and Sheeds had knocked a few back and started goading big Martin, who had been drinking Coca-Cola all afternoon. Martin wasn't biting, so Sheeds changed his tactics. Martin's brother was out with us and he'd turned up a little overdressed in a shirt and tie.

'And another thing,' Sheeds said. 'Your brother is a dickhead!'

That was the straw that broke the camel's back. The next minute, fists were flying. Martin was stone-cold sober and got much the better of the scuffle – although I don't really think his sobriety was a contributing factor in the outcome of the fight.

Back on the field, I just kept on doing my best, although the goals just weren't going in for me. I ended the season with just six League goals from thirty-three appearances, although one of them was a record-breaking effort against Crystal Palace: I scored past Nigel Martyn at Goodison in a 4–0 win in the March, which put me on 106 League goals – a post-war record.

A welcome diversion from my frustration was the announcement that I was to be granted a testimonial the following season. It had been part of the deal I'd signed the season before. I asked Ray Parr to chair my committee. He'd done a good job when he'd looked after Kevin Ratcliffe's benefit year, so I knew he'd do all right for me. He organised a great launch when he invited the 1966 Everton FA Cup-winning team to attend a special dinner. That was the night my old Rangers hero, Willie Henderson, turned up.

We had another FA Cup marathon that season, first taking three games to defeat Middlesbrough in the third round, then we overcame Sheffield Wednesday before losing to Oldham in the fifth round after another three ties. To add insult to injury, I was fined £500 by the Football Association following comments I made after the first game at Boundary Park that ended 2–2.

I'll never forget the referee that day. He was called Tony Ward and he had a shocking game. Colin had a right go at him after the match, too, but it was my quotes to which the FA took exception. He booked *nine* Everton players in the first two ties and after the Goodison replay I claimed that '36,000 people couldn't all be wrong' after the fans had joined in the condemnation of Ward's performance.

I may have been in trouble, but I'd like to think that at least someone paid attention to me at Lancaster Gate: for the second replay, Roger Milford was installed as the referee.

Oldham won the third game 1–0, and I always look back on that defeat as the beginning of the end for Colin as manager. I took some calls the following morning from the local press lads who said that it was a disgrace to the Everton name. The papers were suggesting that the team was at a low ebb. The knives were being sharpened for Colin from that day.

I played in all bar five of our League games and was therefore happy that I must have been playing reasonably well. Norman Whiteside was one of our stars of the season. He really was a great acquisition for the club.

I remember at one point in the campaign that we were both injured and had to do some cycling. We were told to go from Bellefield to a gymnasium in Knowsley that was owned by a man called Terry Phillips. Norman and I rode the bikes to the gym every day and when we got there we were royally entertained. Liverpool comedians Mickie Finn and Jackie Hamilton were using the cycle machines inside the gym and their banter had Norman and me in pleats of laughter. On the way back, Norman used to pop into a local pub for a full English breakfast and a couple of beers! It was unbelievable, but that was Norman. He fitted in well – it's just a shame that his injury problems prevented him from having a better Everton career.

One player who was never in a million years going to have anything like a good career at Goodison was Mike Milligan, who Colin signed from Oldham during the summer of 1990. Mike was a lovely lad and always gave of his best, but things just didn't go well for him at Everton. The punters could see it as well and he had a nightmare spell at the club. I felt it was a mistake by Colin because it was a transfer that was never going to work out.

The other big summer signing was Andy Hinchcliffe, who had a bit more about him. He was a loner and kept himself very much to himself. Unlike the player who had gone the other way in the deal: Neil Pointon.

Andy did well for Everton, but I never really had time to get used to playing in the same team because, although I didn't know it at the time, I was starting my last season at Goodison Park.

For me, the best recruit of that summer was the return to the club of Jimmy Gabriel. Jimmy is a fantastic man, who lived quite near to me, and I had a lot of time for him. I didn't know him until he came back to the club, but he was a diamond. You could talk to Jimmy about football for hours.

We played Galatasaray in a testimonial for their goalkeeper during our pre-season campaign. It was my first time in Istanbul and I thought it was an unbelievable city. We stayed right in the middle. When we got to the stadium, I couldn't believe that it was jam-packed to capacity. There wasn't an empty seat in the house. About 20 minutes into the game, the referee blew his whistle for no apparent reason. On the whistle, all the Galatasaray outfield players swarmed around the keeper and carried him shoulder high on a lap of honour. There were still 25 minutes of the first half to go but that got the supporters even more excited – the atmosphere was already electric.

We beat them 3–1, which maybe wasn't the wisest thing to do under the circumstances. On the team bus en route back to the hotel, we got stuck in the Istanbul traffic and were spotted by a group of local supporters who were none too pleased that the tribute match to their goalkeeper had ended in defeat and smashed all the windows on the bus! Bang, bang, bang! One by one the windows gave way under a barrage of bricks and stones – and this was supposed to be a friendly match.

Our next match was in the more tranquil surroundings of Glasgow. Whoever planned that pre-season schedule must have had a grudge against the lads! We played Celtic, where I got plenty of stick from the home fans because they knew that I was a Rangers supporter, but it was the first time I had played at Parkhead and it gave my family a chance to come and watch. We drew 2–2, with Newelly scoring two good goals for us.

The 1990–91 season itself got off to a bizarre start when we lost at home to Leeds United on the opening day. It is a game that will forever be remembered for Neville Southall spending the half-time interval sitting against the goalpost although the rest of the lads didn't know about that until after the game. It was a friend who gave me all the details. We honestly hadn't noticed that Nev wasn't in the dressing-room. We were 3–0 down, but I thought it was a stupid thing to do. I think he was merely making a public statement, which was totally unnecessary. But that was Nev and you could never legislate for him.

We lost each of our opening three games and were rooted to the bottom of the table. The writing was on the wall for Colin. We didn't win our first game until the end of September when we defeated Southampton 3–0 at Goodison. The football club was on its knees and it was heartbreaking for someone like me who had been a regular when we were the best team in Europe.

By the end of October, we had still only won one League game; we were third from bottom and we had been dumped out of the League Cup by Sheffield United. The board of directors had lost patience with Colin and he was dismissed.

Although, if I am being honest, I could see it coming, I was still very upset about Colin's departure because I had grown up with him at Everton and he had been such a huge influence on me. When he left the club, I gave him my first Scotland cap as a thank you for everything he had done for me. Colin was taken aback by my gesture. He refused to take it off me at first, but I insisted and told him that without his help I would never have got the cap in the first place. I am pleased to say that he eventually accepted it. Colin has since given me his shirt from the 1966 FA Cup final, which bowled me over. He didn't have to do that, but, to this day, it is one of my most valued possessions.

I was really gutted when Colin left. And I must admit I wasn't exactly jumping for joy when his successor was revealed as . . . Howard Kendall. I thought that it was the wrong appointment to make and I still stand by that assessment. I am a great believer in never going back. Howard was fantastic during his first spell at the club, but it didn't happen for him the second time around – he was never going to emulate the team he had crafted in the mid-'80s.

The supporters were ecstatic, but I had an inkling that his re-appointment wouldn't exactly be the best thing for my Everton career. As far as I was concerned, the only plus point to emerge was the appointment of Colin as his number two. Everyone connected with the club was delighted to see him back where he belonged.

Results didn't get too much better until the Christmas and New Year period and I reached a personal landmark at Stamford Bridge against Chelsea on 1 January when I scored in our 2–1 win. It was my 111th League goal for the club, which put me second in the all-time list behind the immortal Dixie Dean – in fact, that strike put me within just 238 goals of Dixie's tally! In all seriousness, I was very proud indeed to look at the record books and see only the greatest centre-forward of all time ahead of me in the Everton goal list.

Two other significant goals were the brace I bagged against Liverpool in the famous 4–4 FA Cup replay in February: the last two goals I scored for Everton. The simple fact was that I wasn't enjoying my football. I was putting my heart and soul into every match because I didn't know any other way, but things just weren't going well for me. And Howard's return had scarcely inspired me.

Once again, Aston Villa loomed large in my story. It was at Villa Park on 30 March 1991 that I pulled on an Everton jersey for the 446th and final time. There was no fanfare and no emotional farewell to the supporters because there was no indication at the time that I would never play for the club again. The Everton side that earned a 2–2 draw in my last game was: Southall, McDonald, Hinchcliffe, Ratcliffe, Keown, Milligan, Warzycha, McCall, Sharp, Cottee, Sheedy. Youds and Nevin were the substitutes. There were just four survivors from the team that won the title in 1985 and, unsurprisingly, not one who had appeared in my first game eleven years earlier.

Like I say, I didn't know at the time that I'd reached the end of the Everton road and I certainly had no inclination that my love affair with the club would end in such a sloppy and distasteful manner.

SHARPY

I didn't get selected for the Zenith Data Systems Cup final against Crystal Palace at Wembley in April, but I didn't really care too much because I thought it was a ridiculous competition. Norman and Snods missed out as well, so we sat at the back of the dugout watching the game. We decided to move indoors in the end because Norman was coming in for some awful abuse from nearby Palace supporters. We made our way to the players' bar and got ourselves so comfortable that we stayed there for the duration of the second half.

Palace thrashed us 4–1, but we had a laugh watching it on a big screen, drinking a few beers. What we didn't know was that an Everton director had spotted us and on the Monday morning we were summoned to Howard's office. He accused us of not bothering to watch the game, but, of course, we'd seen it all and we managed to describe all the goals in fine detail. Howard wasn't having it, though, and he fined all three of us!

Everton finished 1990–91 far better than we'd started it and managed a comfortable mid-table berth in the end. I was forced to admit that my goalscoring record hadn't been the best at the close of the season, but I was looking forward to having a good rest and recharging my batteries. Things may not have gone as well as I'd hoped, but I was still confident in my ability to perform at the highest level.

I took Ann Marie and the children to America for three weeks during the summer. It was the longest we'd ever been away and we all thoroughly enjoyed it. We stayed at Walt Disney World in Florida for a fortnight and then spent a week on the coast in Clearwater, where we met up with Rats and his family. It was just the sort of complete break that I needed. I also met up with goalkeeper Jim Leighton, who was then with Manchester United, and we went for a meal with his family.

The day before we were due to return home a telephone call was put through to my room. It was my pal, Dave Sheron, back home.

'Sorry to bother you, Sharpy,' he said, 'but I've had Phil Black on the phone and he was asking about you moving to Oldham Athletic.'

Phil Black was a mate of Joe Royle's. I knew him because he owned a clothes shop in Manchester that I went to from time to time.

'Oldham?' I queried. 'Why would I want to go to Oldham? I'm on holiday, I'll speak to you when I get back.'

I really didn't think any more of it. I just assumed that someone, somewhere had got the wrong end of the stick. I knew of Joe Royle, obviously, and I had great respect for him, but I had no intention of signing for his football club.

We finished our holiday and, having heard nothing more, I reported for pre-season training as normal. On the first day, though, I was summoned to Howard's office at Bellefield. He told me that he had reason to believe that I had been discussing a move to Oldham with Joe Royle.

I was quite taken aback and, quite naturally, denied the allegation.

He was having none of it and I had to stress over and over again that I had not had any sort of conversation with Joe. It was unbelievable. I felt like a schoolboy who was being accused of a misdemeanour by an angry headmaster.

'Look,' I said, 'I haven't spoken to Joe about anything and if you've heard something, then just pick up the phone, ring him yourself and tell him that I don't want to sign for Oldham Athletic.'

He refused to do so.

The conversation reached an uncomfortable stalemate. I left Howard's office convinced that he did not believe me.

I spoke to Kevin Ratcliffe and told him that the club was plotting to sell me on. He couldn't fathom it out and neither could I. I went home that night with my head in a whirl. I spoke to Ann Marie about it, but before we had finished our discussion the telephone rang. It was Joe Royle. He'd got my number from Howard.

That was my first contact with Joe and he was great about it. He told me that Howard had given him permission to approach me, but I repeated that I wasn't really interested in joining Oldham. Joe simply said that he understood, but that he would like to come across to my house to have a chat about things. Out of respect for Joe, I agreed and he drove to Birkdale to meet me.

Joe is a lovely man and we had a nice chat about his plans. Oldham had been promoted to the First Division and, although I was impressed at the way he tried to sell the club to me, I could only re-emphasise that I wouldn't be a part of his rebuilding. He left after asking me to give the move some serious consideration.

'Just think about it, that's all,' he said. 'If you still don't want to come, then fine. I won't fall out with you and we'll just get on with things, but I'd love you to say yes to us.'

He was a very persuasive character, but when I went to see Howard the next day I told him that I'd be going nowhere.

But Howard had another card up his sleeve. He told me of his intention to sign Dean Saunders from Derby County.

'That's fine,' I answered, 'but I can guarantee that I'll be back in the side within ten games because I've got nothing to fear from Saunders or Cottee.'

I actually remember thinking that a signing such as Saunders might be the kick up the backside I needed to rekindle my enthusiasm because, if I'm honest, I'd gone a bit stale and had been a bit disillusioned with Everton. The competition would sharpen me up again and I was convinced that I would soon force my way into the reckoning.

Howard left me in no doubt that I would not be a first-choice striker in his team, but that was his prerogative as no player was ever guaranteed a place at Everton.

I was more than willing to prove myself and battle for a starting position, but I got the distinct impression that Howard didn't want me to. I didn't like the way it was being handled one bit. The accusation that I'd spoken to Joe when I hadn't and the fact that Joe told me that he had got my phone number from Howard left me perplexed.

My mind was finally made up when Howard told me that Everton would not match the wages that Oldham were willing to offer me. That was the last straw. It was just pathetic. If Everton genuinely couldn't match what a little club like Oldham were willing to offer me, then it really did confirm that I had no future at Goodison Park. The manager wanted to sell me, pure and simple.

I spoke again with Ann Marie and I told her that I would be going to Oldham. Joe had assured me that I wouldn't have to move house and that was a big factor. I still didn't drive at this stage, so travelling to Oldham was a problem that I still had to solve, but I had no intention of staying at a club that evidently didn't want me. I telephoned Joe at his house and informed him that I would like to sign for Oldham. He was absolutely delighted and we arranged another meet.

The next morning, I told Howard that he could have his way and that I would be off. However, to my surprise, his stance appeared to have changed. He indicated that he couldn't afford to let me go because he had agreed to sell Mike Newell to Blackburn Rovers. 'I don't care. I've told Joe and I'm going,' I said. Things had taken another twist, but my mind was made up. I didn't feel that I was being treated with anything like the respect I deserved after all the service I had given to the club.

I was hurt and disappointed at the way Howard had handled my departure. If he had been upfront and informed me that he was signing Saunders and that the decision to stay and fight for a place was mine, then I'd have had no problem. But the whole affair was messy. I felt it was a scandalous way for my Everton career to end. Howard's record as manager speaks for itself and the club owes him a huge debt of gratitude for the success he brought to Everton, but it took me a long time to forgive the way that he, in my opinion, engineered my exit. We'd shared some wonderful times over the years, but – and I don't say this lightly – I lost a lot of respect for him during the summer of 1991.

The club got £500,000 for me, so they did very well out of the deal, but they didn't put the money towards the Saunders transfer because at the last minute he decided to move to Liverpool. I had a wry smile about that.

There was no opportunity to say a proper goodbye to the fans or the lads. I simply asked Sheeds to get my boots and some of my stuff and bring it round to my house after training one day. The way Howard Kendall treated me broke my heart, but the passage of time has diluted any ill feeling. We get along fine now, but my opinion on the way he conducted my departure from Everton Football Club will never change.

FOURTEEN

ROYLE CALLING

Joe Royle could have forged a successful career as a salesman. He has that natural charm and persuasiveness about him, but I had still deliberated long and hard before agreeing to join his football club. One of the main issues was the Oldham pitch. There was no way I would have ever contemplated moving there if they had kept the artificial playing surface, but Joe assured me that the plastic pitch was to be dug up and replaced by traditional turf.

In the event, it didn't make too much difference, to be honest. They removed the plastic pitch all right, but it seemed to me they just replaced it with a thin layer of grass. I had started to feel twinges in my back after games and as the pitch was very hard all season, it wasn't doing me any favours.

As for the actual playing side, Joe was very enthusiastic about leading Oldham into the First Division for the first time in almost 70 years. He told me that he had assembled a very good young team and that he preferred to play with two wingers who both liked getting balls into the box, which, for a centre-forward like me, was very pleasing to hear. Joe wanted me to knit things together a bit and use my experience to help the younger players through what was bound to be at times a testing season.

I couldn't help but like Joe. An ex-Everton centre-forward like myself, he was as honest as the day is long. The contract that Oldham had offered me – a three-year deal – was good, but Joe was the significant factor in my joining the club.

SHARPY

After the heartache of leaving Everton had subsided, I couldn't wait to throw myself into the pre-season and begin a new chapter in my career. The training was hard to start with, but such was my determination to prove to Howard Kendall that I was still a top-flight player that I approached it with real gusto – I even enjoyed it . . . well, most of it. When Joe told me that he was also signing big Brian Kilcline, I thought, 'Jesus Christ, what do you want him for?' Big Brian had a reputation for being a no-nonsense centre-half whose priority was to prevent the centre-forwards from playing – and he wasn't overly fussed about what methods he used! But Killer was great for us.

Joe had been right. Oldham did have some very promising young players. Paul Gerrard in goal later signed for Everton, Paul Bernard won England B honours, Darren Beckford from Norwich City had cost a fair amount of money, Richard Jobson, Earl Barrett and Nicky Henry all went on to have very good careers, and Rick Holden was something of a cult hero at Boundary Park. They also had older heads like Roger Palmer, who was a marvellous character, Andy Holden at centre-half and Andy Ritchie. Joe had the right balance between youth and experience and he treated everyone accordingly.

They were a great set of lads and they made me feel very welcome. I don't know what they expected when Joe first signed me, but I have never been one for putting on airs and graces and I felt right at home very quickly.

I remember one of our early training sessions when Willie Donachie, Joe's assistant, lined us all up in two ranks and instructed us to pass to each other over a distance of twenty yards. This went on for about half an hour and I was very quickly bored witless by the monotony of it all. It was just passing, passing, passing and only from 20 yards.

'What's going on here, gaffer?' I asked Joe.

'You've been spoilt, Sharpy. You've come here from Everton,' he replied.

I never carried on the conversation, but I did wonder why First Division footballers had to pass a ball again and again over such a short distance.

That was Willie's way and I felt the training could often be quite repetitive at Oldham. Willie is a really nice man, but I thought he could be a bit dour, and he had this way about him that rendered him hard work at times. Despite this the training had gone very well. One fly in the ointment at the time was the daily trip from my home in Birkdale to Oldham. I still couldn't drive, so it was a chore just getting to the ground each day. Once again, though, Joe was magnificent and he would take me to one side at times and tell me to have a couple of days off. The rest of the lads would give me stick about it, but it was most welcome and Joe knew that I would never abuse his goodwill. He had a great line that he'd use from time to time after he let me off: 'Just make sure you're 100 per cent on a Saturday.' I felt very fit as the season approached and, if anything, the training was tougher at Oldham than it had been at Everton.

My Oldham debut came against Liverpool at Anfield – you can imagine the welcome I received from The Kop that afternoon – and we nearly won the game. We had led 1–0 for such a long time before they snatched it with two very late goals. That was a blow, but I remember feeling very positive after the game. We'd given a good account of ourselves and, although we were still a lot of people's favourites to go straight back down again, I thought we had a chance.

My first goal came in September against Torquay in a 7–1 win in the Rumbelows Cup. It was a relief to get off the mark after not scoring in our opening few games, but I never felt under any pressure. It was refreshing for me to know with absolute certainty that I was wanted and that I was a first-choice striker at the club. That hadn't always been the way at Everton.

Four days after opening my Oldham account, I scored two more in a great win at Maine Road against Manchester City. Peter Reid was the manager at the time and Neil Pointon, my old pal from Everton, was in their side. Points and I were chatting away to each other during the match and, unbelievably, he gave me some advice that was to prove detrimental to his new teammates: he advised me to attack the far post if we looked like getting the ball into the box from wide positions. He explained that Steve Redmond, who would be my likely marker in such a scenario, had a tendency to daydream and that I would get a good goalscoring chance. He was right about that! My first goal was a header at the far post after I managed to get in front of Redmond.

We beat City 2–1 and I was really pleased with myself because I had shown the Oldham fans just what I was capable of. The only negative was that Oldham wore all red as their away strip and that was always a difficult colour for me to put on!

My form in my first season was good and in April I scored four goals in one match against my old Everton foes, Luton Town. A former teammate, Alec Chamberlain, was in goal, and Chris Kamara marked me (or at least tried to!). Mark Pembridge, later to join Everton, was also in the line-up. It was one of those days when everything I tried came off. By the way, I believe I am still the only player to have scored four goals in one match for two different teams in the top flight.

At the end of my first season with Oldham, I was proud to have been an ever-present in both League and cup matches, which is something I never achieved in my 11 years at Everton. The tough training clearly agreed with me.

Having confounded the critics and finished in 17th position in the First Division, Oldham Athletic proudly became founder members of the brand new FA Premier League for the 1992–93 season. We were sitting at football's top table and to give us every chance of staying amongst the elite, Joe and Willie formulated an even tougher pre-season regime. We had to be at the public swimming baths in Oldham by 8 a.m. every morning. The baths were opened especially for the players and it was hard going. It wasn't for relaxation; it was very much geared towards increasing our stamina. We'd do length after length, above and below the surface, and lots of energetic exercises. After that we'd make our way to a hotel in the city centre for some breakfast and then it would be off to Boundary Park to get changed before heading to the nearby hills for more training.

There was no shortage of hills in the area either. When I first encountered a local hill, I refused to run up it because it was so steep and there was only one route with access to the top. I pointed out, with all sincerity I hasten to add, that my back was not up to that type of running. Thankfully Joe agreed and drove me up in his car. You can well imagine the reaction of the lads as I cruised past them in the passenger seat of the manager's car. I had no qualms about running when we got to the top of the hill but negotiating the steep climb wasn't for me. Joe evened it up a bit when he paired me in the sprints with Earl Barrett – he could catch pigeons he was so quick.

After the hill training, it was back down to the stadium for a shower and change before making our way to the gymnasium for some weight and conditioning training.

This was the routine every single day and it was very, very tough. It was probably the hardest I had ever trained in my life, but I enjoyed it, I have to say, and felt great for it. But poor Dave Munro, the friend who was driving me to and from Oldham, had to wait for me all day, which was a nuisance for him. Even though I was paying him, he soon got fed up, quite understandably, and packed it in.

So I began to use public transport again. I'd get the 7 a.m. train from Southport to Manchester and then change to catch the Oldham connection. I got into a routine whereby I'd buy a load of the morning papers and then sit and read them on the train. I became friendly with the drivers and the guards and it didn't bother me as much as you would think it would.

Ann Marie was also involved in driving me around, but it all became a bit too much for her during my second season with the club and she booked some driving lessons for me. At first

I refused to take them, but she insisted and so I finally began to learn to drive at the age of 32. I had lessons in an automatic and I took to driving so well I passed my test first time. It made such a difference to my life – I wondered why on earth I had never done it before. I looked back on all the years that I'd had to arrange lifts everywhere. I must have been mad. I can't really explain why it took so long for me to bother to learn: my dad always drove a car and my two brothers learned when they were young. I had just never got around to it.

On the football side of things, I didn't agree with everything Willie tried to introduce in training, but I always had to concede that everything was well thought out. Joe had shares in a gymnasium in Oldham that the lads would use. One day we were in an empty room on the premises when Willie walked in and introduced us to an aerobics teacher.

'We are doing some aerobics today, lads,' he said. 'There may be some of you that don't want to do it and that's fair enough, you can leave the room right now.'

That was my signal and I got up and walked out. I fully expected there to be at least half a dozen boys behind me, but when I turned around I was on my own. I wasn't bothered too much. I just sat behind the glass screen that backed onto the room and watched the lads going through their paces. I hadn't been sitting there long when Joe walked in and clocked me. His face broke into a huge grin.

'How did I know you wouldn't do aerobics!' he said.

Another of Willie's ideas was to bring in Lennie Heppell. I had met Lennie when I was at Everton. He was a movement coach who had taught us how to be a bit livelier on our toes. Lennie was a lovely man. When he came to Oldham, he must have been in his 80s, but he was still as fit as a fiddle. He'd been a champion ballroom dancer. When I saw him, I started laughing. Lennie made straight for me, saying, 'Hi, Graeme, nice to see you again. How are you?' I could sense the rest of the players looking at me and thinking, 'Aye aye, what's going on here?'

Lennie brought his wife into the gym and they started ballroom dancing in front of us. It was all the lads could do to stifle their giggles, but they soon straightened their faces when Willie told them they'd all be having a go at it themselves. We had to do the moves because Willie thought we'd benefit from it.

He also brought along two psychologists. They asked us all to write down five things that we thought we were good at and five things we felt we could improve about ourselves. I thought it was nonsense, but Joe and Willie believed in it and told the players that the psychologists would be willing to stage sessions every week if there was sufficient interest. I politely declined, but some of the lads fancied it and put their names down. As the weeks went by, those lads were coming into training with bigger and bigger folders filled with reams and reams of notes and printouts. They even started getting homework.

I may sound like an old-fashioned sceptic, but I genuinely didn't think I needed any mind training. Colin Harvey summed it up beautifully when I spoke to him about it later on. 'Sharpy,' he said, 'weak people need a crutch to lean on and that's what these psychologists are for.'

To be fair to Willie, who, I must re-emphasise, was a smashing man, he was using all the tools he possibly could to get the very best out of the players he had at his disposal. And if speaking to a complete stranger about one or two problems helps anyone, then who am I to dismiss it? It just wasn't for me.

We only lost one of our opening half-dozen Premiership games – against Arsenal – so our start was fairly solid. I was still enjoying my football and, with wide men like Rick Holden and Neil Adams supplying regular crosses into the box, why shouldn't I have been? I was still motivated by the desire to prove certain people wrong, so I took a lot of satisfaction from playing my part in a 1–0 win over Everton in October at Boundary Park. I attacked a corner at the near post and got a flick-on for Richard Jobson to head home. It was a tactic I'd used countless times at Everton and Andy Gray, who was sitting in the commentary box that afternoon, said he could not believe that Howard had failed to tell his defenders to watch for a Graeme Sharp run to the near post.

I enjoyed that result, though I had nothing against Everton. I still socialised with a few of the lads. I'd see Snods and Rats from time to time and would also meet up with Maurice Johnston when he signed for the club. We all used to drink together in the Fisherman's Rest. I would also take my dad there for a couple of pints when he was down from Glasgow, as it was only a ten-minute walk from my house. We knew the landlord very well and there was never any problem until one night Mark Ward and Maurice came in together. They had been drinking and, unbeknown to us, Wardy was attracting attention from all the girls who were going to the ladies toilet. Some of them were with boyfriends and, inevitably, it led to a spot of bother when one of them had a go at Wardy. We all piled in to help out and it was mayhem. The landlord went ballistic. The police were called and we were all barred. It had been my local for a long time and here I was on the 'unwanted' list.

I have always got on with Wardy. He was on Everton's books when I first came down to the club and he was a great little footballer. He was a hard player, too. He put Steve McMahon straight into a wall with a ferocious tackle that earned him a stern rebuke from Colin Harvey. But he was a good lad and it was really unfortunate that he went off the rails so badly later in his life. I was saddened to learn that he had been jailed for eight years in 2005.

My Premiership season ended in January 1992 when I required surgery on my back. Oldham used to train a lot on the pitch at Boundary Park and, as I have already explained, it was a very hard playing surface that did my back no good at all. I was forever having hot baths before and after training and I was a regular customer for the club masseur. We were due to play Blackburn Rovers in the middle of January and were training during the week when I felt a strange warm sensation in my back. It started when I had kicked the ball during shooting practice at the end of the session and when I tried again, the feeling got worse.

I reported it to the physio, who made me lie down under a heat lamp, but when that treatment was over I couldn't get off the table without assistance. I somehow got myself dressed and asked Neil Pointon to drive me to the chiropractor. He prescribed a few days of complete rest, but after 48 hours I felt even worse and was given an appointment to see a top surgeon, Dr Banks, at the private Beaumont Hospital in Bolton.

I had an MRI scan and, after assessing the results, it was suggested that I have an epidural. I was quite happy to go along with that . . . but then I had no idea what an epidural was! When I saw the size of the needle, my first thought was, 'Bloody hell, what's that?' To make matters worse, they couldn't get it into my back at first, which made me even more edgy. The sweat was streaming out of me. I nearly crushed the nurse's hand, I was squeezing it that hard. At the end of it all, the epidural made not a jot of difference to the pain. They diagnosed a prolapsed disc in my back that needed to be removed. The problem was eventually sorted out, but there is no doubt that I was never the same player again.

One good thing was that the Beaumont Hospital was like a five-star hotel. I had a few regular visitors who would think nothing of ordering from the wine list while they were there. Anyone visiting the hospital to see a patient was perfectly entitled to order themselves a meal and a glass of wine, but my pals turned it into a daily party. Quite where the catering staff thought all the bottles of Chablis were going is anybody's guess – I would even join my guests some days. One of the nurses caught me having a few wines one afternoon and she went mad, claiming that she would be sacked if the senior staff found out. I laugh about it now, but I was in a lot of pain and it was actually a very worrying period for me.

A phone call one night did little to calm my troubled mind. In between my MRI scan and my eventual operation, the phone went at one o'clock in the morning and I instantly feared the worst, which is everyone's natural feeling when you get a call late at night or in the small hours. I wasn't too far wrong, either, although at least it wasn't bad news about any of my family. It was Dr Banks.

'How long are you thinking of continuing playing professional football, Graeme?' he asked. What a question to pose at that hour of the morning!

'Ideally, I would like to play until I touch 40,' I replied.

'Hmmm, well, we've seen your scan results and I wouldn't think you'll get much beyond 35,' he said bluntly.

I was shattered by that bombshell and didn't sleep another wink. I feared the very worst and thought my career was over there and then. There I was with a wife and two young children and football was all I'd ever known. I considered the coaching option, but I wasn't overly keen on taking all the required courses and obtaining the badges.

As it happens, all my fretting was premature. I did play at the top level again, although I never felt 100 per cent fit again.

Thankfully I was able to take part in my own testimonial match at Goodison Park in November 1992, though I was bitter that things hadn't panned out the way I had hoped. For a start, I was having my benefit match at Goodison some 16 months after I left Everton and, regardless of how well you've done for a team, you lose your appeal after that length of time. In fact, I think the only reason I got a game at all was because the club were contractually obliged to give me one.

The initial idea was for Everton to play Celtic, who had agreed to come down for the game. That was great for me because they are a big draw being the best-supported away team on the planet. We were scheduled to play the game on a Sunday but because Liverpool had a home match the day before, Merseyside Police said they couldn't cover both events. They claimed that the policing of the city centre on the Saturday night would be made extremely difficult because of the volume of Celtic fans that would have been around. Reluctantly, and with no small annoyance, we were forced to cancel the game completely and it put a dampener on everything.

My committee was terrific and they came up with the idea of having a Merseyside eleven against a Manchester eleven. It was a novel suggestion – I don't think anybody could arrange such a contest now because the rivalry between the two cities has descended into virtual hatred – and the response from the players was more than I could have asked for. I was overwhelmed by the level of support from the lads: Bryan Robson played, as did Kenny Dalglish, Andy Gray, John Barnes, Steve McMahon, Peter Reid and Bruce Grobbelaar.

It didn't have the lure of an Everton–Celtic clash – we only attracted something like 12,000 supporters, whereas Celtic would have brought that many on their own – but I was very grateful indeed to all the players who gave up their time. The weather was against us, as it was a bitterly cold day, but I enjoyed the game. It was a good day for my family, too, because Chris and Emma were the mascots.

Being in the Everton dressing-room again with Andy was great. He always had so much to say in the dressing-room and, typically, he automatically started to pick the team himself – and we were happy to let him do so. He called Kenny over and just said to him, 'Play to your capabilities, son!' It was really funny, as it was when Reidy came on for Manchester and starting tackling anything that moved. Typically he gave the game a competitive edge. John Barnes only intended to play the first half, but he stayed on for the full 90, which was great.

My season at Oldham had ended in January and I knew because of the operation on my back that I was unlikely to be able to play at full throttle again, so it wasn't long before disillusionment started to set in. The travelling started to became more of a bind, too. At one stage in the season, I was linked with Tranmere Rovers, which would have suited me. Johnny King was the manager and I'm sure I would have enjoyed playing alongside a natural-born goalscorer like John Aldridge.

In August 1993, I asked Joe to put me on the transfer list. He had brought in Ian Olney from Aston Villa for big money the previous year and, with all due respect to him, I didn't think he was the best striker in the world. I'd also stopped enjoying my football and that wasn't like me at all. All my life I'd gleaned so much pleasure and enjoyment from playing the game that it was something of a shock to my system when I began to fall out of love with it.

I didn't think Oldham was a football club that was looking hard enough to move forward. I still had the utmost respect for Joe and he knew that I would still run through a brick wall for him, but there was an air of expectancy about the 1993–94 season. It was as though Oldham had done the hard part by surviving two seasons in the top flight but that this would be the year when they finally slipped out of it. I had trained as well as I could and I was ready for the new season, but I wasn't sure how many I had left in me.

Only a miraculous three-wins-out-of-three finish against Aston Villa, Liverpool and Southampton had saved us the previous season, but when the opening twelve games of the 1993–94 campaign yielded just one win, the writing was on the wall. We were stuffed 5–0 at Tottenham in September when poor old Paul Gerrard had a nightmare. He was struggling to get used to the new back-pass rule, which decreed the keeper could not pick up the ball when it was played back to him by one of his own teammates. Three of the Spurs goals came from sliced clearances from him after his defenders had rolled the ball back to him!

For me, a lot of the satisfaction had gone, although we did have some good times that year. We beat Chelsea at Stamford Bridge and then again at Boundary Park, for a start. It will be a long, long time before Oldham play Chelsea in a League fixture again, let alone beat them twice in the same season!

I also had a day to remember in March 1994 when we played Everton at Goodison Park. We lost 2–1 but of significance to me was that I was sent off for the one and only time in my professional career. What a place for it to happen! And it was all Ian Snodin's fault!

Richard Jobson had possession for us, but Snods challenged him. In my opinion, Snods fouled him, but David Elleray waved play on at which Everton broke clear and scored. I told Elleray that his decision was 'scandalous'. Within minutes, I won a throw-in by the corner flag after I tackled Andy Hinchcliffe and the ball came off him and went out of play, but the linesman indicated an Everton throw-in. I lost my rag completely. I called him every name I could think of and he stood there waving his flag like a demented railway guard trying to attract Elleray's attention. After a brief discussion, I was sent off. I must be the only player in history to get sent off playing for the away team yet still get a thunderous standing ovation from every single home supporter!

Far and away the best thing we achieved that season was to reach the semi-final of the FA Cup. We played Manchester United at Wembley and came within a whisker of beating them after Neil Pointon gave us the lead. I was dreaming of another, wholly unexpected, FA Cup-final appearance when Mark Hughes volleyed home a fantastic equaliser in the way that only he could do. That was also the day a Wembley official knocked on the Oldham dressing-room door ten minutes before we were due to go out onto the pitch and asked to speak to me. He said that my brother was with him, asking for his ticket. That confused me because I knew that neither of my brothers had planned to come down for the game, but I went with the official anyway. It was my mate Joe Farley! In typical fashion, he had blagged his way through security to the dressing-room area.

I had to confirm that he was my brother, then the official said, 'OK, Mr Sharp, we'll look after him for you.'

Joe gave me a big wink as he was escorted to the directors' box from where he watched the match in just about the best seat in the house.

After the disappointment of conceding a last-gasp equaliser, we were always going to struggle in the replay and United beat us easily 4–1. Once again, though, the difference in mentality between Oldham and the successful Everton teams I'd played in was brought into focus. There were too many players saying, 'Oh, well, never mind, we did well to get this far.' I hated that attitude. It was an FA Cup semi-final, for goodness sake, and some of them were highly unlikely to ever get that close to the final again. I'd sensed a bit of it during my last couple of seasons at Everton, but at least they were more likely to reach cup semi-finals than Oldham.

A couple of weeks later, we lost 3–0 at Wimbledon. I had a furious row with Willie in the dressing-room after the game. He was walking around patting players on the head and telling them that they had been unlucky, but I didn't want to hear talk like that.

'This is every fucking week we're getting this,' I raged. 'We're not unlucky, we're just not good enough, and if we play like this every week, we can be as unlucky as you want, but we'll be fucking relegated.'

Willie had a go back and we had a right ding-dong nose-to-nose argument in front of the rest of the lads. I told him that I found his training boring and that the team weren't playing well enough.

When we got on the bus Joe just said to me, 'Have you calmed down yet?'

'No, I haven't,' I replied. 'Your mate's daft, he hasn't got a clue.'

That was wrong and I regretted saying it.

On Monday morning, I went to Willie's office and apologised

to him, and to his credit he didn't hold a grudge. We were relegated on the last day of the season after failing to win any of our final eight games.

I was injured when relegation was confirmed at Norwich on the same day that Everton had to beat Wimbledon at Goodison to have a chance of survival. I knew a few people in Liverpool and I had heard a whisper that there was no way that Everton were going to lose that match. I conveyed this to Joe, but he wouldn't have it, especially when news filtered through that Wimbledon were two goals ahead.

We concentrated on our own match, but a 1–1 draw wasn't enough to save us (in the end, even a win wouldn't have kept us up). We didn't find out the full details of Everton's great escape until later. Joe just shook his head in bewilderment when he was told that Everton had fought back to gain an incredible 3–2 win.

'Sharpy, it looks as though you were right,' he said. 'Everton scored a dubious penalty, Barry Horne scored from 35 yards and then the keeper dived over one towards the end.'

I just laughed, but it wasn't long before Joe Royle was taking more than a passing interest in the fortunes of Everton Football Club.

FIFTEEN

BOUNDARY PARK HOT SEAT

Despite my back surgery, I had played in 35 of Oldham's League matches when the team suffered relegation and, against my better judgement, I declared myself ready for the following season, which would be my first outside the top division. It was a new experience for me playing at the likes of Port Vale, Southend United and Bristol City.

Usually when a team is relegated from a higher division there is always a good chance that they will get themselves right back up again at the first time of asking, but that wasn't the feeling around Boundary Park as the 1994–95 season kicked off.

We battered Charlton 5–2 on the opening day, but just look how the fortunes of the two clubs have contrasted since then. We are only going back 12 years or so, but Charlton are an established Premiership club whereas Oldham are largely forgotten as they struggle to hold their own in the lower leagues. The way the two football clubs were run is hugely significant. One club was very forward thinking and wanted to get into the top echelons of the game; the other was content to just plod along and maybe save a few quid en route.

Other teams in the division were making big signings because they knew that this new Premiership was the place to be and they were structured towards reaching it. But I didn't sense any desire at Oldham to gain promotion.

We lost at Port Vale in our second game – the day that a talented footballer called Billy Kenny made his debut. Joe had taken a chance on Billy because the boy had had real problems at Everton and he'd eventually been shown the door. He was a fabulous footballer, who had every attribute that a top-class midfielder needed. I found him to be a nice lad, too, but he lost his way, got involved in the wrong crowd and never got anywhere near to reaching his enormous potential.

In November, Everton sacked Mike Walker. Walker had taken the reins after Howard had resigned for a second time in December 1993. It was the worst-kept secret in the game that Joe was the favourite to take over. He had turned down chances to leave Oldham in the past, but, like me, Everton was his club and the opportunity to try and rebuild it was too tempting to refuse. Nobody blamed him for leaving Oldham and he went with the best wishes of everyone with any sort of connection to the club, but his departure left a vacancy that needed to be filled.

We had a game against Luton Town on the Saturday. I was injured at the time and was therefore unlikely to be playing, so the chairman, Ian Stott, called me in and asked me to take the team for the match. I agreed because management was something I had tentatively considered when my surgeon warned me that my playing career wouldn't last long past 35. I knew, however, that I couldn't approach it in the same manner as a permanent manager. I couldn't go too hard on the lads because there was every chance that the board would appoint a new man and I'd soon be back in the dressing-room as a player. All I did was pick the team, speak to the press, have a word with the lads and prepare them as best I could.

The game ended in a 0–0 draw and speculation was rife about Joe's successor. I'd enjoyed the brief experience and after the match I'd spoken at length with Ann Marie about the prospect of applying for the job. Only with her backing did I complete my curriculum vitae and hand it in to the chairman. Andy Ritchie did the same and I heard that Howard Kendall was also in the frame. I wasn't expecting to get the job, but I didn't see the harm in throwing my hat into the ring because the end of my playing days was in sight.

I had to go for an interview with the chairman and the board, and I felt it went well. They asked me whom I'd bring in to work with me because Willie had obviously gone with Joe. Without hesitation I'd told them I'd like Colin Harvey.

Not long after the interview, I was formally offered the job. I was also informed that they'd approached Colin and that he was willing to come in as my number two. It was as smooth as that, although I know that, when asked about me, Joe Royle had been very complimentary.

Being a player-manager is not the easiest job in the world, especially when you're in charge of the same bunch of players you've had as teammates. One of my first tasks was to phone Andy Ritchie. He was an Oldham legend and the fans' favourite to take over from Joe, so I knew he'd be disappointed. I said that I was sorry he hadn't got the job but that I was in charge now and I hoped there'd be no hard feelings or animosity. I assured him that he'd be in my plans and I asked him to give me 100 per cent. He wasn't happy, but he appreciated the call.

I had no problems with any of the lads. I'd spoken to them all as a group before my first training session and asked them to call me boss or gaffer instead of Graeme or Sharpy. Colin organised most of the coaching because that was his forte. We had Billy Urmson and Jim Cassell to help us out and Andy Holden was the reserve coach. I had a good backroom staff but brought in Alex Moreno as a replacement physiotherapist.

My first full game as manager of Oldham Athletic was at the Hawthorns against West Brom when we lost 3–1. Despite that, my opening record was good. We won five of our next six matches, including an excellent 4–1 drubbing of Wolves, who finished fourth in the table that season. Things were going well.

We lost a great game against Leeds United at Elland Road in the FA Cup. They were a Premiership team, but they only beat us by the odd goal in five and we gave a great account of ourselves.

Colin always urged me to keep playing, but my days on the training ground and then in the manager's office were long and it was tiring for me, so I only picked myself sporadically. I scored against Reading in the FA Cup and kept myself in the team for a match against Sunderland on Saturday, 14 January 1995. It was at Boundary Park and we drew 0–0. It was my last ever game as a professional footballer. With everything else that was going on, I had lost my appetite for the playing side.

It was clear from a long way out that we wouldn't be troubling the promotion or even the play-off positions. We were 15th when I took over and we finished 14th, so at least I'd stopped the early rot and stabilised our position, which wasn't bad for a novice manager. I'd quite enjoyed it, but it was an eye-opening experience because, as I very quickly discovered, a manager is involved in many, many aspects of running a football club. I recall being taken aback when I was first given the players' contracts to have a look over. I couldn't believe some of the money the lads were earning. They had clearly signed lucrative contracts when Oldham were in the Premiership and I knew that there would be trouble brewing because we couldn't run a First Division club paying top-flight wages.

At the end of my first season, I went to see the chairman for a review of the situation and he told me, quite bluntly, that I had to get rid of a lot of players. I questioned his decision because I wanted to try and build a team that could push for a Premiership return, but he had already prepared a list of the players that he wanted me to offload.

They were all of my best players! Paul Bernard, Richard Jobson, Rick Holden, Chris Makin, Gunne Halle and Paul Gerrard were all there.

'These are the highest earners at the club and I want them off the books,' said Stott.

It didn't matter that they were also the best players and

represented our best chance of promotion. He had formulated a cost-cutting plan and he wanted them out. Stott did all the deals with the other clubs and, quite quickly, the squad was taking on a thoroughly depleted look.

Amidst all this, I had to dispense with the services of Billy Kenny. Billy would fail to turn up for training and I could never make contact with him. Sometimes he would go missing for days on end and we wouldn't hear a word from him. After an unauthorised absence of ten days, Colin and I called him in and offered him one last chance.

'Get yourself together, do the training and you'll be in my team,' I said. And I meant it because the lad could play and Colin had a lot of time for him. He'd been terrific at Everton when he first broke into the team, but I felt that unwelcome distractions in his private life had ruined him. He squandered that last chance and, in my heart of hearts, I always knew he would. I had to sack him. He was a dreadful example to the young players and I couldn't have one rule for him and one for everyone else. He'd moved into a house in Oldham, which I thought was a good thing, but he was hardly ever in it. He spent most of his spare time in Liverpool.

It was a great shame, but he was too far down the wrong road for us to be able to help him out. I just never knew what he was up to.

I knew that my own first full season as manager was going to be hard, but I accepted the situation. I urged Stott to be honest with the punters and explain that because of the financial situation we were going to have to sell our best assets and we were unlikely to get back to the glory days we'd enjoyed under Joe Royle. I told him the supporters wouldn't be happy, but I was sure they would acknowledge and appreciate our honesty. Stott was horrified at the mere suggestion.

'No, no, no, we can't possibly do that,' he said. 'That will dampen their enthusiasm. We need to tell them that promotion is our priority.'

'Promotion?' I said. 'You're selling all the best players, so how the hell do you expect to win promotion?'

'We need to keep everyone positive,' he said.

I couldn't believe my ears because there was only one person who was going to get the blame for any substandard performances and that was me. I should have known then that things weren't going to work out, but I was inexperienced and surmised that it was just part and parcel of being with a smaller club.

Stott had organised a 'Fans Forum' before the start of the season and once again I suggested that honesty was the best policy. He still wouldn't have it and in front of more than 100 supporters at Boundary Park I was hung out to dry. Not unnaturally the fans were concerned that their football club, with the supposed ambition of hauling itself back amongst the elite, was selling too many good players. I couldn't answer them.

Stott could, though, and gave them a load of blether that I could scarcely comprehend. I honestly felt that he was misleading the supporters. I should have got up, spoken my mind and walked out of the door there and then.

He had let me down in public, but I vowed to carry on with Colin and work to the best of our abilities with the lads we had left. Stott encouraged me to bring in free transfer players. Joe had done it and had done it well, but times had changed since his day. I don't think the chairman could see that.

An agent telephoned me one day about a full-back called Simon Morgan who had been playing for Blackpool. He was a decent player and we talked figures. The lad was only on £750 a week at Blackpool and he wanted a £20,000 signing-on payment because he was available on a free transfer. That sounded like good business and I approached Stott. He liked the idea of paying someone £750 a week, but he baulked at the prospect of the twenty-grand signing-on fee.

'We're not doing signing-on fees any more,' he said.

'Not doing signing-on fees?' I answered. 'Then how are we going to bring anyone in? Do you actually know how free transfers work?'

That was when I realised that I had no chance of attracting any players to Oldham. If we couldn't fork out £20,000 to get a decent player, then what hope was there?

Stott kept telling me to blood the youngsters at the club. He reasoned that the public would like to see youth given an opportunity. That's perfectly true of any club, but the reality was that the kids at Oldham just weren't good enough. Again, he wouldn't hear of it. He wanted the kids in the team. Eventually, because we didn't have anybody else, I was forced to put some of the young players into the first team, but I was right: they were nowhere near good enough for the First Division.

I was always fighting an uphill battle. Every single board meeting had one main topic: finance. There was no ambition at the club other than to cut corners and reduce the debt. The board stopped the team travelling to away games the day before and staying in hotels unless the journey was more than four hours away. They would even go through the bookings that the lads had picked up to see if they had a legitimate reason to fine them. A club official once questioned me about a booking that he claimed one of the players had received at Swindon Town.

'He didn't get booked,' I pointed out.

'Yes, he did, I recall it,' was his reply.

I thought about it and I was sure that the player concerned had not been booked in the match. In fact, I was certain. 'If you think he was booked, can you describe the incident?' I challenged him.

'Well, no, because I was only listening on the radio,' he said.

That's what I was up against. To a certain extent, I could understand the need for the club to cut its cloth accordingly, but it was the lack of honesty with the supporters that I found increasingly difficult to handle.

I brought across a centre-half from Finland who I'd heard good reports about and I offered him a trial. His name was Sami Hyypiä and he did very, very well. He played in a specially organised 'behind closed doors' friendly at Boundary Park and had a great game. Colin agreed with me that he was better than anyone we had and I asked the chairman to follow up the interest and bring in the player.

Ten days or so passed with no word from the chairman, then he informed me that Sami had joined the Dutch team Willem II. That was a blow because the lad had sounded keen to come to Oldham and experience English football, but Stott told me that because his close friend had signed for Willem II then he did, too.

It wasn't until many years later that I met Sami at Anfield. He remembered me and laughed that I'd missed out on him. 'You didn't want to take a chance on me,' he said.

I assured him that I had wanted very much to bring him over but that my chairman had told me about the Willem II situation. I was left with the impression that Stott just hadn't been prepared to pay Sami the money he wanted – which wasn't a great amount, by the way – and Oldham lost out on a defender they could have sold on for a massive profit.

Just about the last player who cost a decent fee was Stuart Barlow from Everton. We paid £350,000 for his services, rising to £450,000 once he had completed 50 League appearances. But Barlow was a disappointment to me.

Colin had been convinced that he was going to be a good acquisition because he had plenty of pace. We thought that would be a big attribute at First Division level, but he didn't meet our expectations as often as we needed him to. When he was on top of his game, he was a threat, and I remember him scoring a hat-trick at Bradford. I felt his attitude wasn't spot-on, either: defeat didn't seem to hurt him enough and I don't think he had the drive or determination we needed.

One of the best bits of business I ever did was signing

Snods from Everton. I'd kept in touch with him after I'd joined Oldham. I knew that he'd had a falling out at Everton and that he wasn't getting a game, so I met him in Southport one night and sold Oldham to him. He was fantastic for me. He'd had his fair share of injuries and he wasn't a regular trainer, but you could guarantee that once you got him onto the pitch on a Saturday he would give you everything he had for 90 minutes. He was a great example to the younger players around him and I know he went through the pain barrier by playing when he really shouldn't have done. Whenever we lost games, I could legitimately point the finger at several players in the team but never at Snods. He would never let me down, so I made him my captain.

I wish I could have said the same about Darren Beckford. He was a good player and he had everything you wanted in a top-class centre-forward, but I thought he was lazy. I always felt that he didn't actually like playing football. He loved the lifestyle, but he was always injured. I needed him because we were really struggling, but he didn't seem to want to go the extra mile for the team.

I eventually confronted him about it. 'I don't know when you're fit and when you're not,' I said. 'I never know exactly what your injury is. I think you've got it within you to be a great player, but you don't want it enough. You want to live a footballer's life without putting the hours in. Well, that's not happening any more. Not here. You either liven up or you'll be on your way.'

He thought I had been a bit harsh and accused me of not fancying him as a player. I told him that I rated him highly, but the way he was behaving was wasting both his time and mine. I was under pressure to get results and I needed everyone pulling together. 'Get yourself fit, sort the attitude out and you'll always be in my team,' I said. I was honest and upfront with him, but he didn't take it on board and he didn't change his ways. He should have had a much better career than he did because he was a player, no doubt about that. It was a pity because he's a nice lad. I still see him from time to time.

I had to release Andy Ritchie at the beginning of August 1995, which went down like a lead balloon. I always felt that he had too much to say in the dressing-room and around the town. He lived in Oldham and he was a hero to the punters, so I could have done with him firmly on my side, but word reached me that it was the complete opposite and when his contract was up for renewal, I decided to let him go. That was a shock to a lot of people and the fans went mad, but I had to do things my own way and make decisions that I knew weren't going to be popular. Andy was also one of the highest earners, so it made financial sense to allow him to move on, but, of course, the chairman would never come out and say as much.

We finished a thoroughly miserable season in 18th position and, given the circumstances under which we were operating, I think Colin and I did well to stave off another relegation.

We had some decent results along the way, especially at home. We beat Crystal Palace 3–1, Leicester City 3–1, and Stoke City 2–0 at Boundary Park and each of those teams made it to the Premiership play-offs at the end of the season. In fact, it was Leicester who got promoted and our home record was actually better than theirs in that 1995–96 campaign.

Before the start of my final season in charge, I took the team to play a few games in Scotland. We stayed in a hotel in Stepps close to where I lived as a boy. We played Airdrie and Clyde and, while we were there, I took the opportunity to show Snods a few of my old haunts.

We got off to the worst possible start in 1996–97; in fact, it was the worst in the club's history, with us failing to win any of our opening ten League games. My frustration boiled over when we played Manchester City at Boundary Park in January in a match that, ironically, we won 2–1. The referee had had a poor game and at one point he wouldn't let our physio on to treat a stricken player. I went in to see him in his dressing-room after the match – I had already been in trouble with the FA for my condemnation of match officials, so I was determined to be on my best behaviour when I went to have a word with him. For safety reasons, there was always a policeman on the door of the ref's room and I politely knocked before asking for a few minutes of the official's time.

I queried some of his decisions but not once did I raise my voice or use foul or abusive language. We had a fairly convivial conversation in front of the policeman and I returned to the home dressing-room. I thought nothing of it until I got a letter from the FA charging me with misconduct. I couldn't believe it.

I showed the letter to Stott, who was on an FA committee, and told him I wanted a personal appearance at Lancaster Gate and that I wanted the policeman with me because he saw the entire incident. Stott didn't like it, but down to London I went with the policeman, who had very kindly agreed to give evidence, and a solicitor provided by the League Managers Association.

It was a kangaroo court. It was a total disgrace and, although we gave our evidence clearly and concisely, my appeal against the charge was thrown out. I was found guilty and ordered not only to pay the original fine but also the costs of the appeal. The sergeant was every bit as annoyed as me. He'd appeared in full uniform and answered questions under oath but had been virtually branded a liar.

I was furious and wanted to take the matter further with another appeal, but it was pointed out to me that if the subsequent appeal failed, and there was every likelihood that it would, then I would be hit with further costs. With a great deal of reluctance, I let the matter drop. The system had let us down, and by all accounts things haven't changed. The FA is still the prosecutor, judge and jury, so what chance do the clubs, managers and players have?

This unhappy episode further soured my mood. We had spent the entire season languishing in the relegation zone and there was little chance of us escaping it and I was becoming difficult to live with at home. We had a beautiful new home, but I wasn't happy with life because there seemed to be so many obstacles in my way. I was under pressure and I wasn't seeing as much of Ann Marie and the children as I would have liked. The support of my family was, as ever, completely unswerving, but Ann Marie could see that it was all getting to me and that I wasn't the same person.

Oldham lost 3–0 at home to Grimsby Town on 8 February 1997 and afterwards I told Colin that I'd had enough. 'I don't need this any more,' I said. 'I'm handing my notice in on Monday.'

He advised me not to be hasty, but, after speaking to Ann Marie about it, my mind was made up. I knocked on the chairman's door first thing on the Monday morning and informed him of my decision. I cited a lack of backing from him and a total absence of honesty with the supporters. And that was it. I just cleared my office and drove away, never to return.

Snods rang me that night and told me that the lads were gutted about it. He said they wanted to say goodbye properly and that they were all willing to come over to Liverpool for a night out. I appreciated that and we did have a good time when we arranged it. The players knew what I was up against because I had always kept them informed of what was going on.

Neil Warnock came in to replace me with 17 games to go, but he couldn't turn it around and the team was relegated again.

I had been in charge from November 1994 to February 1997 and in that time I had released and sold no fewer than 22 players. A debt of £1.5 million had been turned into a profit of £307,012, but the heart and soul of the place had been ripped out in the process.

Looking back on it, I think I made the wrong move in joining Oldham Athletic in the first place. I loved working with Joe Royle, I made a lot of good friends at the club and I enjoyed proving that I could still score goals in the Premiership, but if I had my time all over again I would not have left Everton for Oldham. Joe was a very persuasive man, but maybe I should have waited a bit longer and a different, more beneficial move may have materialised. It might not have done, and I know that, but I still regard signing for Oldham as a big mistake on my part. The travelling, the injuries I suffered whilst I was there and the troubles I had as manager have doubtless clouded my memories of the place, but I just didn't enjoy the latter stages of my playing career and I certainly didn't enjoy being in charge in the most trying of circumstances.

It's safe to say that I felt a massive relief when the time came for me to walk away. The night I resigned, I slept soundly in my bed for the first time in months.

SIXTEEN
THE DAY WE WENT TO BANGOR . . .

After my Oldham experience, I was a bit disillusioned with football and I decided to take some time out and get my golf handicap down a bit. One of my playing partners was a local councillor called Tony Sharps and we were in the golf club bar one evening when he introduced me to a car dealer friend of his called Ken Jones. Ken had just bought a house in the area and he was a director at Bangor City. He asked me if I wanted to come down and get involved at his football club, but I was reluctant to do so.

The manager at the time was Kevin Langley, who had been a teammate of mine at Everton when we won the Championship in 1987. I genuinely wasn't interested in getting involved and I had no intention of showing my face around the club because it would have put Kevin under a bit of pressure. I did say to Ken that if Kevin wanted me to help out in any way, then I would be more than happy to do so, but the call had to come from the manager. I wasn't going to turn up on a Saturday or at a training session on the invite of one of the directors. Ken kept on at me, so one night I went with him to Farrar Road to watch a game. It was basically just to see a bit of football and keep Ken off my back. I can't even remember who Bangor played or what the score was. I thought that would be it, but at the end of the 1996–97 season Bangor dispensed with Kevin's services and Ken asked for my advice when they started to look for a replacement. I knew what was coming next and, sure enough, he asked me if I fancied it. Again, I declined, but Ken is nothing if not persistent and he badgered me into getting involved. It didn't seem to matter to him how many times his invitation was politely refused, he kept coming back for more – so I told him that he couldn't afford me!

'How much? How much?' he kept asking, so I plucked a figure out of the air, thinking that it would finally put the issue to bed.

'£25,000 a year,' I said.

He considered it for a moment and said, 'Yes, that's no problem. I think we can do that.'

I was quite surprised, but we had further discussions and I eventually agreed to give it a go. Our relationship was solid enough, but I knew that I was very much entering into the unknown. I didn't know the first thing about the League of Wales – I didn't know the teams, I didn't know the players – and I knew that I'd need some local knowledge alongside me. You often find at non-League level that when a manager moves on, it's not uncommon for a large section of the squad to move on with him, so I was fully aware that I would probably have something of a rebuilding job to do as soon as I took over.

Ken was one step ahead of me and said that they'd already had similar thoughts and that they'd approached a man called John Hulse to come in and work with me. John was at Conway and he'd done a good job, so Ken arranged for the two of us to get together and have a chat. I didn't know John, but we had a good meeting, made easier by the fact that he's an Evertonian, and he agreed to come along. He knew the League of Wales inside out and had all the contacts we needed to bring in players.

He did most of the recruitment and we started planning for the 1997–98 season. We only trained twice a week and because the majority of the squad were based in Merseyside we used a high school in Ellesmere Port for our training sessions on a Monday and a Thursday night.

We assembled a very good squad of players. Our key signing was Kenny McKenna, my old adversary from Telford United. He had Football League experience and was the highest-paid player on Bangor's books while we were there, but he was like a breath of fresh air around the place. He had a fantastic attitude and kept himself unbelievably fit. His career was winding down, but he was still very professional in the way he approached training and playing and his attitude rubbed off on some of the other lads.

I also brought a player called Neil Sang to the club. Sangy had been a young reserve during my latter years at Everton, but he hadn't managed to break through into the first team, which was a bit of a surprise because he had all the attributes to be a class footballer. He'd been doing the rounds at the lower levels and he came in and did a very good job for us. He's still in the game now, working as an agent to a number of young players.

John and I had our own ideas and we enjoyed implementing them. On my first night in charge, I spoke to all the players, even though I didn't know many of them, and assured them that everyone was starting with a clean slate. They were a smashing set of lads and, as many of them were Scousers, there was always plenty of Everton and Liverpool banter. It was an eye-opener becoming involved in a non-League outfit. I was determined to be as professional as I possibly could, but all the time I was mindful that some of the lads had done a full day's work before they arrived for training. Especially where discipline was concerned, it was essential to bear in mind they were working men, so, for instance, we wouldn't hit them too hard in the pocket for any transgressions.

My first competitive match in charge was away to Welshpool. We met the team bus in Chester at the Post House Hotel. It was a beautiful day there, a typical August afternoon, but as we journeyed deeper and deeper into Wales, the fog began to descend. It got worse and worse by the minute and when we arrived at the ground it was really thick. I didn't think there was any way the game could be played, but we got off the bus and headed for the dressing-room. Then, out of the mist, a young couple approached me pushing a pram. The guy was very excited to see me and explained that he'd been waiting for a long time for our bus to arrive because he was a mad Evertonian.

He called his wife across to meet me and he revealed that his baby was 'a bit different'. I wondered what on earth was coming next and to my utter disbelief he peeled back the blanket in the pram, took the baby's little socks off and said, 'Look – he's got six toes!'

So I am standing in the middle of Welshpool in thick, thick fog, peering into a pram to look at a six-toed infant! 'What on earth have I let myself in for with all this,' I thought to myself as I signed a few autographs for them. I tried to catch Ken Jones's eye, but he wouldn't look at me.

The day actually got better and I was pleased to start my Bangor City reign with a comfortable 5–1 win. I knew we had some very good players and I knew we'd get plenty more good results than bad ones, but I didn't expect us to win the title because the best team in the League of Wales at the time was Barry Town. They had the most money by far and could pay good wages for the top players.

In the event, they strolled to the title, remaining unbeaten throughout their 38-match League campaign, with a goal difference of +103. They finished 26 points clear of second-placed Newtown.

Another time we were travelling away I noticed that some of the players weren't treating the football as professionally as they should have been. We were playing down in South Wales and when we stopped at the service station, some of the lads spent a fortune on sweets, crisps, chocolate and lemonade. I couldn't believe it. After the game, I told them that I didn't expect that sort of behaviour before we played.

Lee Noble was one of the worst culprits and when I confronted him about his eating habits, I expected him to be a bit sheepish, but he popped a wine gum into his mouth and said, 'I've always done it!'

He was a good player and agreed to try to cut down on future trips – he'd buy a normal bag of Maltesers rather than a family-sized bag.

I tried to alter a few little things, but I knew that I couldn't march in there and start shouting the odds, changing everything that I didn't agree with, and to be fair they were a really good set of lads.

I had a good centre-forward called Marc Lloyd-Williams, a local boy who was at the club when I arrived. He was capable of scoring spectacular goals and, although he could find the net for fun, he could also be sloppy and lazy in his play. I used to take him to one side and work on those negative aspects of his game. To be fair to the lad, he listened, learned and became a better footballer.

I always stressed to all the players that it was never too late to be spotted by a bigger club and it happened in Marc's case. I'd left Bangor when he rang me to say that Stockport County had made him an offer and he wanted my advice. I told him to accept the challenge, which he did, and he went on to play for Halifax Town and York City as well – both League clubs at the time. I was pleased for him because he'd taken on board what I'd told him and I was delighted that he respected me sufficiently to seek my advice.

We got through to the League Cup final and played Barry Town. We were underdogs because they had already beaten us twice in the League – 4–1 at our place and 5–0 at Barry. The final was played at Farrar Road and we gave them a really good contest. Lloyd-Williams scored for us in a 1–1 draw, but Barry beat us on penalties. We were by far the better side on the night and after the game their manager agreed that the best team lost.

There was no time to brood over that defeat because six days later we had the Welsh Cup final. It goes without saying that the Welsh Cup is the biggest competition as far as the clubs are concerned and there had been great excitement in Bangor as we progressed through the rounds. We had beaten Welshpool, Flint Town United, Aberystwyth Town and Caernarfon Town before meeting Newtown in the semi-final. They took us all the way through to extra-time, but we managed to score to beat them 2–1. Lloyd-Williams got both our goals.

The final against Connah's Quay Nomads was played at the Wrexham Racecourse ground. It was screened live on television and it was a great day, although we got off to the worst possible start when we had Johnny Whelan sent off in the very first minute for a bad tackle. Johnny is married to one of Colin Harvey's daughters. He left us down to ten men for virtually the whole game that day and I wasn't best pleased with him. If Connah's Quay had changed their system to take advantage of the extra man, I'm convinced they would have beaten us, but as it was we trailed by one goal until the last minute when Kenny McKenna scored an equaliser. Both teams had chances to win the game in extra-time, but it went to penalties and a lad called Nick Brookman slotted in the winning kick for us. I was delighted for everyone connected with the club and especially for the supporters because we had taken a great following to Wrexham that day.

As it happened, that was the last ever match of my football career and so it was good to go out on a high with a trophy and get the team into Europe. Strangely enough, after spending my career enjoying famous nights of celebration, this one was comparatively low-key. I had a couple of drinks with everyone in one of the lounges at the racecourse, then went home to let the lads get on with it. Perhaps I had a premonition of what was to follow.

Managing Bangor was tough going at times and I had to put up with a lot of petty jealousy from certain members of the board. They wanted me to bring in more local players and not have so many Scousers in my teams. I could understand their grievance to a certain extent, but, as far as I was concerned, they were paying me decent money to win football matches and I could only do that by selecting my strongest possible team week in, week out. I used to tell the board that if they got me some local players who were better than the lads I already had, then they would play, simple as that. I wasn't going to put anyone in the side just because they were local.

One of the directors kept going on about these two Bangor lads who were playing in the reserves. I did have a look at them, but, with all due respect, they were nowhere near good enough. They lacked the mental toughness of the Scousers and I just couldn't play them. Certain club officials, naturally, didn't agree with me and although they never said anything to my face, I knew they were being quite vocal about me behind the scenes. I was aware they were voicing strong opinions about who they thought should be in and out of the team, but there was no way John and I would tolerate any interference from people who just didn't know the game. When I was present during such conversations, I could only understand two words – 'Graeme' and 'Sharp' – because they normally took place in Welsh.

If I needed anything or I wanted something doing, I would speak to Ken Jones or the president, Gwynne Pearce-Owen, a nice man who I thought looked like Harry Secombe. Ken and I would speak regularly – he only lived down the road from me, and he and I got on fine and, I'm happy to say, we still do now. In fact it's come around full circle because during the 2005–06 season when my son, Chris, was playing for Rhyl in the League of Wales, Ken was badgering me again to get him to sign for Bangor City.

After the 1998 Welsh Cup final, John and I were summoned to Ken's car showroom in Anglesey in North Wales for a review of the season with the board. We'd won the Welsh Cup and I was fairly happy with our League form. They wanted to see John and me separately and I was in first.

They told me that they felt we could have pushed Barry

Town a bit more. I gave them my reasons why we didn't: we just couldn't compete with them financially. That led them nicely to their next point. I was informed that they had been assessing the financial side of the football club and they told me that I had to get rid of John Hulse. John and I had worked very well together, the team enjoyed playing for us and I told the board in no uncertain terms that John would be going nowhere. They were adamant and insisted John would have to go. It wasn't even up for discussion. I was livid.

'If that's the way it's going to be, then I don't want to stay myself either,' I said. 'I don't want the job. If that's your final word on the subject, then you need to get yourself a new manager because I'm not having that.'

I looked straight at the two directors with whom I had never seen eye to eye and suggested that they might like to do the job themselves, as they clearly thought they knew better than me how to run the football team. And, I added, their appointment would keep the costs down.

They didn't say a word.

I stormed out of the room and John walked straight in, though I had to sit and wait because we'd travelled in the same car. Not five minutes had passed before John walked out of the door.

'You won't believe this, Graeme,' he said. 'They've just offered me the manager's job.'

I shook my head and smiled at him. They'd only just been trying to sack the man and now they were offering him my job. Needless to say, John was disgusted and insulted at the offer and he told them as much. He more or less said the same things that I had, but his choice of words was a touch less diplomatic!

It was an uncomfortable situation for Ken and he was upset enough to resign from the board. He's back there now because he loves the club and couldn't stay away, but I know it left a sour taste in his mouth for a while.

I knew enough about the non-League game to understand that clubs need to cut their cloth accordingly but to even suggest that I get rid of John showed that they certainly didn't know me very well. John had brought in some excellent players for Bangor City and together we had delivered the Welsh Cup to the club, which got them into Europe, don't forget. The way they treated us at that meeting was scandalous and I had no intention of hanging around after that.

In all honesty, I had enjoyed managing Bangor, but I was fortunate that I could just walk away when the internal politics got too much. Unlike my stint at Oldham, I wasn't losing any sleep after Bangor matches, although to be fair we won more than we lost. Don't get me wrong, I was still as professionally competitive and still wanted to win, but I had only taken the job as a favour to a friend and so my head was held high and my conscience was crystal clear when it all came to an end. Incidentally we finished sixth in the table that year. In the following three seasons after John and I left, Bangor finished 11th, 9th and 14th.

The 1997–98 season was also the one in which Everton came so close to relegation from the Premiership under Howard Kendall. I may have been managing Bangor City, but I was obviously well aware that things weren't going well for my old team. It may sound as if I am being wise after the event, but I looked at some of the players that Howard brought in to play for the club that season and I thought they should have been nowhere near the place. They should not have been playing for the club, simple as that. That's possibly something that all ex-players think about teams that follow their own era – I'm sure that some of the lads from the 1970 Championship team would look at our title crop of '85 and think not many of us would have made their team; even so, I could see that Everton were really up against it in 1998 and I just didn't think that Howard had players who were good enough to prevent the team from slipping out of the Premiership. I managed to get to some of the matches and they were poor. I didn't speak to Howard at all that season because I figured he didn't need any former players telling him how to do his job, but

I was very relieved when they drew 1–1 with Coventry City on the last day to preserve their status.

My departure from Bangor left me with more time on my hands and I was able to pick up work in the media again. When I left Oldham, I had received a call from Radio City, asking me to cover the odd game for them and I was pleased to do so because it had kept me involved and given me the chance to meet up with a few old faces around the grounds. Of course, I had to stop when I went to Bangor, but when that finished, Radio City were straight back in touch, asking me to be the Everton match summariser. It was very enjoyable and, again, it allowed me to watch Everton home and away. I would sit in the press box alongside the match commentator and offer my views during the game before hosting a phone-in chat show along with Ian St John afterwards. Wherever Everton and Liverpool were in the country, the studio back on Merseyside would link up with Saint and me and we had a great show. Saint's a smashing fellow. We get on very well and the banter between us and the punters was wonderful. It made for a very popular radio programme.

Things were going very well until one day I received a call from Dominic Johnson, who was then the head of sport for Century FM in Manchester. They wanted me to do five days a week as well as the usual football stuff on a Saturday afternoon. There was the prospect of my own show and the money, I have to say, was very good, so I was tempted. I met with Dominic, liked what he had to say and agreed to join them. It was a shame to leave City because I had really enjoyed my time there, but this was an opening that was simply too good for me to turn down.

As well as me, Dominic recruited Mickey Thomas, Gary Owen and Alan Kennedy to host a daily phone-in. At the time, the station covered every team in the North-west and they invested heavily in football, which made it an exciting time to jump aboard. I did Everton most weeks, but if they didn't have a game, I would be sent to Blackburn Rovers or Bolton Wanderers.

My own proposed show only lasted a week because they had overstepped the 'chat threshold' and so needed more music, but losing that slot wasn't a problem for me because we were doing the phone-in every night anyway.

Gary, Mickey, Alan and I all get on together and the atmosphere on the show is terrific. We don't always agree with each other and some of the debates can get a bit heated, but that's what makes it work. We all stick up for our own respective clubs but there are no grudges held and we don't fall out.

Gary, who everyone remembers from his days with Manchester City and West Bromwich Albion, is a great lad and we hit it off immediately. I admit I didn't know too much about him and I certainly didn't know that he'd played for Sheffield Wednesday against Everton during the run of FA Cup ties that took four games to settle in 1988. He told me that he didn't play in the last game, which we won 5–0, and he reckons that his absence was the difference after three drawn matches! He had actually nearly become a teammate of mine back in 1983 when Howard Kendall made enquiries about bringing him to Goodison from West Brom.

Mickey T is a one-off! I knew him from his brief spell at Everton when Howard first joined the club and he's a real character. We do very well to get Mickey to sit in his seat in the studio for two hours because he is the biggest fidget I have ever met in my life, but he's a bundle of fun. He has a wealth of stories from the time when he went off the rails a bit.

Then there's Alan Kennedy, who has won everything there is to win in the game and the mix between us is ideal.

The listening figures are very good and if ever the programme is going a bit slowly, one of us will throw in a really controversial opinion and the calls will come flooding in – which is usually a good thing, but it wasn't midway through last season when the four of us were in the studio in Manchester trying desperately to operate a new system. It was like Fred Karno's Circus! We had been given no training and were putting the wrong callers through, getting all the names wrong and pressing buttons that played jingles halfway through a call. We also kept microphones open during commercial breaks so callers could hear everything! We got used to it, but it was an inauspicious start for the new equipment.

The show is good fun but it is a really big commitment for the four of us. It's two hours a night every weekday and makes for a very long day when I'm leaving the house at half-eight in the morning to get to Goodison.

People have been kind enough to say that I sound very good on radio and I just think it's something that you pick up with experience. Even as a player, I was very comfortable dealing with all arms of the media. I think the fact that my dad had always worked in newspapers gave me a certain empathy with reporters. I knew the effort they had to put in to get their stories and I was always willing to help them . . . the ones I trusted anyway!

I didn't particularly enjoy that side of the profession when I was a young player, but then I don't think many do. There was no media training for us: we just had to get on with it and learn as quickly as we could. These days you can see the difference that some media coaching can make when you look at how comfortable someone like Wayne Rooney is when he faces the press. He was a normal tongue-tied kid when he signed his first big contract with Everton and he looked terrified in front of the cameras, but he looks far more relaxed when you see him now. It takes time to build up your communication skills. You can't just walk out of school, make a name for yourself as a footballer and expect to be a fluent speaker in front of a microphone.

We didn't have press officers at the club when I played. Most of the journalists had your home number and would ring you if they wanted to check something or if they wanted to conduct an interview. I had reporters I liked and to whom I was perfectly happy to give my phone number. We had the 'Mersey Mafia' in my day – a group of local journalists who always got together at press conferences and matches and who could be very influential within the game. I always had a lot of time for John Keith, Colin Wood, Matt Darcy, Mike Ellis and Chris James. I got on well with these lads and they were always good to me; I can't recall ever having any problems with them.

I couldn't say the same about Ian Hargraves, of course, who seemed to have it in for me. Every footballer knows when he's had a bad game and he fully expects to get a less than complimentary write-up in the newspapers, but Hargraves would hammer me even when I didn't think I'd done too badly. He really went for me for a while. I never gave him the time I'd put aside for the other lads I've mentioned.

It's something I try to remember now when I'm analysing matches for the radio. Yes, I have to make honest assessments and I have to call things how I see them, but I'd like to think I'm never less than 100 per cent respectful to professional players.

SEVENTEEN

EVERTON AGAIN!

Winning the Welsh Cup with Bangor City was an appropriate way for me to finish my football career. I'd always prided myself on being a winner and to bow out with a trophy was nice. I had my radio and other media work, but for the first time in just on 19 years I didn't have any football club commitments to consider when planning my life. It was a strange feeling because although football had been my life, I really didn't miss it too much and I enjoyed having time on my hands.

A few people were advising me to update my CV and circulate it, but I never fancied doing that. I had the opportunity to spend a bit more time at home with Ann Marie and the children, and getting back into football wasn't a necessity for me. I know some people who post off their application to every job that crops up and fair play to them, if that's what they want to do. But that wasn't me. I've always been laid-back and my philosophy at that time was that if something came up, then so be it – but I had absolutely no intention of chasing anything.

I was advised to take my coaching badges, but, again, the enthusiasm wasn't there. I don't necessarily agree with the concept of coaching certificates because I consider a vast part of management to be the ability to deal with players: basically to be a good man-manager. I've seen too many men armed with certificates and diplomas who haven't got the first clue how to work with the players.

I took my preliminary badge when I was at Oldham after

Ian Stott told me that the Football Association were going to introduce a rule that decreed every manager needed the right qualifications. Ironically the course I attended was held at Everton and Paul Power was one of the regional coaches, but I didn't enjoy it.

So I carried on playing lots of golf during the day and I had my radio work at weekends, but, other than that, I was taking a complete break. Eventually, and probably predictably, Ann Marie got fed up with me being around the house all the time and I was contemplating my next move, when, out of the blue, Everton contacted me.

They had become one of the first clubs, if not *the* first, to appoint a former player as an official fans liaison officer. Joe Parkinson, who had retired early through injury, had been the first man in the job but when he decided to pack it in, the club contacted me to see if I knew anyone who may fancy the role. My first reaction was that I wouldn't mind having a go myself because I was getting a bit bored being at home all the time. Bill Kenwright, the Everton chairman, rang me and confessed that he hadn't considered me for the position because he didn't think it would appeal to me.

We had a couple of further discussions at Goodison when I pointed out that I wasn't going to give up my media work, but Bill was fine with that. In fact he was great about everything. He stressed that the position was mine to shape and make my own. Every day was bound to throw up different issues and it was never going to be a run-of-the-mill Monday-to-Friday nine-to-five job.

We fine-tuned a role for me and on my 40th birthday, 16 October 2000, I returned to Everton Football Club. It was great to be back. Even when I left the club to sign for Oldham Athletic, my heart remained at Goodison and I loved watching the team home and away as a radio analyser.

Joe had done a great job, but the concept of a fans liaison officer was still in its infancy. Bill saw it as a crucial link between the football club and the supporters. I think it's a very good idea because the fans can all identify with a former player – particularly one like me or Joe, who both had a good relationship with them when we played. I've developed the position to encompass the hundreds of charity requests we receive every week. As you would expect, we can't possibly send out signed merchandise in response to every letter we receive from charitable organisations, but we read them all and then make a decision. And what I can state with all certainty is that every letter, phone call or email gets answered either by me or my assistant, Val.

We often get items sent to us to be autographed by the players, but the most bizarre request came from a group of nurses who were organising a charity night. They sent us a large pair of knickers for the players to sign! Val took them to Bellefield and, despite some funny looks from the lads, she came back with a fully autographed pair of knickers. I have to say that the Everton lads are fantastic when it comes to charity requests. I can't speak highly enough of them.

Towards the end of the 2005–06 season, the club introduced a new initiative that we called 'Sharpy's Surgery', which gives the fans the opportunity to book an appointment with me and come to Goodison to air a grievance or make a point about a club issue. Obviously I am in no position to actually provide an immediate answer to every query, but I can pass the comments or complaint on to the relevant department and the supporters are gratified that they have been given the opportunity to express themselves. I like meeting the fans and, judging by the feedback we get, they enjoy it too. I've always been comfortable talking to people and some of the chats I have at the Surgery meetings can overrun.

One aspect of the job that I've never got used to, and probably never will, is the requests to attend funerals. Again, I couldn't possibly attend every funeral to which I am invited. It wouldn't be possible in terms of both time and emotions. I am aware that my presence can be a source of comfort for the bereaved families and I am glad to be able to make that small, if brief, difference, but it can be hard. It is at these times that I realise just how much the football club means to people.

Stan Tyrell, who passed away in 2005, had been voted the Everton Fan of the Year after battling with cancer whilst still attending games and organising trips for his fellow Blues. Stan's funeral was an incredible spectacle. I attended and so did Duncan Ferguson and David Moyes, along with several members of Everton staff. The streets around the church were lined with hundreds of Evertonians. Stan was buried in a royal-blue coffin and his pall-bearers wore the club's home shirts. It was an Everton-themed funeral, and it was a very emotional occasion for his wife and young family.

It is impossible not be affected by such events, even when they are in memory of someone you never knew, which is often the case. Some of the charitable requests can be touching, too, but generally my job is an enjoyable one.

When I first returned to the club, I was invited to Bellefield by the then Everton manager Walter Smith. Walter and I go back a long way and it was nice to see him and catch up. He was terrific and was very supportive of anything that we needed him to do. I also met up again with Richard Gough, a former Scottish international teammate of mine, who was enjoying a tremendous last chapter of an excellent playing career. But – and this may surprise some people – my visits to Bellefield have been few and far between.

I was never one for going back to the training ground after I'd left the club as a player in 1991. I am a great believer that once you've had your time, you shouldn't go back. The training ground is very much the current players' territory and the last thing they want is ex-players hanging around the place. Not every former player shares that point of view, but if I'm not specifically invited or I haven't got a special reason for being at Bellefield, then I never go.

SHARPY

When David Moyes first became manager in 2002, he also asked me to pop down for a chat. He knew that I'd watched a lot of Everton matches and that I knew the club better than he did. He just wanted to pick my brain about a few things over a cup of tea and a bit of lunch. David had joined the club from Preston and was interested in the opinions of a few people connected with Everton, which I thought was wise of him. Whether he took things on board or not, I don't know, but he respected my opinion enough to ask me in the first place.

Even before I'd returned to Everton, I had been involved with the former players' foundation. The EFPF is a terrific initiative that raises money for the sole purpose of aiding those ex-Everton players who need assistance. They contacted me to put my name to the list of patrons when the idea was first formulated and I help them out with functions and golf days whenever I can. The foundation has grown unbelievably over the years and it does some fantastic work to help the former heroes of the club.

Evertonians love to support any of the former players' functions and our teams from 1984 to 1987 are still held in very high esteem. I am often asked to coordinate reunion events involving my own former teammates because I've got most of the lads' telephone numbers.

We still have a fabulous time whenever we get together. People are surprised at the strength of the camaraderie between us, but we were just a group of ordinary lads who formed a great team together and had a great time doing it: nobody was ever allowed to get above his station. The banter can be as ruthless now as it was all those years ago.

We had a really big reunion dinner for the team of '85 in Liverpool a couple of years ago and it was a truly wonderful affair. We all met up in the afternoon and had a few drinks together before getting ready for the evening. It was a black-tie event and we even had the team bus collect us from our hotel and take us to the venue. It was just like old times. The team spirit we had will never diminish and I'm fairly confident that the atmosphere between any current players from any current club will not be as good in 20 years as ours is today, though friendships between all ex-footballers, not just Everton colleagues, are something special.

Howard Kendall was in great form and he stood at the front of the bus and asked for some quiet while he named the team. He deliberately left out Bails and Inchy! We had the European Cup-Winners' Cup and the League Championship trophies on board with us that night and it was great because virtually every member of our squad was there. Ian Atkins didn't play too often for us, but he always goes out of his way to make it to any reunion events. When I rang him about that one, he was delighted. He went into his loft and found his European Cup-Winners' Cup-final jersey so that he could bring it for all the lads to sign – his daughter tried to do him a favour and iron it, but sadly all she succeeded in doing was leaving a large triangular hole in the shirt because the iron was too hot!

After the dinner, we were all offered the use of a private room for a few more drinks together and the stick was soon flying again! Andy Gray and I were winding Trevor Steven up about his claim that he'd gone to Rangers for European football rather than the money.

We shot that suggestion down and gave him some earache. 'You went for the money, Trev, so don't try to flannel us!' said Andy.

That was a late night.

I am fortunate enough to get invited to a number of golf tournaments around the world where corporations and business people pay to have a few rounds with some ex-players. Terry Mancini, the former Arsenal and Queens Park Rangers defender, organises two superb ones. One of them, the Footballers' Golf Classic, gets played in La Manga every June and it's brilliant. So is the other, played every November in Dubai.

I've been playing in Terry's tournaments for seven years or

so and there is always something in the region of forty former professional footballers at each one. The La Manga event is run over five days and the going can get a bit tough at times. The social side is very enjoyable, but you can sometimes pay for it the next morning when you're on the first tee! But the punters love it because they really enjoy mixing with former players.

Phil Parkes, Tony Gale, Francis Lee, Alan Ball, Pat Jennings, Chris Nicoll, David Speedie, Gordon Hill, Sammy Nelson, Frank McLintock and Alan McInally are superb company. And some of the stories are terrific! That's why punters pay good money to go on Terry's trips.

But, as I say, the bond between the lads is in a different class. I had some real ding-dong battles with Paul Miller when he was at Tottenham, but after not seeing him for years we bumped into each other at a PFA Golf Day in Worsley and had a few beers together. The next day he was walking up the fairway with his group of golfers when he spotted me and shouted, 'Hey, Sharpy! I must have been marking you again last night because my head is banging!'

Footballers are a special breed because you can obviously be fully aware of someone without actually knowing them. I will see ex-pros whom I have never met before but will always say hello because I know who they are.

I remember being on holiday in Portugal a few years after I'd retired from playing and I was approached in a shop by Alan Curbishley. We'd never had a conversation in our lives, but he came over, asked how I was and we had a nice chat.

I also play a fair bit of golf with Andy Gray. He takes a group of friends over to Spain for a few days' golf and he really looks after us. Andy may have a high-profile position these days with Sky television, but I don't think he's changed one jot. At heart he's still the lad who left Glasgow many years ago.

As well as meeting up with old colleagues and adversaries, I also take a great deal of pleasure from playing golf with my friends and neighbours from the area in which I live. I moved to North Wales when I was at Oldham and I think it's one of the best things I've ever done. We love it out there. We are in the country, but we're not too far from the coast, and I've met some lovely people, none more so than Ken Davies.

A close friend, Ken is the type who would do anyone a favour . . . and he tells some wonderful stories. He was a very talented footballer in his youth and was once selected for North Wales Boys. He told me he was so excited in the dressing-room that he wasn't paying any attention to the coach and he missed all the lads being asked to provide their dates of birth. When his concentration returned, he was bemused by each young player shouting out a set of numbers. '12–10–48', '24–1–49' and so on until the boy next to him said, '11–9–48'. As Ken didn't have a clue what was going on, he merely repeated, '11–9–48'.

The coach was absolutely flabbergasted. 'In all my years in football,' he said, 'I have never known two players from the same team with exactly the same date of birth!'

He told the committee members and had plans to alert the local paper, but still Ken didn't realise what all the fuss was about! He's a really down-to-earth guy and we have some very entertaining Sunday afternoons with a group of great lads.

As well as watching Everton, whenever I can I also watch my son playing football. By the time this book hits the shelves, Chris will be 20 years old and he's a good centre-forward. At the time of writing, he is playing in the Welsh League for Rhyl and played his part in helping the team to win the 2006 Welsh Cup final at Wrexham. Being involved in the game myself makes it hard for me to watch him play as often as I'd like, but I enjoy seeing him in action.

He was at the Everton Academy when he was only seven years old, but I took him out because I felt that the little kids were already being put under too much pressure. Of course being the son of a professional footballer automatically brings a bit of added pressure, but he copes with it very well. Once when he played for Vauxhall Motors in the West Cheshire League, the opposition supporters would regularly have a go at him because of who I was and it would drive me nuts. I had many a row on the touchline over it.

My daughter, Emma, is also doing well for herself. She's at nursing college, which she enjoys. Every father will understand this when I say that I worry more about my daughter as she grows up than I do about my son, but Emma's doing smashing. I'm very proud of both my children.

Ann Marie and I have tried to bring them up in the correct manner and teach them what's right and wrong and hopefully that will stand them in good stead.

*

So there you have it. That's my story.

What happens now? The answer to that is I don't really know. I love working at Everton and I enjoy the media work I do, but no one can predict what will happen in the future. What I do know is that I consider myself to have been extremely fortunate to have enjoyed such a fulfilling and rewarding life so far. It's a life that I'm still enjoying immensely. I've got a wonderful wife, two fantastic children, a happy and close-knit family, and a lovely group of close friends. Nobody can ask for more than that and to everyone who's helped me along the way . . . thanks very much.

EIGHTEEN
TRIBUTES

You don't spend a lifetime in football without making some very good friends along the way and during the compilation of this book a number of the sport's personalities were happy to pay tribute to Graeme Sharp.

GARY LINEKER

Former Everton and England striker

'Good footballers are always easy to spot, but I didn't really know the type of player Graeme was until I joined Everton. I knew enough because Everton had been successful and I knew he was someone I would enjoy playing alongside because he was similar in many ways to Alan Smith, the striking partner I was leaving behind at Leicester City.

'It was difficult for me at first because Andy Gray was an Everton hero, and quite rightly so, but playing alongside people like Graeme gave me a chance. It took two or three games as I was feeling my way, but when the goals starting going in, from both of us, we really began to develop as a partnership. Graeme was brilliant in the air and he took a lot of weight off me. I was more of a box player, looking to get in behind the defenders, and I think we complemented each other very well. The only unfortunate thing is that it was only for one year. It would have been lovely to have had a few more years playing alongside him. But the one season we did have was terrific and I've never forgotten it.

'I left without any medals, but I know that had I stayed a bit longer I would have won quite a few.

'Graeme is certainly right up there with the best I've ever played with. My best partnership was probably when I played alongside Peter Beardsley for England, but that was different to the way Graeme and I were. If you're talking about big centre-forwards, he was as good as any. He had good close control, he was powerful and if you add unselfishness and a willingness to work hard, then you've got a tremendous centre-forward.'

KEVIN SHEEDY

Former Everton midfielder

'I had a great relationship on and off the field with Sharpy. I used to travel in with him every day. I only lived around the corner and I would pick him and Pat Van Den Hauwe up. Sometimes Pat wouldn't be there, but Sharpy always was!

'We had lots of good characters in the team and he was one of them. He was a very influential player for us because you knew what you were going to get. He gave quality displays week in, week out. Even when things weren't going his way he would work just as hard. He could play alongside anyone. He would unsettle defenders and even when he knew he couldn't win the ball he would make sure that his marker never got a free header. He'd win some great challenges in the middle of the park and that enabled the likes of Peter Reid and Paul Bracewell to get the ball and knock it about.

'Sharpy always knew that if I ever got half a yard on the defender, I would whip a cross in and he would always be there waiting for it. I knew the areas that he liked to attack and I would always try to put the ball into them.

'I watched one of his early games for Everton when he gave Kenny Burns a torrid time. I was at Liverpool at the time, living in digs close to Anfield, but I'd often cross the park to watch matches at Goodison and Sharpy really caught my eye. I knew Everton had some great young players and that made my decision an easy one when Howard Kendall asked me to join the club.'

IAN SNODIN
Former Everton teammate

'When I came to the club from Yorkshire, Sharpy and Sheeds were the two who really made me feel welcome. Sharpy knew that I played golf and invited me to play with him and his pals. He really helped me to settle. When I was looking for somewhere to live, he told me that all the good lads were in the Southport area and he helped me find a place. I can't thank him enough for how good he was to me when I first came to Everton.

'When I first signed for the club, I knew that I was joining a squad of great players, but it wasn't until I actually started training with them that I realised just how good they were. And it wasn't until I moved into the back four that I truly appreciated Sharpy's fantastic ability. As a defender, you could play any ball forward to him: you could knock it high and he'd win it, you could give it to him at chest height and he'd control it, or you could keep it on the deck and he was just as comfortable. His touch was magnificent and he had just about everything . . . although his pace wasn't the best!

'I remember one day against Sheffield Wednesday when he ran alongside Mel Sterland for the full length of the pitch. The move broke down and he had to turn and chase Mel the full length again in the other direction. We won the ball back and clobbered it back into their half.

'"Get after it, Sharpy," I shouted.

'His reply isn't suitable for this publication!

'I always remember that Sharpy had a bit of style about him. He loved buying new clothes and loved having all the latest fashions. He always paid good money for his gear . . . unlike myself!'

KEVIN RATCLIFFE

Former Everton captain

'There's only about a month between us in age and we hit it off straight away when he came down from Dumbarton. We've had some great times over the years. I also spent too many long flights sitting next to him on the plane and he's not the best passenger when he's snoring down your earhole on a 12-hour journey!

'Sharpy was an all-round striker who could win the ball, hold it up and also run the channels, as well as score goals. He had a great touch for a big fellow and he could control the ball superbly well with his chest, which is a difficult skill to master.

'I played against him once when Wales met Scotland. It was hard for both of us because we were such close mates, but luckily enough Sharpy spent more time up against Pat Van Den Hauwe than me.

'He used to demoralise centre-halves. I used to room with Ian Rush for Wales in the '80s and he used to say that Paul McGrath was the toughest defender he ever played against. But Sharpy used to tear McGrath to shreds whenever we played Manchester United. He always did very well against United. He used to terrorise Nottingham Forest as well and the lad Chris Fairclough at the back for them used to dread playing against us. There was nobody better than Sharpy when he was angry. He really did make things happen.

'As a centre-half, I would have hated to have played against someone like Graeme Sharp every week.'

COLIN HARVEY

Former Everton manager

'When Graeme first came down from Scotland, it took him a little while to settle, but the potential was there for everyone to see. I can't take any credit for spotting that he had something. He had an ability to work hard, he was very determined and he was a great lad to work with. And, apart from the fact that he was a very good player, he loved his football and was always interested in the game. Having said that, you wouldn't have guessed that he would turn out to be one of the strong dressing-room characters when Everton were a very successful team.

'We worked together at Oldham and I had no hesitation whatsoever in teaming up with him because I knew exactly what he was about. He wanted players to work hard and achieve their full potential, which is what he'd done himself. He was a top-class footballer and he matured into a top-class man. He was always disciplined and well mannered and clearly came from a good background. I've got a great deal of time and respect for Graeme and his family.'

HOWARD KENDALL

Former Everton manager

'You could see the talent, but you could also see that he needed time after coming down from Scotland. I used to think that if a centre-forward had no stitches or scars then there was something wrong: he was too good-looking!

'Graeme was the best of his type and if I had to liken him to another striker, then Frank Stapleton was probably as close as anyone. I don't think Stapleton was as brave as Graeme, though.

'He had a tremendous art at jumping early and getting free-kicks. It was something he developed himself because he was being dominated a little bit during his early days. He picked up a lot from Andy Gray. He had such respect for Andy. They shared the workload and that's the way it should be.

'I still say to this day that he could have been better. Had he got simpler tap-ins we would have had the perfect centre-forward because he had everything else. I was always on to him about scoring goals in the six-yard box. He had a great record, but I still wanted him to improve in front of goal.

'I would have loved to have taken Graeme to Athletic Bilbao and I would have loved to have taken quite a few of the others as well, but there was a Basque-only tradition and I had to respect that completely.'

DAVIE WILSON
Former Dumbarton manager

'I first saw Graeme when he was just 16 years old and he stuck out like a sore thumb. I remember watching him play for Eastercraigs in one particular match and I spotted a scout from Glasgow Rangers there. My heart sank because I thought there and then that he would sign for Rangers and that I wouldn't get him. He had a bit of everything. He was only very skinny at that time, but he was already brilliant in the air. He had a fantastic attitude to the game as well and as soon as he came to us he wanted to learn everything as quickly as you could teach him.

'We had some experienced players who kept an eye on him, but he was an easy boy to handle. He was never going to be the sort to go off the rails because he came from a very good family. I knew his dad because once I'd seen Graeme play I kept in touch with him. We became good friends. His dad knew that sending Graeme to me was the right thing to do because it was the best place for him to learn.

'I knew that he would go on to achieve bigger and better things, although not everyone shared my judgement. I nearly got the sack from my chairman because I had offered Graeme a new contract fee of £750! The chairman went mad, saying, "Why are you giving a boy who's just 17 all that money?"

'Seven months later, I reminded the chairman that he was going to sack me over £750 when we started to get enquiries about Graeme from all over the place. He just laughed and said, "Ah, well, that shows what I know about football!"

'Graeme was a jewel and you just don't find players like him coming along very often. He became stronger when he turned full time and he learned how to hold off the big centre-halves that were trying to come through the back of him.

'I was friendly with the Everton manager Gordon Lee and after Graeme had signed for the club, Gordon would ring me and tell me that the boy was everything I said he would be. I had every confidence that he'd make it in England.

'I haven't seen him for a long time, but I see his picture in the newspapers from time to time – he's certainly not as skinny as he was when I first brought him to Dumbarton!'

JOE ROYLE
Former Oldham Athletic manager

'Graeme was exactly what I was looking for because I wanted somebody who knew his way around. I'd got wind of the fact that he was maybe leaving Everton. There were rumours flying around that one or two other clubs were interested, so I made contact with him straight away and went to see him at his house. Oldham had just been promoted and I had always admired Graeme as a player. We were a young team with the likes of Earl Barrett, Andy Barlow, Nicky Henry and Ian Marshall. There weren't many veterans in the squad and Graeme gave us a bit of know-how. We needed someone who wasn't going to be fazed about going to places like Anfield or Highbury or Old Trafford . . . or even Goodison Park!

'As he got older and he got to know the game a bit more, he got better and he was just what we needed. He could hold the forward line together for me and he was capable of scoring goals. I knew he was the right man for me.

'Colin Harvey is one of my closest friends in football and when I spoke to him he confirmed that Graeme was just the right type. He told me that Graeme cared about the game and that he was a great professional. He had a keen sense of humour and played with a smile on his face. He was never scared to voice an opinion either, which I like in a senior player. I was delighted with him. He was our leading goalscorer in our first season in the Premiership.

'When I left for Everton, the chairman told me that he was going to ask Graeme to look after things for a bit and I said that I could see where he was coming from. He didn't want to put another member of staff in charge and so he asked Graeme to take the team for the first match after my departure. I spoke to the chairman after that game and he was really pleased with how things had gone and at how Graeme had conducted himself and looked after everything. They had other people in mind, but I told them that the man you know is often the best bet. And that man was Graeme.

'It's over the top to suggest that I recommended him for the job, but I did endorse what they thought of him. Although I had a great relationship with the chairman, the club wouldn't have appointed a new manager on my say-so. The chairman was impressed enough with Graeme to make his own mind up.

'I never had a minute's regret about bringing Sharpy to Oldham. He was smashing for me.'

WALTER SMITH

Scotland manager

'I actually played for Dumbarton just before Graeme joined the club. I left for Dundee United a couple of years before he came along and when I was the coach of the Scottish youth team, we called Graeme into one of our squads only for him to pull out through injury. Graeme's great attribute was his approach to the game, which was always superb – and I don't mean to detract from his magnificent all-round ability when I say that. He had a terrific attitude to go with his ability and he could cause any type of defender a problem. He used all his assets to the full and you can never ask for more than that.

'He had the best football education when he came through from Eastercraigs because the standard of the amateur game was very high in Scotland. It wasn't unusual for players to progress through to the professional ranks having not been regular starters for their amateur team. Eastercraigs and Drumchapel Amateurs were the best around and it was never a slight on anybody's ability when they struggled to get a game for these teams, yet Graeme always played. They were great grounding areas and he was from a good family.

'I played against his older brother Richard when he was at Kilmarnock. He was a good player himself and Graeme obviously benefited from him along the way.

'Graeme was perhaps unfortunate that, in the 1980s, Scotland had some fantastic players, especially in the striking positions, and that made it very difficult for any one forward player to nail down a regular place. Everton were a very successful side, Graeme was scoring lots of goals for them and the fans down there must have wondered why their star striker wasn't getting a game for Scotland. The competition was tremendous and although it was great for Alex Ferguson and me, it was obviously frustrating for the players. But not being selected all the time was no slight on Graeme's ability and it was no reflection on how highly we rated him. He was a terrific centre-forward and he proved that time and again throughout his career.'

KEN JONES

Bangor City chairman

'Getting Graeme was one of the biggest coups that this club ever had. I went to every game that Bangor played under Graeme and it was great craic. It was something new for us to get off the team bus and be greeted by autograph hunters! It was great fun. I remember one time we were preparing for a game against Marine and we were having a training session. Our goalkeeper was late arriving, so I offered to go in goal for a bit. The lads were only warming up at this time so it was a bit light-hearted, and Graeme had the ball by the halfway line. He looked up, saw me in goal and let fly with everything he had. I tell you, I was lucky that I managed to jump out of the way of the ball as it shot past me!

'When Graeme left, I left. We'd won the Welsh Cup, but it came down to economics. If I'd had my way, he and his assistant would have stayed. I still see Graeme from time to time and we are still good friends.'

ALAN HANSEN

Former Liverpool and Scotland defender

'Even though he was right at the top of the tree, I think, strangely enough, that he was still underrated. A lot of people didn't realise how good Sharpy was. But the players did. People tended to talk about his goalscoring record, which was exceptional, but he was also a great provider of goals. He was unbelievably difficult to play against and he was a tremendously intelligent player. Whether the ball was coming towards him on the ground or in the air, it was very difficult to get above him or get around him. I used to have a ploy against big centre-forwards, like Mark Hughes, for example, where I would try to get in front of them or jump all over them early on just so that they wouldn't really know which way I was going to come at them.

'But Sharpy was impossible to do that against!

'In that great Everton side, there were a lot of very, very good players and I would say that Graeme was right up there with the best of them. He should have got more caps, we all know that. But at that time there was a feeling that if you came down south, the Scottish media would be after you. I was told early in my career that if you were a Scottish international based in England then it wasn't worth looking at the papers when Scotland lost!

'Without sounding disrespectful to Scottish supporters, I

think maybe that Graeme was too intelligent a player for them to really take to. The Scots liked their centre-forwards to be real "battering-ram" types, like Joe Jordan or Andy Gray. Graeme wasn't their type of player, but, ironically, he probably would be now. He'd be a superstar in the modern game because he had such good positional sense.'

DUNCAN McKENZIE

Former Everton striker

'I was very fortunate to play alongside some very good centre-forwards. I had Neil Martin at Nottingham Forest, who was a very underrated striker, then Allan Clarke at Leeds United, who was a fantastic finisher, as was Bob Latchford, who I played with at Everton. I didn't think I'd see a better one than Bob, but I did . . . Graeme Sharp. When Howard had that great team in the '80s, Everton had great forwards such as Adrian Heath, Andy Gray and Gary Lineker, but what impressed me most was that Sharpy could play equally well alongside any of them. Andy would head crosses that other people would half-volley, Gary was the best goalscorer in the country but Sharpy, for me, was the complete centre-forward. He led the line so well, had a fabulous touch and still managed to score plenty of goals himself. People thought he was a big 6 ft 4 in. lad, but he wasn't. He was just so good in the air. Scotland have had no one like him since, that's for sure.

'He's a bit tasty on the golf course, too! We played in an absolute gale at Wallasey for charity once and he shot a two-over par. Great player – although the handicap he claims needs keeping an eye on!'

KENNY DALGLISH

Former Liverpool player and manager

'Sharpy was as successful as the Everton fans like their number 9s to be. When you score a winning goal in a Merseyside derby, your supporters don't forget you . . . but neither do the opposition fans, as Sharpy has doubtless discovered over the years! He played as big a part as anyone in Everton's success at that time and nobody could ever say that his career was anything other than successful. Unfortunately for me, it was Liverpool on the receiving end at times.

'He was always a handful, but if you play in a derby game and you don't want to compete, then you've got a big problem. You can understand the frustrations of the players who are losing, but that's the way derby games are played and at the end of the day you shook hands and there was no animosity carried forward in any way, shape or form.

'I wouldn't have minded playing alongside Sharpy a few more times for Scotland, but I don't know whether he would have fancied being alongside me! I never had the pace of Gary Lineker, so I may not have got on the end of his headers! But there were a lot of good Scottish centre-forwards about then. The competition was very fierce and if he could have had his career at another time, he probably would have got a lot more caps. Anyone would have enjoyed playing alongside him.

'I never actually played against him at amateur level. He's much younger than me! Eastercraigs were a very strong club, but I played for Glasgow United against them once in a Scottish Cup final and we battered them 6–0! It was before Sharpy's time, but they were always a traditionally strong team.'

CLIVE TYLDESLEY

ITV football commentator

'When I think of a "target man", I think of Graeme Sharp – some football phrases and terms immediately conjure up images in your mind. Whether that means Sharpy is the best target man I've ever seen or not, I don't know. But he would be one of them. A combination of a strong and aggressive striker that can also hold the ball up and play is rare. Graeme could look after himself and he could look after the ball as well.

'How many centre-forwards of his ilk are remembered for truly spectacular volleyed goals? Not just the derby winner at Anfield, but I remember a brilliant goal past Ray Clemence when he was the Spurs keeper earlier in Graeme's career. It was a stunning effort, one of the great Goodison goals. There were some crackers against United, too. He also got some of the most important goals of that era. The first in the '84 Cup final, the first against Bayern, the extra-time goal in the FA Cup semi against Sheffield Wednesday. And maybe, just maybe, most importantly of all, a really scruffy goal in front of 9,000 at Goodison that kept Everton in the League Cup a couple of months before Adrian Heath scored at Oxford. If I remember correctly, it was the night that the infamous "leaflets" were handed out expressing the black mood of the time.

'He was a stubborn bugger. Still is! I remember him refusing to go to a beckoning referee that was about to book him. He stood his ground four or five paces away and dared the official to send him off. That wasn't the only card of his career either. He gave every bit as good as he took. Ask Chris Fairclough. The only opponent that ever roughed him up was his dog. Didn't he once miss a match because it bit his hand? And while we are talking about embarrassments, what about the day he waltzed round Grobbelaar at Anfield, then missed!

'But I've said it many times to many people. In my opinion, Graeme Sharp was one of the three or four most important

SHARPY

Everton players of the '80s success story. Two players in one. A fearless and fearsome leader of the line from the old school of Everton number 9s, but also a modern striker with the touch and the technique to knit an attacking unit together and score fabulous goals. The archetypal target man.'

RAY STUBBS

BBC Match of the Day *presenter*

'I remember sitting in the Manchester United manager's office at The Cliff, their old training ground, with Ron Atkinson. Ron was on the phone, talking it large, as he always did, and when he put the phone down, he had an agonised look on his face. "There's just no way Everton will sell me Graeme Sharp." I didn't think there was and quite rightly so. But it reinforced just what a top striker Sharpy was.

'I will always be biased about Sharpy because I know him and I class him as a friend, but I do think that he was the complete centre-forward. I think he was underrated by certain people in the game, but if you speak to people like Hansen and Lawrenson, they still get a twitch when you mention Graeme Sharp! That's because he made things so difficult for them. Sharpy was a great character and what a guy to have around any club. I can't speak highly enough of him. The club has a great tradition of number 9s and you have to be more than just a good player to wear that shirt, you have to have a stature about you.'

MARTIN TYLER

Sky Sports commentator

'Graeme Sharp and I shared the "John Lacy experience". I was a hopeful amateur centre-forward and Lacy played against me for both Kingstonian and London University before he became a professional with Tottenham Hotspur. He made me look really dreadful, but I later saw him play against Graeme

Sharp. Graeme made him look very ordinary! Lacy was a very good player, but Graeme, on his day, was a terrific centre-forward.

'One of my first truly great Goodison Park moments as a commentator was Graeme's goal against Tottenham in 1981. I had only recently joined Granada from Yorkshire Television and he scored a wonderful goal with a strike that not many centre-forwards would have been capable of.

'His mobility was terrific. I think it was a bit unfair when it was claimed that he would deliberately jump early for the ball to win free-kicks. I just think he was very confident in the air. Graeme always struck me as being a Corinthian-type player and everyone who knows him is aware that he is a real gentleman.

'It all really clicked into place for him when Andy Gray joined Everton and I know they used to jostle a lot over the ownership of the number 9 shirt! They really liked each other a lot, too, and that helps on the football field. It's great to see them together nowadays. There's so much mickey-taking between them.

'In our different ways, at different times, I think both Graeme and I have acted as surrogate fathers to Andy because we both love him to bits, but he gets himself in the odd scrape! I have spent a lot of time with Andy over the last 15 years and neither of us has ever heard anyone say a word against Graeme as either a person or a player. It's been a privilege for me to know him and I still enjoy seeing him at Goodison on match days. Over the years, we've got to know each other really well and I'm delighted to say that I know Graeme Sharp.'

ALAN STUBBS

Everton defender

'Everyone knows that I was an Everton regular when I was a kid, but they always assume that my favourite players were the defenders. Of course, I loved watching Kevin Ratcliffe, Mark

SHARPY

Higgins and Mike Lyons, but Graeme Sharp was always one of my heroes. I liked my Everton players to give 100 per cent to the cause and Sharpy was certainly one of them. And anyone who liked nothing better than roughing up Liverpool in the derby could do no wrong in my book!

'One of my great memories is of actually playing against Sharpy when I was at Bolton Wanderers. It was January 1989 and he was coming back from an injury lay-off and was playing against Bolton in the Lancashire League for the Everton A team. The game was at Bellefield and I had no idea I'd be facing one of my heroes until the teams ran out onto the pitch. I have no recollection of the score, but I do know that Sharpy played for an hour and that I was terrified of injuring him because all my Evertonian mates would have killed me! He had everything that you wanted in a centre-forward and although I felt honoured to have played against him that day, I wouldn't have fancied marking him when it really mattered!'

HANS KRANKL

Former Rapid Vienna centre-forward

'I remember playing against Everton in the 1985 European Cup-Winners' Cup final. I was aware that Everton had been the best English football team throughout the whole year. I knew about Graeme Sharp and I knew that both he and Andy Gray were very good goal-getters and that they were extremely good headers of the ball too.

'We had seen Sharp play very well against Bayern Munich in their semi-final, so we knew that he was a dangerous centre-forward. His partnership with Gray was excellent and very important to Everton. Sharp may not have scored in the final, but he was a handful to our defence all night and did well to set up the important opening goal for Gray. He was a very good centre-forward; they both were.

'It was disappointing to lose the game, but it was good that it was a very nice, friendly final and we could see that the fans of both teams even exchanged scarves and caps afterwards.'

BILL KENWRIGHT

Everton chairman

'Sharpy' – six of the best letters in the dictionary to any Evertonian. OK, no one will ever emulate the five letters that make up 'Dixie' in our folklore, but Graeme Sharp certainly can take his place amongst the all-time legendary Everton centre-forwards in the hearts and minds of the blue-and-white disciples of Goodison Park.

'It's not easy to pinpoint the real strengths of Graeme's game – but one word that constantly sticks in my mind is "elegant". He was elegant on the field and he remains just as elegant off it: a real gentleman and a real son of Everton, who first adopted him as a raw teenager from Dumbarton almost three decades ago.

'Part of Sharpy's greatness was that he always seemed to be able to fine-tune his game to accommodate the strengths of those he played alongside at the business end of the Everton attack. I know for a fact that allies as diverse as Inchy, Andy Gray, Gary Lineker and Tony Cottee extol his virtues to this day – and enjoyed huge success playing alongside him.

'Sharpy never scored an easy goal when a spectacular one would do! None of us will ever forget Anfield in 1984 when he scored that thunderbolt from way, way outside the penalty area – nor that famous ear-to-ear smile when he made us believe that this really was to be "our year" with his goal against Watford in the victorious FA Cup final.

'It's often been said that Everton gets into your bones, even when footballers move on. The great thing about Sharpy is that he never truly "moved on". After a brief sojourn down the East Lancs Road, when he played for and managed Oldham Athletic, Graeme returned to Goodison to take an executive role as the fans' liaison officer – a role he has since performed with his customary skill, dedication and, yes, elegance. He is a hugely positive and popular figure around Goodison Park and the club continues to be enriched by his presence. But we do long for one of those thunderbolts from the halfway line in the odd pre-season friendly, Graeme!

'A great centre-forward, a great footballer, a great Evertonian – and a great guy.

'Respect, Sharpy!'

DARREN GRIFFITHS

Co-author of Sharpy: My Story

'When Graeme smashed home the winning goal at Anfield in 1984, I was in the Kemlyn Road Stand. Had somebody suggested then that I would play any part in the compilation of his autobiography, I would have thought they were mad. But here we are and what an absolute pleasure it's been.

'Whether we were sharing a few beers in a hotel or a Chester wine bar, sitting in Graeme's living room or chatting at Goodison Park, all the sessions were great fun. Of course, most of them were punctuated by autograph hunters and well-wishers, but then Graeme is such a popular figure it's something all his friends have grown accustomed to.

'I am indebted to his father, Jim, for patiently maintaining scrapbooks of his son's terrific career and also to all the people who were more than happy to help out along the way.

'And that's another thing. Not only did I discover a willingness to help, but I found that people were perfectly happy to go out of their way to contribute. It served as a reminder of just how highly Graeme is regarded within the game.

'In all honesty, my little tribute has no right whatsoever to be in the same section as the ones from the more illustrious contributors, but forgive me a bit of self-indulgence. People can claim that better footballers than Graeme Sharp have worn the royal-blue shirt of Everton and I would probably concede that, yes, they may be right. But have any better *men* played for the club?

'I doubt it.

'A legend and a gentleman: that's Graeme Sharp.'

Index